The Roots of Southern Writing

The Roots Of Southern Writing

Essays on the Literature Of the American South

———————— ❖ ————————

C. Hugh Holman

———————— ❖ ————————

University of Georgia Press
Athens

Library of Congress Catalog Card Number:
74-184774
International Standard Book Number:
0-8203-0290-2

University of Georgia Press, Athens 30601

Printed in the United States of America
by Heritage Printers, Inc.
Charlotte, North Carolina

SPECIAL ACKNOWLEDGMENTS

The author and the publisher acknowledge permission by Holt, Rinehart and Winston, Inc., to reprint ten lines from "The Gift Outright" from *The Poetry of Robert Frost*, edited by Edward Connery Lathem (New York, 1970). Copyright 1942 by Robert Frost. Copyright © 1970 by Lesley Frost Ballantine.

To
Marshall W. Brown
a great teacher . . .
a true friend

Contents

Acknowledgments
ix

Preface
xi

The Southerner
as American Writer
1

Simms and the Wider World
Views and Reviews
16

William Gilmore Simms's Picture
of the Revolution as a Civil War
35

The Influence of Scott
and Cooper on Simms
50

Simms and the British Dramatists
61

William Gilmore Simms
and the "American Renaissance"
75

The Novel in the South
87

The View from the Regency Hyatt
96

Ellen Glasgow: The Novelist
of Manners as Social Critic
108

The Dark, Ruined Helen of His Blood
Thomas Wolfe and the South
118

The Loneliness at the Core
134

Europe as Catalyst for Thomas Wolfe
139

The Unity of Faulkner's
Light in August
149

Absalom, Absalom!
The Historian as Detective
168

Her Rue with a Difference
177

Literature and Culture
The Fugitive-Agrarians
187

Three Views of the Real
194

Notes
201

Index
223

Acknowledgments

I am grateful to the following publishers for their generosity in allowing me to reprint the essays in this volume:

American Literature and the Duke University Press, for "The Influence of Scott and Cooper on Simms," *American Literature*, xxiii (May 1951), 203–218. Copyright 1951 by Duke University Press.

Fordham University Press, for "Her Rue with a Difference: Flannery O'Connor and the Southern Literary Tradition," from *The Added Dimension: The Art and Mind of Flannery O'Connor*, edited by Melvin J. Friedman and Lewis A. Lawson (New York: Fordham University Press, 1966), Copyright © 1966 by Fordham University Press, pp. 73–87.

Harvard University Press, for "Simms and the Wider World," which first appeared as the introduction to *Views and Reviews in American Literature, History and Fiction*, by William Gilmore Simms, edited by C. Hugh Holman. The John Harvard Library. Cambridge: The Belknap Press of Harvard University Press, 1962. Copyright © 1962 by the President and Fellows of Harvard College.

The Mississippi Quarterly, for "William Gilmore Simms and the 'American Renaissance,'" *Mississippi Quarterly*, xv (Summer 1962), 126–137. Copyright 1962 Mississippi State University.

The Journal of Southern History, for "Simms's Picture of the Revolution," which originally appeared as "William Gilmore Simms' Picture of the Revolution as a Civil Conflict," *Journal of Southern History*, xv (November 1949), 441–462. Copyright 1949 by the Southern Historical Association. Reprinted by permission of the Managing Editor.

The Modern Language Association of America, for "Simms and the British Dramatists," *Publications of the Modern Language Association*, lxv (June 1950), 346–359. Copyright 1950 by The Modern Language Association. And for "The Unity of Faulkner's *Light in August*," *Publications of the Modern Language Association*, lxxii (March 1958), 155–166. Copyright 1958 by The Modern Language Association.

The New Republic, for "The Loneliness at the Core," *The New Republic*, cxxiii (October 10, 1955), 16–17. Reprinted by permission of *The New Republic*, © 1955, Harrison-Blaine of New Jersey, Inc.

Louis D. Rubin, Jr., for " 'The Dark, Ruined Helen of His Blood': Thomas Wolfe and the South," from *South: Modern Southern Literature in Its Cultural Setting*, edited by Louis D. Rubin, Jr. and Robert D. Jacobs (Garden City, N. Y.: Doubleday and Company, 1961), pp. 177–197. Copyright © 1961 by Louis D. Rubin, Jr., and Robert D. Jacobs.

Preface

These seventeen essays about southern writing have been selected from a little more than twice that number which I have written over the past twenty-five years. They represent my several efforts to relate the work of southern writers to their physical, social, and moral environment and to the history of their region. None of them was written with the idea of its finding a place in such as book as this. When the idea of assembling them was broached to me by friends perhaps more generous than critically astute, my first response was to dismiss the notion. But such an insidious seed once planted tends to grow, and I went back over about thirty-five pieces that I have written about literary matters connected with the South and saw what I thought was a common pattern emerging from them. My reaction then was to think of rewriting them and reshaping them into a book. However, when I set out on that task, I found that the virtue, if any, which the separate pieces had was being lost in the revisions, and that whatever value they had was in what each individually said. I concluded that they supported and reinforced each other, despite the fact that they repeat the same ideas from time to time and that they are not interwoven into a single argument.

A word about how they came into being is in order, I think. Of the seventeen only three—all dealing with Gilmore Simms's Revolutionary Romances—were called forth by the desire to write an article setting forth a discovery or a position. The other fourteen were "occasional" in the sense that some occasion or other was responsible for their being written. They were talks or papers presented to meetings or symposiums, often on invitation, or they were chapters or essays written to be parts of series or portions of books; all of these essays were done on invitation. Thus the bulk of these pieces are responses of a southern student of the novel to certain aspects of his own culture viewed through the frames of idea or subject matter imposed by the occasions that called them forth.

A further justification for assembling them in the present form is that, although they have all been published in some form, they have appeared in books or journals of a very disparate character. Nine of the fifteen have been published in different books. Seven have appeared in some form in six different journals, with *PMLA* the only journal represented twice, and in such esoteric (at least for literary studies) places of publication as the *Journal of Southern History* and *Social Forces*. If any one should wish to peruse them in their earlier published forms, he would be hard put to it to assemble them in one place. If the assumption that such perusal is desirable is made, bringing them together here is then desirable. Hence I am submitting them now to the public in the forms in which they were originally published, with brief headnotes explaining how they came to be written and in some cases how they fit into the general pattern which I think I sense in them. I have decided to present them without major correction or updating. Here the reader may see them warts and all.

Perhaps I owe that reader a few words about myself, so that he can see where I stand in this twenty-five-year endeavor. I was born in South Carolina; educated there, in New York City, and at the University of North Carolina; and have lived most of my life in the two Carolinas. I have been teaching at the University of North Carolina at Chapel Hill since 1949. My adolescent and adult life has chronologically overlapped with the literary movement often called, without great precision, "The Southern Renascence." And I have inevitably been spectator and participant in the great social and moral revolution in the region. I have felt the strong affection for the soil of my native region that is, I think, a fairly common quality for southerners of my generation. I have felt, too, a revulsion and a distress over many of the aspects of the morals and mores of the South. Henry James once said that it is a complex fate to be an American. It is an even more complex fate to be a southern American, and few of us have escaped the moral tug-of-war that it represents. I also have what I now recognize as a characteristic southern concern with history—a desire to know how something came to be, a tendency to see the past as emblem if not as allegory, and a belief in the forces of history and tradition.

I never decided to specialize in southern American literature, and I do not think of myself as a worker in that particular field. I am interested in the novel—an interest of very long standing and some intensity. I am particularly interested in the novel in English, and most particularly interested in the novel written in America. A concern with history strong enough to lead to a double major in English and history in college has given me an interest in the interrelationships of history and fiction.

My critical faith leans toward that of Hippolyte Taine, although I am aware, I think, of his inadequacies and his oversimplifications; and I find particularly illuminating the work of critics like Edmund Wilson, Georg Lukács, and F. O. Matthiessen—and in the field of southern literature Louis D. Rubin, Jr. Thus when I come to examine a literary work I am likely to find one of its most fascinating aspects to be its relationship to the world out of which it came. Hence I have wondered why southern writers write as they do and whether they are in a tradition of some kind, and these essays represent my efforts to come to grips with that question

The Roots of Southern Writing

in quite specific terms. I think I have glimpsed from afar off and from time to time a shape into which southern writing tends to fall, and in these essays I have tried to describe that shape with regard to quite specific works.

The essence of that shape is in unresolved but still existent contradictions and in the ability to see life in terms of sharp contrast. If southern writing is a metaphor of a social and spiritual experience, it is also a vast figure of speech which, like the oxymoron, is a condensed paradox which unites for the moment in harmonious accord incongruous or dissimilar things and like a riddle tells the truth in hidden ways.

I wish to express my gratitude to a number of people who have done much to make these essays and this volume possible. The editors of the various journals and volumes in which these essays appeared have earned my undying gratitude for the assistance they have given me. Certain people by inviting me to participate in programs, series, or symposiums have set my mind working in new patterns, among these have been Louis D. Rubin, Jr., Robert Evett, Carl Dolmetsch, Lewis A. Lawson, Arlin Turner, George Tindall, Howard Mumford Jones, Robert E. Spiller, Rinaldi Simonini, Benjamin W. Griffith, Jr., and George Core. Miss Sue Fields Ross has been of great help in assembling the manuscript. Grants from the Research Council of the University of North Carolina and a fellowship from the John Simon Guggenheim Memorial Foundation have been of assistance in the research that has gone into some of these papers. To George Core, editor of the University of Georgia Press, my gratitude is deep and sure. Were it not for him, this volume would probably never have been assembled.

C. Hugh Holman

Chapel Hill, North Carolina
October 20, 1971

The Southerner
as American Writer

Approach it however you will, you will find at the heart of the southern riddle a union of opposites, a condition of instability, a paradox. Calm grace and raw hatred. Polished manners and violence. An intense individualism and intense group pressures toward conformity. A reverence to the point of idolatry of self-determining action and a caste and class structure presupposing an aristocratic hierarchy. A passion for political action and a willingness to surrender to the enslavement of demagogues. A love of the nation intense enough to make the South's fighting men notorious in our wars and the advocacy of interposition and of the public defiance of national law. A region breeding both Thomas Jefferson and John C. Calhoun. If these contradictions are to be brought into focus, if these ambiguities are to be resolved, it must be through the "reconciliation of opposites." And the reconciliation of opposites, as Coleridge has told us, is the function of the poet.

The poet's method is remarkably congenial to the southerner; for the southerner lives, as Robert Penn Warren has pointed out, in "the fear of abstraction . . . the instinctive fear . . . that the massiveness of experience, the concreteness of life, will be violated."[1] This use of the concrete, this pluralistic tendency to see the immediate, the experiential, is the way of the artist. It is little wonder, then, that the paradoxes at the core of southern life, although they have produced misery and catastrophe on many levels, have formed the materials for a literary expression uniquely powerful in our time, and have found in that expression their only effective reconciliation.

The South, however defeated it may feel itself in other areas, has triumphantly taken possession of the American literary world. William Faulkner, John Crowe Ransom, Allen Tate, Katherine Anne Porter, Erskine Caldwell, Robert Penn Warren, Caroline Gordon, Carson McCullers, Eudora Welty, Flannery O'Connor, Truman Capote, William Styron, Shirley Ann Grau, and that loosely defined group called the "New Critics," who in the last two decades have soundly trounced the historical scholars in the battle for the classroom—such a body of writers is unrivaled in a single region of America since the New England transcendentalists in the second third of the last century made Concord, Massachusetts, for a while the intellectual capital of the nation. Few today would argue with the London *Times Literary Supplement*'s assertion that "the literature [of the South] ... has solidly established itself as the most important, the most talented, interesting, and valuable in the United States."[2] This is a group of writers who are not only able to live at ease with a paradox; they are able to value paradox as a primary element of art. Cleanth Brooks sees the depths of meaning in poetry in the paradoxes that are found in word, image, and structure.[3] Allen Tate finds meaning in the "tension" of the poem.[4] These writers have presented the paradoxes and the dilemmas of southern life and thought in the only way in which they can ultimately be comprehended—in concrete and particularized terms. They have dramatized the contradictions, the ambiguities and intolerable couplings in individual cases and have made of them high art as well as accurate statement.

Southern writing from its beginnings, although it produced few works of true distinction and received small critical shrift before the twentieth century, has been consistently centered on the concrete, the particular, the actual, and, with varying degrees of excellence, has busied itself with the representation of reality as seen through southern eyes. That reality has been, until recently, at serious variance with the reality witnessed by other Americans, and southern writers have suffered in reputation and attention the consequences of the difference.

As late as 1710 Cotton Mather, belatedly speaking the sentiments of seventeenth-century New England, could declare that schoolmasters should "let it be [their] grand design to instil into their [pupils'] minds the documents of piety. . . . The sanctifying transformation of their souls would be infinitely preferable to any thing in Ovid's metamorphoses."[5] The first literary work of significance produced in the South was a translation of Ovid's *Metamorphoses*, by George Sandys, made while he was treasurer for the colony at Jamestown and published in London in 1621 —a translation praised by Dryden and Pope.[6] In the first half of the nineteenth century the New England mind fell captive to German Transcendentalism; but Southerners, although interested in German literature,[7] disliked transcendental philosophy. When the German scholar, Dr. Robert Henry, of South Carolina, died, the *Southern Quarterly Review* reported, "Though ... well versed in German literature, he had no taste for the German philosophers. His estimate of Kant was precisely that of Dugald Stewart, and as to Kant's successors, we do not believe that Dr. Henry could ever be induced to read a line of their writings."[8]

As a result of these differing attitudes, the southern writer has functioned as an American with a difference, and that difference has been his unique—and very valuable—contribution to the character of American art and life. It has expressed itself in three major ways: in his conception of nationalism, in his artistic method, and in the picture of archetypal man which his art has portrayed for Americans.

The concept of regionalism as a sound basis of art has been so generally accepted today that it is difficult to see that the importance of region or even of nation in literature could once have been a serious question. Yet it was, and the southern writer and critic tended in the first half of the nineteenth century to adumbrate the future rather than stand with his present on the matter. New England writers, although courageous voices were raised from time to time demanding a native strain, tended to distrust American qualities in art and to feel that nationalism should not manifest itself in our literature with any vigor.[9] In the 1840s a literary war broke out between the group associated with the *Knickerbocker* magazine and those associated with the Duyckinck brothers and the *Literary World* over the issue of nationalism, the *Knickerbocker* writers attacking the idea and the Duyckincks and their followers, known as the "Young America" group, supporting a vigorously patriotic literature. The two most noted southern writers of antebellum times joined the Duyckincks in this war; they were Edgar Allan Poe, certainly the most important writer that the South produced in the nineteenth century, and William Gilmore Simms, who as novelist, poet, dramatist, essayist, critic, and editor was the representative man of letters of the Old South. Yet their position was significantly different from that of the other "Young America" critics.[10] Their idea can be best expressed, I think, by a few lines from Robert Frost's poem "The Gift Outright":

> The land was ours before we were the land's.
> She was our land more than a hundred years
> Before we were her people. She was ours
> In Massachusetts, in Virginia,
> But we were England's, still colonials,
> Possessing what we still were unpossessed by,
> Such as we were we gave ourselves outright . . .
> To the land vaguely realizing westward,
> But still unstoried, artless, unenhanced,
> Such as she was, such as she would become.[11]

Simms wrote E. A. Duyckinck, on July 15, 1845: "If the authors of Am[erica] will only work together we can do wonders yet. But our first step will be to disabuse the public mind of the Eng[lish] & Yankee authorities. . . . Longfellow, a man of nice taste, a clever imitator,—simply an adroit artist. W. Irving is little more than a writer of delicate taste, a pleasant unobtrusive humor, and agreeable talent."[12]

The Southerner as American Writer

Repeatedly throughout his career, Simms was to declare that a nation was "denationalizing" itself if it modeled its art on foreign forms or neglected to treat its native subjects. In a letter to the editor of the *Magnolia* (August 12, 1841), he said, "It is the literature of a country which preserves the language and represents the morality of a period. . . . They preserve all that is preserved."[13] Yet Simms was one with Poe in decrying "puffery"—the praise of a work because it was American—and he almost parted company with his friend Duyckinck because Simms could find only faint praise for the work of Cornelius Mathews and none at all for Melville's *Moby-Dick*, despite these authors' high standing in the "Young America" group.

This was the age when the critical cry was for the "Great American Novel," the book that would encompass the breadth and depth of America in one volume. And here Simms stood sharply aside, for he saw in sectional writing the basis for a national literature. Because he was active as editor, author, and critic in the movement for a distinctively southern literature between 1830 and 1860,[14] Simms has often been accused of fostering a sectional literature at the cost of a national one, and indeed such charges were made by the editor of the *Knickerbocker* magazine during his lifetime. However, Simms praised Cooper's novels for their "Americanism,"[15] and they were as "sectional" as his own and certainly not southern. In 1839 he praised James K. Paulding for his novels of Dutch life in New York as "one of the earliest pioneers in the fields of American letters . . . who has never made any concessions to that foreign sway."[16] He viewed the northern monopoly of book publishing without great alarm and believed that New York would become the publishing center of America without American literature suffering as a result.[17] As late as 1856, when the fires of rebellion were flaming and Simms as southern patriot was talking secession and a Caribbean Empire, he wrote in the Dedication to a new edition of *The Wigwam and the Cabin*: "One word for the material of these legends. It is local, sectional —and to be *national* in literature, one must needs be *sectional*. No one mind can fully or fairly illustrate the characteristics of any great country; and he who shall depict *one section* faithfully, has made his proper and sufficient contribution to the great work of *national* literature."[18]

Simms followed in practice in his fiction the theory here enunciated. His novels were motivated in large measure by his desire to help in creating a literature indigenous to the spirit, events, and character of America by faithfully working with those distinctively American materials which were his local and sectional heritage.

In the period after the Civil War, when the local color school captured American fiction, the average critic and reader arrived at a view of

The Roots of Southern Writing

sectionalism much like that of Simms. The Middle West became the focus of sectional talent, and the modern southern writer, finding "regionalism" everywhere noised abroad as a virtue of incomparable stature, moved on from Simms's position to a new one. In 1945 Allen Tate, writing on the occasion of the twentieth anniversary of the *Virginia Quarterly Review*, asserted, "Picturesque regionalism of local color is a by-product of nationalism. And it is not informed enough to support a mature literature.... Yet no literature can be mature without the regional consciousness." Then he went on to define *regionalism* as opposed to the *provincialism* of local color: "I mean the writer who takes the South as he knows it today or can find out about it in the past, and who sees it as a region with some special characteristics, but otherwise offering as an imaginative subject the plight of human beings as it has been and will doubtless continue to be, here and in other parts of the world." [19]

The national impulse in the southern writer reached perhaps its most intense expression in the works of Thomas Wolfe, who, like his character Eugene Gant, sought to find and to express the meaning of his nation, and one night in Dijon had awakened in him

> a suddenly living and intolerable memory . . . of a life he had lost. . . . The memory of the lost America—the America of twenty years ago, of quiet streets, the time-enchanted spell and magic of full June, the solid, lonely, liquid shuffle of men in shirtsleeves coming home, the leafy fragrance of the cooling turnip-greens, and screens that slammed, and sudden silence—had long since died, had been drowned beneath the brutal flood-tide, the fierce stupefaction of that roaring surge and mechanic life which had succeeded it.
>
> And now, all that lost magic had come to life again here in the little whitened square, here in this old French town, and he was closer to his childhood and his father's life of power and magnificence than he could ever be again in savage new America; and as the knowledge of these strange, these lost yet familiar things returned to him, his heart was filled with all the mystery of time, dark time, the mystery of strange million-visaged time that haunts us with the briefness of our days. [20]

Wolfe goes on from this moment of revelation to attempt the representation of the nation through the experiences of an archetypal self, and yet in the closeness with which he confines himself to immediate experience, in the degree to which the concrete fact is the material of his expression, he is at one with the regional impulse, when it is viewed as a method of giving expression to the nation. When Wolfe concludes his exploration of his land, "I think the true discovery of America is before us. I think the true fulfillment of our spirit, of our people, of our mighty and immortal land, is yet to come. I think the true discovery of our own democracy is still before us,"[21] he speaks both as southerner and as American. Here, indeed "the land vaguely realizing westward, / But still unstoried, artless, unenhanced" has become ours. That is the goal of the regional writer, and that persistent pushing forward at the frontier of art which the southerner has made—sometimes, perhaps, for ignoble reasons—has ultimately made him loom large as American, and has taught him and through him others the dignity and the beauty and the terror of the land to be possessed.

If the southern writer seems a little out of step with the national literary scene through the earliness and the intensity with which he espoused the representation of the nation as a proper aim of art and the use of the region as the tool for such representation, he is even more out of step when the methods and materials of his writing are examined.

Fundamentally the ways of looking at art may be considered to be two —Aristotelian, in which the art object is examined with an eye to finding its values and its meaning within it, and Platonic, in which the art object acquires value and meaning in relation to something else, something extrinsic to it. Although the use of the names of Aristotle and Plato here represents the grossest of overgeneralizations, the tendency of criticism is toward examining the work of art either in itself, as Aristotle does in the *Poetics*, or in terms of its service to something else, as Plato does in the *Republic*.[22] In these terms American writing in the nineteenth century was Platonic, and much twentieth-century American writing has been, too. And in sharp contrast southern writers were more likely to take an Aristotelian view of literature. Poe, for example, wrote often of the "heresy of the didactic," and declared that a poem dealt with beauty rather than "truth." He studied seriously the emotional effect produced upon the reader by the separate elements of the poem, and tried to establish an objective standard for evaluating works of art; he was concerned with the psychology of the audience and the technical qualities of versification. The line which connects him with the "New Critics" is a direct one.[23]

For Simms, the great novelist is a professional man of letters, producing work whose utility rests on its satisfaction of man's desire to tell and hear stories, on the creation of myths to raise the real into the realm of the ideal, and on the building of national character.[24] Simms's criticism was analytical and objective; as Bernard Smith—who is fundamentally unsympathetic to Simms—noted, "He had a decided interest in the mechanics of composition—plot, invention—a greater interest by far than the famous critics of New England."[25] This interest in the intrinsic qualities and the technical aspects of literature continued in southern writing, a notable instance being Sidney Lanier's book-length study, *The Science of English Verse* (1880). Throughout the nineteenth century this tendency of the southern writer met with little approval outside the region. Poe was the "jingle man"; his "Philosophy of Composition" was discredited as a hoax; and his "Rationale of Verse" was never read. Simms's criticism accumulated dust in unread periodicals, and Lanier's *Science of English Verse* was taken as proof of the madness of mixing music and letters.

In our time the wheel has come full circle. A group of southern poets and critics, the "New Critics"—among them John Crowe Ransom, Allen Tate, Donald Davidson, Robert Penn Warren, and Cleanth Brooks— have triumphantly carried the gospel of the self-contained and self-sufficient art object across the land. These critics in true southern style have never formulated a system and have written comparatively few general statements. As Allen Tate says, "there was no Southern criticism; merely a few Southern critics."[26] The New Critics have usually exercised their judgment upon particular works of art, not indulging in abstract theories very often. Yet the teaching of literature in the colleges and universities of the nation and the criticism of literature in critical quarterlies and in scholarly journals have undergone a profound revolution as a result of the persuasive insistence of these men that the values of art are intrinsic, that literature is a valid way of knowing and expressing something rather than a mere ornament to something else, and that nothing can replace for the reader the painstaking analysis of the work itself. Small though it may seem in one way, it may be ultimately true that the poet-critics who founded the *Fugitive* and fathered the "New Criticism" will have had a more profound effect upon the thinking of a larger number of Americans than any other single small group of southerners in history. Yet what they assert, with astringent wit and calm grace, is essentially what southerners have been saying about writing for a hundred and fifty years. The southern critics have not only functioned as Americans; they have made an indelible impact upon the America in which they have functioned.

The southern sense of the particular and the southern distrust of the abstract early expressed themselves in a concern with reality as immediately discerned by the senses. As early as 1827, when fiction in America walked a genteel way, even on Cooper's frontier, Augustus Baldwin Longstreet began publishing the sketches of frontier Georgia life which, as *Georgia Scenes*, have given him abiding fame. When they appeared in book form in 1835, Poe praised them, but the realism and the aesthetic distance at which Judge Longstreet stood when he sketched a violent and impolite society found few imitators. As early as 1833 Gilmore Simms began publishing novels based on life on the "Border," rough tales of violent men of harsh actions and untutored tongues. The polite press of America found them shocking, as did his biographer as late as 1892.[27]

In 1841 Simms published a story, "Caloya; or The Loves of the Driver," in the *Magnolia* magazine. The story was attacked as obscene, low, vulgar, impure. In a spirited defense Simms wrote:

> It is a tale of low life—very low life—that is true.... There is nothing surely very attractive in Negroes and Indians; but something is conceded to intellectual curiosity; and the desire is human, and a very natural one, to know how our fellow beings fare in other aspects than our own, and under other forms of humanity, however inferior. No race is so very low, as to deprive them of the power of exciting this interest in the breasts of men ... there can be no substantial moral objection to the mere agents in the narrative. Their modes of life, passions, pursuits, capacities and interests, are as legitimately the objects of the analyst, as those of the best bred people at the fashionable end of London; and possibly, considering their superior wants, are more obviously the objects of a higher moral and Christian interest....
>
> Nearly all of the great writers that ever survive their day ... employ the deadly sins of man, as so many foils to his living virtues and whether he falls or triumphs, the end of the moralist is attained, if he takes care to speak the truth, the whole truth, and nothing but the truth! In this, in fact, lies the whole secret of his art. *A writer is moral only in proportion to his truthfulness*. He is and cannot but be immoral, whose truth is partial and one-sided.[28]

This is an attitude toward material that we normally do not expect to see in American writing much before 1870, for it is practically a definition of realism. What Longstreet, Joseph Glover Baldwin, George Washington Harris, and Simms were doing—and what Simms was here justifying —is the same thing that Ellen Glasgow was to do and defend; it is what Erskine Caldwell does when he functions at his best; what Faulkner did and Robert Penn Warren does. In the last third of the nineteenth century this impulse was to fall into the trap of whimsy and sentimentality in the local color school, but the writers of the twentieth century in the South have exercised—sometimes to the southerner's discomfort—the right which Simms asserted to treat all material truthfully. That some excellent realistic writing done in the nineteenth century by southerners fell by the critical wayside should not blind us to the fact that it was done, and that those harsh celebrators of the crude vulgarity of the southern and southwestern frontiers were in a tradition which our age sees as American.

But the way in which the southern writer has been most significantly

The Roots of Southern Writing

of service to his fellow Americans has been as the portrayer of an archetypal man sharply at variance with the standard American view. In holding up this archetypal man the southern writer has presented America with a valuable image of the unique southern experience, and at the same time he has offered himself as a scapegoat for the frustrations and guilts of modern America.

In the broadest and simplest sense the southern writer has shown man as caught in a tragic dilemma, tragic in the older and traditionally European sense. This "tragic sense of life" is, of course, partly the result of the experience of the South since 1860. As C. Vann Woodward has cogently argued:

> The inescapable facts of history were that the South had repeatedly met with frustration and failure. It had learned what it was to be faced with economic, social, and political problems that refused to yield to all the ingenuity, patience, and intelligence that a people could bring to bear upon them. It had learned to accommodate itself to conditions that it swore it would never accept and it had learned the taste left in the mouth by the swallowing of one's own words. It had learned to live for long decades in quite un-American poverty, and it had learned the equally un-American lesson of submission. For the South had undergone an experience that it could share with no other part of America—though it is shared by nearly all the peoples of Europe and Asia—the experience of military defeat, occupation, and reconstruction. Nothing about this history was conducive to the theory that the South was the darling of divine providence.[29]

Such a series of experiences is in sharp conflict with a view of life dedicated to inevitable success, to plenty, to progress and perfectibility, or even to the doctrine of individualistic strenuosity in which man is master of his fate and captain of his soul. If we can set the southerner's experience of life against the perceptive comments of Alexis de Tocqueville on the nature of the poetry that would normally be produced in a democratic nation, the contrast between the southern writer and his nonsouthern American contemporary is almost shocking: "I have shown," says Tocqueville, "how the ideas of progress and of the indefinite perfectibility of the human race belong to democratic ages. Democratic nations care but little for what has been but they are haunted by visions of what will be.... [Americans'] eyes are fixed upon another sight: the American people views its own march across these wilds, draining swamps, turning the course of rivers, peopling solitudes, and subduing nature. This magnificent image of themselves does not meet the gaze of the Americans at intervals only; it may be said to haunt every one of them in his least as well as in his most important actions and to be always flitting before his mind."[30]

In 1840 when Tocqueville was publishing this, long before the catastrophe to which Mr. Woodward refers, southern writers were already viewing man as a limited creature, with evil as an active force in life. Poe was dramatizing in his short stories and evoking through a medley of almost surrealistic images in his poetry the sense of evil and intolerable anxiety at the core of life, and he was casting serious doubts upon democratic processes. Simms in 1859, even when his hopes were high for the successful establishment of a Confederate government, wrote: "We are of those who think that we have very little to do with happiness. We have a certain destiny to fulfill, certain duties to perform, certain laws to obey, and vicissitudes to encounter, with such resources of courage as we have—energy, industry, and patient submission, with working; and, these laws complied with, we are to trouble ourselves no further with the compensative in our lot."[31] In 1842 he had written that "we are ... only so many agents and instruments, blind, and scuffling vainly in our blindness."[32]

Perhaps one source of this sense of imperfection and evil is the fundamentally Calvinistic religious belief of much of the South. Certainly the religious patterns of the region were shaped much more by the Scotch-Irish Presbyterians who settled the back country and fanned out to encompass the region except for the coastal plain than by that plain's essentially Episcopal quality. In any case the view of life which many southerners took was basically grim.

After the Civil War this quality was deepened by the sense of defeat that war brought. Ellen Glasgow said that she could never recall a time when "the pattern of society as well as the scheme of things in general, had not seemed to [her] false and even malignant."[33] And she declared, "For as long as the human race remains virtually, and perhaps essentially, barbarian, all the social orders invented by men will be merely the mirrors of his favourite imperfections."[34]

In the closing years of the nineteenth century and the early years of the twentieth, American writers were generally arriving at a similar disillusionment with the concepts of progress and perfectibility and, bowing to the new voices of science—to Darwin, to Spencer, to Comte, to Marx—were formulating a literature of despair and calling into being an American equivalent of the French naturalistic novel in which man is seen as hopelessly trapped. In the southern writer, by and large, the sense of defeat and of imperfection resulted in a picture rather of tragic strength than of pathetic weakness. Again Ellen Glasgow is a good case in point. She summed up the doctrine of her novel *Barren Ground* in

The Roots of Southern Writing

these words: "One may learn to live, one may even learn to live gallantly, without delight."[35] A confirmed pessimist, confident that the happy end, either in fiction or in philosophy, was false, she was always writing in some form or other the kind of book which she called a "drama of mortal conflict with fate."[36] Defeat was inevitable, but in the "conflict of human beings with human nature, of civilization with biology... tragedy lies, not in defeat, but in surrender."[37] A Greek sense of fate hangs over her world, and nobility is the function not of actions or of effective alterations in the world but of the spiritual qualities called forth by the world's hostility.

She is not alone in this view. Indeed the extensive use of southern history by serious southern novelists has been as a tragic fable of man's lot in a hostile world. From Poe's damnation to Faulkner's myth of the reduplicating tragic history of Yoknapatawpha County, to Wolfe's half-lugubrious "Lost O Lost and by the wind grieved," to the ambiguous calamity of Robert Penn Warren's Willie Stark in *All the King's Men* and the dark destruction of Peyton Loftis in William Styron's *Lie Down in Darkness*, southern writers and their characters have known what it is like to surrender their best hopes to the worst disasters, then pick up the pieces with stoic fortitude, and begin to make another dream that though lesser is equally doomed. Yet man does not lose his tragic stature in the process; he retains, though soiled and common like the Bundrens of Faulkner's *As I Lay Dying*, the potential of being challenged by an obligation and of accomplishing the impossible in discharging it. In this world, dark with evil and torn with bloody violence, over and over an idea of human dignity and responsibility comes. For example it speaks through the words of Ike McCaslin in Faulkner's "Delta Autumn," when Ike says, " 'There are good men everywhere, at all times. Most men are. Some are just unlucky, because most men are a little better than their circumstances give them a chance to be. And I've known some that even the circumstances couldn't stop.' "[38]

In the thoroughness and the consistency with which the southern writer has dramatized this tragic aspect of his experience he has differed most radically from his fellow American writers. It has been only in our time that the average American has begun to sense the possibilities for disaster with which life is filled, to see the likelihood that the path of progress leads to the edge of a precipice, to imagine himself trapped and doomed. In that moment of facing the possible end of his world, when he suddenly hopes that his world can end differently from T. S. Eliot's— "Not with a bang but a whimper"—he finds a previously unsuspected validity in the work of the southern writers.

And, although they are southern and have undergone, at least vicari-

ously, the tragic experience, these writers are also Americans and democratic: they weave their tragedies around common people, sometimes
contemptible people, characters lacking in the social or economic status
that would give them significance. Upon the insignificant shoulders of
an itinerant sawmill worker with a possible trace of Negro blood, William Faulkner in *Light in August* lays the burden of human guilt and
the painful need for expiation. In the frail, middle-class son of a decaying
southern family in *The Sound and the Fury* he finds the sufficient image
for a vicarious (although ineffectual) atonement. Warren's Willie Stark
rises from the soil to almost tragic power in *All the King's Men;* but
Amantha Starr, in *Band of Angels,* who must learn for all of us that no
man is free except in the act of surrendering freedom, is herself a slave.
Erskine Caldwell's decayed creatures, drawn with the humor and detached anger that was in *Georgia Scenes,* can hardly be considered tragic,
except in the sense we have of how far they have fallen; and yet the
outraged sense of human dignity is powerfully present in his harsh tales.

Considered in a broad sense, nineteenth-century America built a democratic dream upon the idea of perfectibility and progress, upon the belief
that the freedom of the individual inevitably meant the building of a
new, healthy, strong state. By the last quarter of the century the drift of
American culture had begun to raise questions in the mind of the most
devoted dreamer of the simple democratic dream, questions which men
like Nathaniel Hawthorne and Herman Melville had raised by mid-
century. Even for Walt Whitman the question of the possible conflicts
of the demands of the social order and the realization of the individual
had validity. In *Democratic Vistas* he wrote: "Must not the virtue of
modern Individualism, continually enlarging, usurping all, seriously
affect, perhaps keep down entirely, in America, the like of the ancient
virtue of Patriotism, the fervid and absorbing love of general country?
I have no doubt myself that the two will merge.... But I feel that at
present they and their oppositions form a serious problem and paradox
in the United States."[39]

The southern writer suggests, along with Hawthorne, that there are
other bases for fellow sympathy and democratic process than man's inevitable goodness, that a commonwealth of mutual respect and common constructive effort can be built upon an awareness of our inevitable
evil rather than upon the realization of our perfectible selves. Like the
lesson the Reverend Mr. Dimmesdale learned—" 'Be true! Be true! Be
true! Show freely to the world, if not your worst, yet some trait whereby
the worst may be inferred!' "[40]—the southern writer's message has often
seemed to be: "Acknowledge your own evil, plumb the depths of dark-

ness possible to you, and then let us join in trying to save ourselves from disaster." He may be formulating a more acceptable basis for democracy than the old one was.

The southern writer has been uniquely equipped by his history to draw the symbol of guilt and to serve, himself, as an example. For there have been few times in southern history, early or late, when the fact of Negro slavery, the inequity of the freedman's case, or the taint of second-class citizenship for the black citizen has not darkened the world of thoughtful southern men. The early writers, down to the 1840s, tended to rationalize the fact of slavery and to point to its final eradication. For instance John Pendleton Kennedy in *Swallow Barn* (1832), the first influential book in the "Plantation Tradition," writes of slavery with a clear sense of its injustice, although he regards it also as a necessary expedient. Meriwether, the owner of "Swallow Barn," explains to the narrator, as they visit the slave quarters: " 'I am sure the Southern sentiment on this question is temperate and wise, and that we neither regard slavery as a good, nor account it, except in some favorable conditions, as profitable,' " and he proceeds to outline a program of gradual emancipation.[41] It would, of course, be a gross error to assume that all southern writers secretly felt slavery to be evil—Henry Timrod, for example, would demolish such a contention—but it is true that throughout the writing of the antebellum period, the southerner knew himself to be a part of a system almost universally condemned outside his own region and often he himself seemed to feel it to be wrong.

Thus the Negro becomes both the cause and the symbol of the southerner's guilt, and the southern writer repeatedly has so used him. Faulkner has one of his characters express it this way: "A race doomed and cursed to be forever and ever a part of the white race's doom and curse for its sins. . . . The curse of every white child that ever was born and that ever will be born. None can escape it. . . . And I seemed to see the black shadow in the shape of a cross. And it seemed like the white babies were struggling, even before they drew breath, to escape from the shadow that was not only upon them but beneath them too, flung out like their arms were flung out, as if they were nailed to the cross."[42] This intense sense of guilt, inherited from the past and demanding powerful expiations that exceed our ability to give, is recurrent in Faulkner. Joe Christmas in *Light in August* believes that he had an infinitely small trace of Negro blood which functions as a symbol of his guilt, and unreasonably it preys upon his mind until he must die in expiating it. Ike McCaslin refuses the inheritance of his fathers in *The Bear*, because it has been bought with human injustice, and yet he is unable to stand upon his repudiation.

In some writers this sense of guilt expresses itself in broader terms. In Robert Penn Warren's poem "Original Sin: A Short Story," it relentlessly tracks the protagonist at home, in Omaha, in the Harvard Yard,

> But it never came in the quantum glare of sun
> To shame you before your friends, and had nothing to do
> With your public experience or private reformation:
> But it thought no bed too narrow—[43]

In "The Wolves" Allen Tate dramatizes this guilty evil as threatening

> wolves in the next room waiting
> With heads bent low, thrust out, breathing
> As nothing in the dark.

And the protagonist must go in fear to open the door and confront the evil—"and man can never be alone."[44]

Time too becomes a frightful entity for many southern writers, whose concern with time reminds us of European rather than American authors. Time is Thomas Wolfe's great enemy. Ellen Glasgow said, "Within time, and within time alone, there was life,"[45] and thus the relentless passage of time is the decay of death. To Faulkner's Quentin Compson in *The Sound and the Fury*, time as symbolized by the watch, is the arch enemy. In one of Warren's most original poems, "The Ballad of Billie Potts," it is time that gives us identity and carries us relentlessly away from lost innocence.

Now certainly it would be an error to assume that in the South and its treatment of the Negro resides the sum total of American guilt, and yet for a hundred and fifty years America has seen in the South its classic symbol of willful injustice. As gradually Americans as a whole have come to question their easy assumptions, to feel uncertainty and inadequacy, to see what Reinhold Niebuhr has called "the irony of American history," I think they have found in the acknowledgment of guilt, in the pervasive sense of evil, in the darkness, the terror, and the despair of twentieth-century southern writing an effective catharsis for their own fear and pity. In the bringing of peace to the soul and in the awakening of the spirit to right impulses and noble actions, religions have employed the symbol of the scapegoat, upon whom, symbolically, the sins of the group are loaded and who through his sacrifice expiates them. In a sense the southern writer has been a scapegoat for his fellow Americans, for in taking his guilt upon himself and dramatizing it he has borne the sins of us all. I believe that the powerful impact which southern writing has made upon the tormented world of the twentieth century is a commen-

The Roots of Southern Writing

tary on the painful extent to which our total experience makes the southern experience intelligible, so that the southern writer, who has faced the bitter paradoxes of his world and found in them the element of tragic grandeur, can speak as brother and friend to his troubled nation. In doing so he sometimes seems to betray the trust of his southern friends and to portray them in anger and harshness, but he does it as an American and in love.

Out of the cauldron of the South's experience the southern writer has fashioned tragic grandeur and given it as a gift to his fellow Americans. It is possible that no other southern accomplishment will equal it in enduring importance. As urbanization and industrialization conspire to write an "Epitaph for Dixie," its greatest contribution to mankind may well be the lesson of its history and the drama of its suffering.

Simms and the Wider World
Views and Reviews

William Gilmore Simms was the most prolific, the most versatile, and the most successful southern antebellum man of letters. Although he lacked the genius of Poe and his works have suffered from the corrosion of time more seriously than have John Pendleton Kennedy's and Henry Timrod's, Simms was from the early 1830s to the Civil War the outstanding southern literary figure and as close to being a representative writer as the Old South produced. In his long career as poet, novelist, critic, historian, biographer, essayist, and dramatist, a stream of words flowed from his busy pen; and as an editor on at least ten southern periodicals, he encouraged and directed the flow of words from other pens than his own.

In his own day Simms's fame rested on his novels and to a very limited extent on his poetry; in ours it rests almost exclusively on two or three novels. Yet in total output Simms probably produced more literary criticism than he did any other form of writing; for he kept a steady stream of reviews, notices, literary comments, and critical essays flowing to practically every southern literary journal from 1825, when he began writing for the short-lived and amateurish *Album*, until his death in 1870, at which time he was conducting a literary section in the Charleston *Courier* and contributing articles to a number of other journals. His last published work was *The Sense of the Beautiful*, an address on aesthetics published as a pamphlet in Charleston in 1870.[1] Most of this prodigious quantity of critical writing remains buried in the yellowing files of the journals in which it appeared; much of it is unsigned, and in many cases the problem of accurate attribution is virtually insoluble; and all copies of many issues of the journals themselves seem to have crumbled away to dust. Thus Simms is less known as a critic than he is in any other role.[2]

The bulk of this criticism shows seriousness about literature, a desire to be honest, a reasonably firm adherence to standards, and adequacy without brilliance. Simms's views of art and life were seldom original: he borrows freely from the general Romantic tenets of his age and at the same time demonstrates clearly that he has gone to school to the British quarterlies and the Scottish "common sense" critics.[3] Typical of his time, he has debts to Coleridge and Carlyle that defy measure and analysis. Edd

Winfield Parks, who explored a large amount of Simms's uncollected critical writing, concluded that "he was a good but not a great critic."[4] Thus it is not surprising that Simms has not found a significant place in the history of American criticism. Furthermore Simms collected his criticism only once—for Wiley and Putnam's Library of American Books. This collection appeared as *Views and Reviews in American Literature, History and Fiction*, First Series and Second Series.[5] These collections are not truly representative of Simms's total criticism,[6] for they were assembled for special purposes and as a part of a heated literary controversy over nationalism in literature.

Views and Reviews, First Series, is the best and the best known of the volumes. Publication of the Second Series was delayed and the volume was greatly shortened from Simms's original plans when it did appear. The first volume assembles a group of Simms's critical writings which were selected, he said, to be "illustrative of our history, our materials of art, the moral of our aims, and the true development of our genius."[7] It is united by common themes and beliefs: the need for a native American literature, the belief that such a native literature should find its subjects in the American past, an adherence to Jeffersonian-Jacksonian agrarianism with an attendant distrust of cities, industry, and capitalism, and a commitment to the idea that literature flourishes best in an egalitarian and not an aristocratic society. Furthermore *Views and Reviews* was a central document—in fact, almost a manifesto—in the Young America literary wars of the 1840s. Thus it is an important document in American literary and cultural history, whatever its weaknesses as criticism may be.

Views and Reviews, First Series, consisted of eleven essays, all originally published in southern literary journals in the 1840s. Five of the essays are examples of the nineteenth-century review article, owing obvious debts in form and manner to the British quarterlies. These essays employ books as the bases for extended comments on the subjects of the books. The other six essays are the parts of a series of lectures on American history as a subject for fictional and artistic treatment.

The first essay, "Americanism in Literature," struck the keynote for the volume. It argues for a distinctively American subject matter and manner in literature and vigorously asks for freedom from both British models and British critical standards, on the grounds that a democratic society can and must produce a native and democratic art.

In the six connected essays that make up "The Epochs and Events of American History as Suited to the Purposes of Art in Fiction," Simms first discusses the kind of truth which the new "scientific" history seeks.

As opposed to this high and exclusive concentration on fact, Simms urges that the artist seek truth to human motives, to human aspirations, to the appreciation of virtue and the admiration of heroes and present this truth as the core and meaning of a nation's history. He then takes up the story of Benedict Arnold as material for historical drama and asks that the dramatic poet, rather than attempt a literal record, seek out a moment of action in which the "ideal of a hero" can be presented. In converting Arnold into the subject matter of such a drama, Simms takes liberties with history that often appear ludicrous; yet, as John Paul Pritchard has pointed out, "Simms's argument anticipates recent theory about artistic process. It derives from Coleridge's concept of the secondary imagination at work together with the fancy, and adds to it the New Critic's emphasis upon the relation between artist and image."[8] Simms next discusses as subjects for art the four periods of American history—the period of exploration from the voyage of Cabot to the settlement at Jamestown, the period from Jamestown to the accession of George III, the period of the Revolution and the early Federal era, and the period from the beginning of the nineteenth century to 1845. He then examines Hernando de Soto and the French settlements of Gaspard de Coligny as subjects for romance, and concludes his exploration of American history as a subject for a vital and native art with speculations on the kinds of paintings that would represent the essence of the Pocahontas story. The six essays taken together form a passionate assertion that there is no paucity of American materials for romance and make an implicit plea that American writers and artists begin to employ them more vigorously.

In the article "Literature and Art Among the American Aborigines," ostensibly a review of two works by Henry R. Schoolcraft, Simms continues his efforts to demonstrate the artistic use of American materials. He sees in the American Indian all the materials of primitive epic art, plus a freedom from the bondage of historical record and fact, a freedom that allows the artist a full use of his imagination.

The essay on "Daniel Boon" is a review of Boone's autobiography. In it Simms elevates the historical figure of Boone to the proportions of a mythic image and sees in him all the virtues of a natural and primitive paradise. In many respects this essay is a biographical sketch but one that seeks the significant meaning in Boone's life and is close in method and tone to Thomas Carlyle's essays in *On Heroes, Hero-Worship, and the Heroic in History*.

This debt to Carlyle becomes very obvious in "Cortes and the Conquest of Mexico," a long review-essay based on Prescott's history and *The Dispatches of Hernando Cortes*. Here Simms sketches in detail

Cortes's conquest of Mexico, emphasizing the attributes that made the Spanish commander an archetypal hero.

The concluding essay, "The Writings of James Fenimore Cooper," is a careful analysis of Cooper's method in his novels, a piece of technical criticism which demonstrates what Bernard Smith meant when he said that Simms "had a decided interest in the mechanics of composition—plot, invention—a greater interest by far than the famous critics of New England."[9] William Cullen Bryant praised this essay as the best and most judicious treatment of Cooper's novels.[10] In this essay Simms also defends Cooper from his Whig attackers and pays tribute to his contributions to the making of a national literature.

None of the themes and ideas in *Views and Reviews* were new in the 1840s, either to American writers or to Simms. One of the principal values of the volume lies in how well it sums up many aspects of Simms's own career and how well it brings together many of the aspects of the movement toward a native and self-consciously national literature in America in the first half of the nineteenth century. It can best be understood in the light of certain events and recurring ideas in Simms's life and in his cultural environment.

One of the basic attitudes in *Views and Reviews* is, surprisingly, a liberal democratic egalitarianism that expresses itself in passionate adherence to Jacksonian democracy and in opposition to the conservative Whig view of the national and artistic life. With Simms that Jacksonianism was an intellectual faith and an emotional commitment.

Gilmore Simms was the son of an Irish immigrant, who failed in a small mercantile business in Charleston, South Carolina, left his two-year-old son in the care of the boy's maternal grandmother, and went west, first to Tennessee and later to Mississippi.[11] In Tennessee the elder Simms became an officer of undetermined rank in the Tennessee Volunteers under General Andrew Jackson, was active in Jackson's campaigns against the Creek and the Seminole Indians, and fought in the Western Army against the British in New Orleans.[12] After the peace in 1815 he settled in Mississippi, and there his city-bred son visited at least twice, traveling over wide ranges of the Indian country and delighting in the rough frontier life he found there. The image of his stalwart father remained in Gilmore Simms's mind throughout his life.[13] Thus one of his early and strong emotional ties was to "Old Hickory," and never did he break it or even desire to.

But the Irish immigrant's son had himself chosen the literary life, after a brief experience with the law, and in the late 1820s he found himself in a proud, aristocratic city, struggling for status against a virtual caste system. In 1848 he was to declare:

Our manners, moulded with the nicest art,
Fit for the court, but foreign to the mart;
Our pride, that points to ancestors of worth,
Whose deeds, perchance, were nobler than their birth,

and a little further along in the poem to say:

The generous youth, in mind and soul erect,
Is on the threshold of performance check'd;
Let him refuse to bend as they demand,
And he becomes a stranger in the land.[14]

In 1852 he wrote of a Charleston lady as one "denuded of vigour by the successive intermarriages of cousins for an hundred years."[15] The egalitarian distrust of the aristocracy was being strengthened by observation. In 1829, after editing the *Southern Literary Gazette* (1828–1829) and publishing a verse pamphlet and three volumes of poetry, Simms invested his small maternal inheritance in a daily newspaper, the Charleston *City Gazette*. The *Gazette*, founded in 1787 and edited at one time by Peter Freneau, brother of the poet, was an avowed party journal, a voice of the party of Jefferson. It was, therefore, also the spokesman for President Jackson and the cause of union in the Nullification Controversy which arose as a result of South Carolina's attempt to nullify the Tariff of 1828. As a party editor supporting "Old Hickory," Simms proved to be vigorous, direct, and tactless, often arguing intemperately and sometimes unpleasantly *ad hominem*. He was a committed Jacksonian and a consistent Jeffersonian. He even supported Daniel Webster in his debate with Robert Y. Hayne and praised his "able and unanswerable defense of the Constitution."[16] He asserted his faith in the good intentions of his fellowmen to the North and was willing to join James Blair when he pleaded with Congress for relief from the "tariff of abominations."[17] He called Secretary of the Treasury McLane's proposed tariff in 1832 a compromise to which neither party could in reason object,[18] and his support of the Adams tariff bill, which passed with the South Carolina Unionists voting for it, brought upon him the charge that he had sold out to northern manufacturers and capitalists, a charge which he repeatedly and angrily refuted. On one occasion he narrowly escaped being attacked by an angry mob of nullifiers.[19] As the nullification sentiment grew the number of subscribers to the *City Gazette* decreased, and its revenue dropped dangerously. On June 7, 1832, Simms sorrowfully sold the newspaper, assuming its large debts himself, and the period of his greatest political involvement was at an end. He was abandoning, he later wrote, "the profession of the patriot and politician."[20] This painful

The Roots of Southern Writing

struggle had annealed his Jeffersonian spirit, although it had not calmed his always intemperate emotions.[21] Simms was to be an ardent supporter of Andrew Jackson, Martin Van Buren, and their party until he defected to General Zachary Taylor, over the slavery issue, in 1848.[22]

It was natural, too, that so intense a Jacksonian democrat should be concerned with an egalitarian literature that had its roots in the American soil and had shrugged off the forms of art and life which aristocratic societies, and particularly that of England, had developed. Almost from the beginning of his career the contrast of American culture to that of England had been of concern to him. One of his very first publications when he turned northward after the debacle of the *Gazette* in 1832 was a long review of Mrs. Frances Milton Trollope's *Domestic Manners of the Americans* in the *American Quarterly Review*.[23] He remained keenly aware of the conflict of attitudes about art between British and American critics throughout his life, often alluding to it in his correspondence and in essays such as his article "Southern Literature" in the *Magnolia*.[24] As the essays in *Views and Reviews* demonstrate, Simms carried the issue back to Thomas Jefferson's patriotic claims in his *Notes on the State of Virginia* in 1787:

So far the Count de Buffon has carried this new theory of the tendency of nature to belittle her productions on this side of the Atlantic. Its application to the race of whites, transplanted from Europe remained for the Abbé Raynal. "One must be astonished (he says) that America has not yet produced . . . one good poet." When we shall have existed as a people as long as the Greeks did before they produced a Homer, the Romans a Virgil, the French a Racine and Voltaire, the English a Shakespeare and Milton, should this reproach be still true, we will enquire from what unfriendly causes it has proceeded, that the other countries of Europe and quarters of the earth shall not have inscribed any name in the roll of poets. . . . As in philosophy and war, so in government, in oratory, in painting, in the plastic art, we might shew that America, though but a child of yesterday, has already given hopeful proofs of genius, as well of the nobler kinds, which arouse the best feelings of man, which call him into action, which substantiate his freedom, and conduct him to happiness, as of the subordinate, which serve to amuse him only. We therefore suppose, that this reproach is as unjust as it is unkind; and that, of the geniuses which adorn the present age, America contributes its full share.[25]

To these remarks, the *British Monthly Review* had promptly replied:

It is but a very few years since the Americans set up for themselves as an independent people, and these *children of yesterday*, with the usual presumption of youth, affect to consider themselves as the most enlightened race existing; and hold the contemporary descendants of their ancestors very cheap!

As to the articles of genius and learning, the Americans do not require our antiquity before they produce a *"Shakespeare or a Milton"*; they had not to undergo the progressive drudgery of emerging from barbarism, for they carried over with them all the knowledge of the age which produced these poets, and have enjoyed regular importations from thence down to the present day. Rural scenery is favourable to poetic inspiration; so that amid the wild novelty which the Americans have for near two centuries enjoyed *"should this reproach be still true"* some other cause must be assigned, for the Muses not having accompanied British freedom when they crossed the Atlantic.[26]

This controversy continued, fed by the heightened feelings of the War of 1812 and its aftermath, revived by the ungenerous remarks by British travelers in America, and intensified from time to time by the lingering sense of colonialism and inferiority in America.[27] The publication in England and America in 1840 of Henry Reeve's translation of Alexis de Tocqueville's *Democracy in America*, Part II, with its discussion of the "Influence of Democracy on the Action of Intellect in the United States," revived and intensified the issues in the 1840s.[28] But in the 1840s an influential group of American writers, critics, and poets were supporting the British position, notable among them being Longfellow.[29]

Thus, when Simms embarked upon a defense of American writing in the essays in *Views and Reviews*, he was engaging in a conflict of long standing and in one in which his emotional and political affiliations had already determined his stance. The vigor with which he defended the richness of American materials for romance was also dictated in part by an active career as novelist, dramatist, and narrative poet in which he had dealt largely with indigenous material. But a large factor was also the persistence in American letters of a tendency to deplore the absence of those elements in American life out of which art of the highest order could be fashioned.

James Fenimore Cooper, who, as Simms pointed out in *Views and Reviews*, did as much as any single writer to demonstrate the usability of American materials for romance, also lamented the absence of such materials. In 1828, in *Notions of the Americans*, he had written:

The second obstacle [the first was competition with unprotected British books] against which American literature has to contend, is in the poverty of materials. There is scarcely an ore which contributes to the wealth of the author, that is found, here, in veins as rich as in Europe. There are no annals for the historian; no follies (beyond the most vulgar

The Roots of Southern Writing

and commonplace) for the satirist; no manners for the dramatist; no obscure fictions for the writer of romance; no gross and hardy offences against decorum for the moralist; nor any of the rich artificial auxiliaries of poetry. The weakest hand can extract a spark from the flint, but it would baffle the strength of a giant to attempt kindling a flame from a puddingstone.... I have never seen a nation so much alike in my life, as the people of the United States, and what is more, they are not only like each other, but they are remarkably like that which common sense tells them they ought to resemble....

All the attempts to blend history with romance in America have been comparatively failures, (and perhaps fortunately,) since the subjects are too familiar to be treated with the freedom that the imagination absolutely requires.[30]

Such an attitude was common in America; for example E. W. Johnston in 1831 asked, "Without fable—without associations—without manners to paint—how can there be imagination?"[31] Hawthorne was to assert it as late as 1860:

No author, without a trial, can conceive of the difficulty of writing a romance about a country where there is no shadow, no antiquity, no mystery, no picturesque and gloomy wrong, nor anything but a commonplace prosperity, in broad and simple daylight, as is happily the case with my dear native land. It will be very long, I trust, before romance-writers may find congenial and easily handled themes, either in the annals of our stalwart republic, or in any characteristic and probable events of our individual lives. Romance and poetry, ivy, lichens, and wallflowers, need ruin to make them grow.[32]

To Simms, who was convinced that a fresh and different material for romantic treatment existed in America, such statements needed refutation, particularly when they came from the lips of the admired Cooper, who had himself "convinced the people not only that there was gold in the land, but that the gold of the land was good,"[33] and from such revered local sources as Hugh Swinton Legaré's Southern Review.[34]

A further reason for his defending the adequacy of American materials for fictional purposes was that Simms's reputation rested primarily on his work as an historical novelist, and his career fluctuated with the vicissitudes of the public attitude toward the historical romance and the market for native fiction.

Simms began his novelistic career in 1833 with a crime novelette, Martin Faber, which owed debts of style, subject, and social attitude to William Godwin. The following year he published Guy Rivers, the first of his novels of the southwestern border, this one laid in the gold fields of Georgia in the 1820s. This romance was the first of the "Border Romances," novels covering the fourth of his periods of American history, that spanning "the progress of interior discovery and settlement."[35] In 1835 he reached what was perhaps his peak as a novelist with *The Yemassee*, a romance of Indian warfare against the white settlements in South Carolina in 1715, and *The Partisan*, the first of his seven romances of the American Revolution, concerned with the guerrilla warfare of General Francis Marion. The second of the romances of the American Revolution, *Mellichampe*, appeared the following year. In 1838 he published another Border Romance, *Richard Hurdis*, a tale of outlaw gangs in Alabama, and *Pelayo*, a romance laid in eight-century Spain. In 1839 appeared *The Damsel of Darien*, a romance of the Spanish conquest of Peru. The next year came a sequel to *Richard Hurdis, Border Beagles*, based on the John A. Murrell gang in Mississippi. The third of the romances of the American Revolution, *The Kinsman* (in later editions called *The Scout*), was published in 1841 and was followed the same year by *Confession*, a Godwinian tale of crime. With the publication in 1842 of *Beauchampe* (in later editions published as two books, *Charlemont* and *Beauchampe*), a novel based on the Beauchampe-Sharpe murder case in Kentucky, Simms's publication of full-length novels came to a stop until 1851.[36] In these ten most fruitful years of Simms's novelistic career he had concentrated most of his attention on his "four periods of American history," and he had not neglected any of them. That the stream of romances grounded in American materials ceased in 1842 was the result of no wavering in Simms's faith in his material, but was the consequence of major changes in the financial structure of the nation and in the methods of book publishing.

The Panic of 1837 was a major financial collapse that continued until it reached its low point in February 1843 and then began a gradual recovery that lasted for four years.[37] One result of this depression was a badly deflated book market. In 1838 books were selling slowly; by 1841 they were selling hardly at all. Furthermore new and rapid printing methods and a new process for manufacturing paper made the production of "cheap books" practical, particularly in the absence of copyright protection for foreign writers. In 1838 the *Great Western* and the *Sirius* crossed the Atlantic by steam. This new and rapid link between England and America quickly resulted in a host of "mammoth weeklies," which reprinted in atrocious form the most popular English writers and offered them for sale at prices sometimes as low as six cents. N. P. Willis's *Corsair*, Park Benjamin's *Brother Jonathan*, Jonas Winchester's *New World*, and George Roberts's *Boston Notion*, which advertised "104 square feet of reading matter," were exploiting the rich popularity of the English novel of the late 1830s and the 1840s.[38] Traditional publishing procedures began to undergo drastic change.

The successors to the illustrious House of Mathew Carey told the story with grave succinctness: "The system of cheap publications ... between 1839 and 1843, rendered general literature less attractive [than before]. It was impossible to sell a work of fiction except in paper, and large stocks of Cooper's novels, bound in cloth and utterly unsalable, had to be stripped of their covers and be done up in paper to find a market. The house [of Lea and Blanchard, at this time] gradually withdrew from enterprises like these; it ceased to publish for Irving, it sold the stereotype plates of Cooper's novels."[39]

In 1841 Simms said: "The publishers are very costive—the sales are terribly diminished within the last few years. You will perceive that Irving now writes almost wholly for magazines and Cooper & myself are almost the only persons whose novels are printed—certainly, we are almost the only persons who hope to get anything for them. . . . In this country an Edition now instead of 4 or 5,000 copies, is scarce 2,000. My Damsel of Darien was 3,000. My Kinsmen not more more than 2,000."[40] In 1847 he wrote: "My income from Literature which in 1835 was $6000 per annum, is scarce $1500 now, owing to the operation of cheap reprints which pay publishers & printers profits only & yield the author little or nothing."[41] The situation was made unmistakably plain in a letter which Simms received from his publishers, Lea and Blanchard, in December 1841:

> "Confession" is a total failure, "The Kinsmen" will do better. We do not see much hope in the future for the American writer in light literature—as a matter of profit it might be abandoned.
>
> The channel seems to be glutted with periodical literature particularly the mammoth Weeklies—besides which we go into the market for $1.50 a copy agt English reprints at 90c.[42]

So Simms turned in the 1840s to biography, criticism, novelettes for the cheap book market and to tales for the annuals and gift books.

Early in the decade he became closely affiliated with the Young America group of writers and critics, and this affiliation was to prove to be of major importance. From 1832 on Simms had been closely associated with the Knickerbocker writers and so nearly a part of their "inner circle" that in his own time he was often thought of as in the New York group. The chief among these friends were the poet and editor William Cullen Bryant, the minor poet John Lawson, and the actor Edwin Forrest. For a while in the 1830s he was a contributor to the powerful *Knickerbocker Magazine*, edited by Lewis Gaylord Clark.

But in the 1840s he became active with a group of new writers and critics who were liberal and radical democrats in politics, ardent nationalists in literature, and committed foes of conservatism in Whig politics and Anglophile criticism. This group, known as the Young America group, had grown out of the Tetractys Club, formed in the middle 1830s in New York City by Evert A. Duyckinck, William A. Jones, J. B. Auld, and Russell Trevett. Cornelius Mathews was soon added as a regular member; George Duyckinck was frequently present at the meetings, and others—notably Herman Melville in the late 1840s—met with the group from time to time. These young men were Loco-foco Democrats, optimistic celebrators of America, believers in its "manifest destiny,"[43] and intense nationalists about art and literature. They wanted a national literature and were willing to see it develop from local and sectional roots; they were willing for their humor to smack rudely of the frontier; and they were committed heart and soul, under the leadership of Mathews, to work for the establishment of an international copyright law. Furthermore, they viewed the revolution in publishing as an opportunity to present good books inexpensively to a growing mass audience.[44]

Their first corporate enterprise was a monthly magazine, *Arcturus*, published from December 1840 to May 1842 with Evert Duyckinck and Mathews as joint editors. They were also active in the *Democratic Review*, Duyckinck serving in several editorial capacities on it from time to time.

To Lewis Gaylord Clark and the *Knickerbocker Magazine* circle the Young America group was anathema. Clark's circle consisted of conservative Whigs, Anglophiles and internationalists, and passionate foes of a copyright law. Clark looked upon the *Democratic Review* and the Young America writers as divinely ordained targets for his scorn and vitriolic attack. Cornelius Mathews, the author of *The Career of Puffer Hopkins* and *Big Abel and the Little Manhattan*, was blasted with malicious glee from the beginning. Simms, although a former contributor,[45] became an object of attack when he began expressing Young America ideas in 1842. Edgar Allan Poe became the object of some of the most telling and poisonous attacks in American literary history after the publication of his "Marginalia" in the *Democratic Review* and his charge in the January 13, 1845, issue of the *Broadway Journal* that Longfellow, the archetypal poet of the Whig critics, was a plagiarist.

At one time Clark had viewed Simms as an important writer and had praised his work.[46] By 1841, however, Simms was publishing in the *Magnolia* a series of articles on "Southern Literature"[47] in which he was arguing vigorously for a national literature on native subjects, attacking Washington Irving as not being truly an American writer, accusing the editors of "the numerous *Soi-disant* literary Journals" of servile, pro-British criticism, and attacking business communities as foes of the arts—"merely trading communities have little or no moral influence," he declared.[48] Clark's recognition of these Young America sentiments was immediate: in the November issue of the *Knickerbocker* he took southern journals to task for "prating" of a sectional literature. "Our remote contemporaries must avoid one thing," he declared. "They must not ask favor for and claim a ready acceptance of, articles which may be ill-written or otherwise objectionable, merely because they are of local manufacture."[49] In April Simms replied; then with its June issue, he assumed the editorship of the *Magnolia*, a post he held until June 1843. Throughout Simms's editorship of the *Magnolia* he and Clark fired away at each other with increasing anger and sharpness. In August 1842 Clark, as was his custom, descended to personal abuse: "Least of all, we may add, do we recognize in *him* [Simms] a competent *arbiter literarum;* his 'lots' of labored romances—upon which Time and the silent indifference of the public, more potential than a thousand censorial voices, are already doing their work—to the contrary notwithstanding...."[50]

Simms was abundantly ready for an alliance with the Young America group when in March 1843 Cornelius Mathews began with him a correspondence that grew into a friendship always rendered precarious by Simms's inability to dissimulate about Mathews's works, most of which he found less than totally satisfactory. That summer he met and liked Evert A. Duyckinck, the true leader of the Young America writers, and became a full-fledged member of the group. By the end of 1843 he had produced four long and serious articles on "International Copyright Law," the chief point of agitation for the Young America group at the time, and arranged for their publication in the *Southern Literary Messenger*.[51] His object in the series was, he wrote Fenimore Cooper, "to show ... that great benefit enures to ourselves [from such a law], and that the chief good of the measure will be to emancipate us from the dictation of British mind."[52] He circulated a Memorial on Copyright to the Senate and the House of Representatives and enlisted the able support of his fellow South Carolinian, Dr. Edwin DeLeon, who contributed an article, "Cheap Literature: Its Character and Tendencies," to the *Southern Literary Messenger*.[53]

In 1844 some of Simms's friends in the Barnwell District, where his residence was located some seventy miles inland from Charleston, requested his permission to put him in nomination for the South Carolina Legislature. He permitted his nomination but warned his neighbors that he was not a candidate, would "neither treat nor speechify—[would] not in short cross the road for their suffrage."[54] Although he did campaign a little during the summer, he went to New York on August 13 to attend to his literary affairs and did not return until October 28, after the election in which he had won. At the same time he was offered the editorship of a new monthly literary journal, the *Southern and Western Magazine*, commonly known as *Simms's Magazine*, which he accepted with alacrity, seeing it as a means toward the establishment of "a manly and proper organ of literature and criticism in the South."[55]

Simms not only made the *Southern and Western Magazine* virtually the southern voice of the Young America group, but he also made it one of the most distinguished southern journals. He published Young America writers like Duyckinck, Mathews, and J. T. Headley and argued the cause of literary nationalism in its pages, and he made it a journal of which Edgar Allan Poe could say, "It is as ably edited as any journal of its species in America—if not more ably edited."[56] In the 135 pages of painfully small type that the "Editorial Bureau" occupied in the twelve issues of the magazine, Simms staunchly maintained the position of the Young America group, praising Poe, questioning Longfellow's originality, liking "bold and manly" Whittier for his "energy and life," preferring Hawthorne to other American writers of prose, expecting great things of Emerson "in spite of his Carlyleisms," and liking Catherine Maria Sedgwick even in the face of her attacks on slavery in *Home*. But the magazine needed a circulation of 3,000 to break even,[57] half of which it had attained by its second issue,[58] and it reached the end of volume two still at least a thousand short of the goal. Before its demise at the end of 1845, however, Simms had made arrangements with Evert A. Duyckinck for the publication of a collection of his essays, including all the long articles which he had prepared for the *Southern and Western*.

Duyckinck, as editor of Wiley and Putnam, Publishers, was not only demanding an American literature and the utilization of modern publishing methods to reach a large audience with inexpensive books; he was also through a series, "The Library of American Books," attempting to present that literature in an adequate form. The series, a portion of the larger "Library of Choice Reading," published material from American writers in well-printed books of from 100 to 250 pages, bound in paper, and offered for sale at prices varying from 31 cents to fifty cents a copy. In many instances two of these paperbound volumes were bound together in cloth for sale at $1.00. The first volume in "The Library of American Books" was Nathaniel Hawthorne's edition of *A Journal of an African Cruiser*, by Horatio Bridge, published in mid-summer 1845. Seven more books in the Library actually appeared in 1845; *Tales*, by Edgar A. Poe; *Letters from Italy*, by J. T. Headley; *The Wigwam and the Cabin*, First Part, a collection of short stories by W. Gilmore Simms;

Big Abel and the Little Manhattan, by Cornelius Mathews; *Wanderings of a Pilgrim under the Shadow of Mont Blanc*, by George B. Cheever; *Western Clearings*, by Mary Clavers [Mrs. Caroline Kirkland]; and *The Raven and Other Poems*, by Edgar A. Poe. Among the 1846 publications in the Library of American Books were: Herman Melville's *Typee*, Hawthorne's *Mosses from an Old Manse*, Simms's *The Wigwam and the Cabin*, Second Part, and J. T. Headley's *The Alps and the Rhine*.[59] A survey of this list of titles indicates that the short-lived library was, indeed, serving the cause of American letters well.

Some time during the summer, Duyckinck apparently proposed to Simms a collection of his critical essays,[60] and on August 7, 1845, Simms accepted the commission, agreeing to prepare "one or two 50 cent vol. of Literary Miscellanies for the American Series."[61] He immediately set to work selecting essays and working toward two fifty-cent volumes to be bound together as the finished book. The first volume was ready and the second under way by October.[62] Then a series of delays began. When Poe's *The Raven* appeared on November 19, 1845, it carried an advertisement stating that Simms's *Views and Reviews* was "just ready." The *Broadway Journal* for November 19, 1845, announcing the publication of *The Raven* and *Western Clearings*, listed *Views and Reviews* for "publication in November." On December 4 the *Broadway Journal* listed *Views and Reviews* for "publication in December."[63] Simms expected the book in November or December, as his letters to Duyckinck show, and by February 1846 he had grown visibly impatient at its long delay.[64] The cause of the delays is unknown, but it was May 1, 1846, before *Views and Reviews*, First Series, appeared, bound in paper to be sold for fifty cents.[65]

Views and Reviews, Second Series, fared even worse. Simms had made plans to include in it a number of his essays from a variety of journals, both northern and southern, as the Advertisement to the First Series indicates. Yet the end of June 1846 came without copy having gone to press. Simms, evidently in response to a letter stating Wiley's intention to drop the Second Series from the library, wrote Duyckinck, threatening suit unless the agreement was carried out; he said, "I cannot suffer my credit to be injured by a failure to publish the sequel of the work begun, and should regard it as certain ruin to the book if the second vol. were not put forth. It will not be sold till complete." And he added ruefully, "Never was vol. put forth with (seemingly) so little disposition on the part of the publisher to bring it properly to the view of the public."[66] The compromise agreement immediately reached was to publish a much smaller volume than Simms had projected. Still the delays continued, for it was July 1847 before the promised volume appeared,[67] paperbound for sale at fifty cents. It contained "The Domestic Manners of the Americans by Mrs. Trollope," "The American Sagas of the Northmen," "The Case of Major André," "Weems, the Biographer and Historian," and "The Humourous in American and British Literature." In all it had 184 pages and was only three-quarters the size of the first volume. It was also a much more heterogeneous book than the First Series, and it did not contain a single essay of the general distinction of the First Series, despite Whitman's liking for "The Humourous in American and British Literature."[68]

Before the second volume of *Views and Reviews* appeared, Duyckinck was no longer editor for Wiley and Putnam; the struggle of the Young America group and the *Knickerbocker* circle had degenerated into invective, innuendo, and insult; Melville and Poe were the centers around which the storm was revolving; and Simms was beginning to turn his eyes homeward, inward, and from the Loco-focos toward Zachary Taylor. If he had felt that the first volume was published with "little disposition on the part of the publisher to bring it properly to the view of the public," he must have felt that the second volume was released surreptitiously. Thus it was *Views and Reviews*, First Series, which attracted whatever critical notice the work was to receive.

Whigs promptly recognized it as a belligerent act by the Young America group. The mighty *North American Review*, usually aloof from these battles, struck the heaviest blow for the conservative Whigs. Cornelius C. Felton, Eliot Professor of Greek Literature at Harvard College, in the October 1846 issue, reviewed the Wiley and Putnam Library of American Books. Mathews's *Big Abel* was bad imitation Dickens; Poe's *Tales* belong to the "forcible-feeble and the shallow-profound" school; Simms's fiction shows no originality. But it was *Views and Reviews* on which Felton centered his scorn: its chauvinism is "without the faintest shadow of sense"; its articles contain "but little valuable criticism; they unfold no principle of beauty, and illustrate no point in the philosophy of literature and art. They breathe an extravagant nationality, equally at war with good taste and generous progress in liberal culture."[69] The following month the *Knickerbocker* quoted this article with sarcastic delight.[70] The Young America group countered such attacks in journals like Mathews's *Yankee Doodle*[71] and Duyckinck's *Literary World*, where the nationalism note was struck hard: "Mr. Simms is truly American. The subjects of this collection, from Americanism, the first paper, to the last, are purely American."[72] The scant notice which the Second Series and the clothbound volume that combined both series received was similar. In November 1847 the *Knickerbocker* quoted the Boston *Morning Post* with obvious relish:

The Roots of Southern Writing

If we understand Mr. Simms and his colleagues, it is necessary that our writers should choose American subjects, in order that their productions, however good, should constitute a real "American literature"; and that they should fill their books with a certain mysterious "American spirit," very difficult to describe and exceedingly hard to imagine.... It is a pity that some one of these gentlemen should not *produce a work* which would serve to show what this singular "American literature" really is....[73]

Clearly Simms was caught up in the Young America group's strident demand for a national literature to accompany an expanding egalitarian society, and *Views and Reviews* was a calculated voice in that demand. As Benjamin T. Spencer has asserted, "The period between 1837 and 1855 ... witnesses a strong movement toward nationality in American literature, deriving much of its impulse from the buoyancy attendant upon the democratic expansion of the time and characterized by its emphasis on the democratic ideal in letters."[74]

But *Views and Reviews* was not only a polemic in a literary war; it was also a piece of literary criticism, subject to judgment in those terms; and its most perceptive and telling criticism came, not from the *Knickerbocker* circle nor in the pages of Duyckinck's *Literary World* but from a fellow affiliate of the Young America writers, a fellow Loco-foco Democrat, and a fellow author in the Library of American Books—Nathaniel Hawthorne. He reviewed the book in the *Salem Advertiser* of May 2, 1846:

This work . . . is made up of able review-articles, chiefly on historical subjects, and a series of picturesque and highly ornamented lectures on "American History, as suited to the purposes of Art."—These are all creditable to the author, and scarcely inferior, in our judgment, to the best of such productions, whether on this or the other side of the Atlantic. Mr. Simms is a man of vigorous and cultivated mind—a writer of well-trained ability—but not, as we feel most sensibly in his best passages, a man of genius. This is especially discernible in the series of lectures above alluded to; they abound in brilliant paragraphs, and appear to bring out, as by a skilfully applied varnish, all the lights and shades that lie upon the surface of our history; but yet, we cannot help feeling that the real treasures of his subject have escaped the author's notice. The themes suggested by him, viewed as he views them, would produce nothing but historical novels, cast in the same worn out mould that has been in use these thirty years, and which it is time to break up and fling away. To be the prophet of Art requires almost as high a gift as to be a fulfiller of the prophecy. Mr. Simms has not this gift; he possesses nothing of the magic touch that should cause new intellectual and moral shapes to spring up in the reader's mind, peopling with varied life what had hither-to been a barren waste. He can merely elaborate what is already familiar. His style, we think, is one which, in a higher or lower degree of finish, is proper to men of his literary stamp. It is composed of very good words, exceedingly well put together; but, instead of being imbued and iden-tified with his subject, it spreads itself over it like an incrustation.[75]

Hawthorne points accurately to both the nature and the weaknesses of *Views and Reviews*, and hence he indicates an important aspect of its significance both in Simms's career and in literary history.

That significance is that *Views and Reviews* is a reasonably detailed statement of the purpose, materials, and method of the historical novel as it was practiced in America from Cooper's *The Spy* in 1821 until the hiatus in the publication of book-length fiction in the 1840s. On such a subject Simms could speak with an authority surpassed only by that of James Fenimore Cooper, for his literary reputation was founded on the historical romances he had written while the genre was at the pinnacle of its popularity in America.

Before 1840 the historical novel had attracted the interest of the best fictional talents in the nation. In the 1830s the fictional successes were by Cooper, Simms, Robert Montgomery Bird, James K. Paulding, and similar followers of the school of Scott.[76] Only Charles Brockden Brown of the significant novelists before 1840 did not use the historical romance as an artistically challenging form, and his career had ended before Scott established the genre and, in his numerous introductions, letters dedicatory, and prefaces to his Waverley novels, produced what still re-mains the largest body of critical and technical comment on the form.[77] Sir Walter was for Simms in this, as he was in most things, a master and a mentor.[78] Although he echoes Scott's formulas and strictures again and again, he adds nothing new to them; his contribution to the subject is his effort to demonstrate that American history and the American fron-tier are rich as subject matter for the historical romancer and form, therefore, an adequate material for artistic treatment. As such Simms was contributing to what ultimately proved to be the fruitless efforts of Americans. During this first half-century of the American novel, the search for the materials and methods of a viable American romance had been pursued. Simms in 1835 in his Advertisement to *The Yemassee*, had tried to distinguish between the novel and the romance, declaring, "Mod-ern romance is the substitute which the people of to-day offer for the ancient epic," and asserting boldly, "The Yemassee is proposed as an American romance."[79] For him and others of his age, as Benjamin T. Spencer suggests, "The genius of European romanticism furnished the imaginative ends; the problem for the American writer was to discover distinctive and appropriate instruments and agencies in the New World toward these ends."[80] Before a truly American romance was to come into existence the imaginative ends supplied by European writers had to give way to fresh and native ends and, as Hawthorne expressed it about *Views and Reviews*, "the same worn out mould that has been in use these thirty years" had to be broken up and flung away.

Between 1840 and 1850 American romance reached its maturity of theme and method, so that it could speak in the 1850s with an authority, a seriousness, and a passionate skill foreign to its earlier modes. The type of romance which *Views and Reviews* attempted to define was, in fact, dead as an artistic form for truly serious writing; and it was calamitous for Simms's career that he did not recognize the fact. In 1850 his romance of the Revolution, *Katharine Walton*, was published serially in *Godey's Lady's Book*.[81] That same year Nathaniel Hawthorne published *The Scarlet Letter*.

After 1847 Simms's attention turned increasingly toward the South and away from the nation. At the center of the issue was slavery; but other factors also contributed. The publication in 1847 of Lorenzo Sabine's *The American Loyalist*, a serious historical study of Loyalist sentiment and activity during the American Revolution, led many northerners to question the part the South had played in the winning of American independence. On this issue Simms was increasingly sensitive. In two articles in the *Southern Quarterly Review*, entitled "South Carolina in the Revolutionary War,"[82] he defended his state against Sabine's view of it. In 1852 he greeted a revised edition of Kennedy's novel *Horse-Shoe Robinson*—a book he had praised in 1835—with a long review taking strong exception to its picture of Loyalist sentiment in South Carolina.[83] These increasingly local and defensive attitudes were in part responsible for his return to the fictional treatment of the Revolution, and he produced in rapid succession four romances emphasizing South Carolina's major role in the winning of the Revolution: *Katharine Walton* (book publication, 1851), *The Sword and the Distaff* (later called *Woodcraft*, 1852), *The Forayers* (1855), and *Eutaw* (1856). He published in book form only two other novels: *Vasconselos* (1853), a Spanish romance of de Soto in America, which he had written much of in the 1830s, and *The Cassique of Kiawah* (1859), a romance of Indian warfare in Carolina in 1685. In all of these books he was still working in the Scott mould.

Thus, in the decade when the American novel had its first great flowering, Simms's critical and artistic eyes remained closed to the revolution that was occurring, and he failed to see that the trappings of the historical past, the posturing of the cloud-topping hero, and the picturesque scenery of the decaying castle had to be abandoned if the American writer was to make epic and romance out of the common man and his average life in a democratic nation. Apparently he read his fellow–Young America writer's *Moby-Dick*, but he did not understand Melville's startling effort to dramatize the romance of the soul through symbol and to define it in wild rhetoric, and he concluded that Ahab's "ravings, and the ravings of Mr. Melville himself . . . are such as would justify a writ *de lunatico* against all parties." [84] Young America's literary revolution had passed Simms by, and he remained caught in the "worn out mould" through which he expressed his steadily narrowing sectionalism.

The standard view of Simms is that he was an ultrasectionalist, steeped in "southern provincialism," a fire-eater of "the Calhoun School," and a blind worshiper of an aristocratic political and social order. [85] Such a view takes the Simms of the 1850s and 1860s and assigns his attitudes at this time to his entire career. Certainly Simms fell victim to the "intellectual blockade" which the defensive South threw around itself, [86] certainly his defense of slavery as an institution was consistent throughout his career, [87] but the intense sectionalism and the political conservatism of his late years were not characteristic of his whole career. Indeed the pattern of Simms's changing social and political thought was strikingly like that of James Fenimore Cooper, for Cooper shifted from the democratic Jacksonianism of *A Letter to His Countrymen* (1834) to the aristocratic conservatism of his last years. [88]

In 1842, however, Simms could write with complete accuracy and candor, "I am an ultra-American, a born Southron, and a resolute locofoco." [89] For in the 1840s he was a part of the first major radical democratic movement in American letters and he did yeoman service in its wars. His *Views and Reviews* remains today an important document in the Young America war, a vigorous expression of the egalitarian ideal in a native literature, and a summary of the ideals of a past literary genre. If in the dark days of the 1860s Simms ever turned its pages, it must have seemed to him to belong to a remote world. But more than a hundred years later it is still a significant reminder that Gilmore Simms marched bravely and fought intemperately in the cause of radical democracy.

William Gilmore Simms's Picture
of the Revolution as a Civil War

William Gilmore Simms expended much of his creative energy during his most productive period in writing a series of novels "devoted to the illustration of the war of the Revolution in South Carolina."[1] These novels present a record of events in the Low Country between 1780 and 1783 "to illustrate the social condition of the country, under the influence of those strifes and trials."[2] Since Simms, a literary figure so representative of the antebellum South that his only biographer calls him "a typical Southerner,"[3] approached his task with a deep respect for historical accuracy,[4] these books have value both for the historian interested in the traditions of the Revolution and for the student of antebellum southern thought. For within their pages is a record of the attitudes of the people of South Carolina about the Revolution and an analysis of the actual issues "which brought some men into doubtful and nearly all men into subtle and obscure relations with their neighbors."[5]

Simms's purpose in these novels was not to add new facts to historical records, but to interpret and to illustrate the impact of events upon men and society. Therefore he strove for a kind of accuracy within the framework of romance that is dissimilar to the later literary manner which Vernon L. Parrington was to call "critical realism."[6] Where the realistic novelist was to deal with average people in commonplace situations, Simms aimed at an accurate portrayal of "a human agent in hitherto untried situations."[7] Yet the extravagance of the historical romance should not blind us to the truthfulness which he always sought to achieve and which he frequently succeeded in attaining. He declared of *Mellichampe* and *The Partisan*, "My object usually has been to adhere, as closely as possible, to the features and the attributes of real life, as it is to be found in the precise scenes and under the governing circumstances —some of them extraordinary and romantic."[8] He pledged himself to "employ, without violating, the *material* resources of the Historian, while seeking to endow them with a vitality which fiction only can confer."[9] *Katherine Walton* he called "the delineation of the social world of Charleston, during the Revolutionary period."[10] *Mellichampe* he declared to be "imbued with the facts and, I believe, so far as I myself may be admitted as a judge, it portrays truly the condition of the time."[11]

Simms was admirably equipped for the task he set himself. He had a historian's interest in the Revolution and an accurate knowledge of the principal sources for its presentation. He wrote biographies of Francis Marion[12] and Nathanael Greene.[13] He knew and used the standard works dealing with the Revolutionary War in South Carolina. In his *Life of Francis Marion*[14] he lists the works which he consulted, and they represent the best sources available at the time that he wrote.[15] He had "read Marion's own letters, had conversed with old men who had served under 'the Swamp Fox,' and had walked or ridden over all the spots that their bravery had consecrated."[16] He had access to General Peter Horry's collection of manuscript letters from officers of the Revolution.[17] He was familiar with B. R. Carroll's *Historical Collections of South Carolina.*[18] He was in frequent communication with the antiquarian David F. Jamison[19] and with Joseph Johnson, the author of *Traditions and Reminiscences of the Revolution in South Carolina.*[20] In the Preface to his *History* he cites as sources consulted the works of Alexander Hewatt, John Drayton, David Ramsay, William Moultrie, John Archdale, B. R. Carroll, Joseph Johnson, James Glenn, William J. Rivers, Abiel Holmes, George Bancroft, James Grahame, and Banastre Tarleton.[21] Certainly when he declared of his novels, "I have followed the best authorities,"[22] it was no idle boast. And when he said, "The events made use of are all historical; and scarcely a page of the work [*Mellichampe*], certainly not a chapter of it, is wanting in the evidence which must support the assertion,"[23] he had the historical background necessary to make such a statement significant.

Simms believed that "the privileges of the romancer only begin where those of the historian cease"[24] and that "Genius dare not take liberties with a history so well known" as that of America.[25] Therefore he employed as a framework for the actions of his fictional characters in these novels the pattern of military events in South Carolina between June 1780 and January 1783 and handled it with accuracy and respect for historical fact.[26] *The Partisan* opens just after Benjamin Lincoln had surrendered Charleston on May 12, 1780, and resistance to British rule had almost completely ceased in the colony. The center of English control was Charleston, protected by an outer ring of forts that swept in a great arc from Augusta, Georgia, to Ninety-Six, to Camden, and to Georgetown. An inner ring was formed by Granby, Orangeburg, Fort Motte, and Fort Watson. Simms's historical framework consists of the series of engagements by which the reviving American forces, unsuccessfully under Horatio Gates and successfully under Greene, forced the withdrawal of British troops into Charleston. In the early chapters of *Woodcraft* the evacuation of Charleston is pictured as an ironic triumph in which the forces of General Marion, the historic hero of the series, were denied participation in the victory celebration. *The Partisan* pictures

The Roots of Southern Writing

the reawakening of armed resistance as a result of Sir Henry Clinton's proclamation of June 3, 1780, requiring all South Carolinians who had taken protection or parole from the British to bear arms in the English cause. It reaches its climax with Gates's defeat at Camden. *Mellichampe* pictures the efforts of Banastre Tarleton's legion to capture and destroy Marion's guerrilla forces. Its action occurs between the defeat at Camden and the return to the colony of the continental army under Greene. *Katharine Walton* also picks up historical events just after the battle of Camden. It pictures the sequestration methods of the English, the administration of Charleston under Nesbitt Balfour, and the underground activities of the Charleston Patriots. *The Scout* is the only one of the novels laid in the Up Country, most of its action occurring west of the Wateree River. Its action begins in the spring of 1781, shortly after the battle of Hobkirk's Hill on April 23, and centers around the siege, relief, and abandonment of Fort Ninety-Six. Presumably it was introduced into the series because of the important effect of Francis Rawdon's retreat from Ninety-Six on the fortunes of war in the Low Country. *The Forayers* opens as Rawdon's forces approach Orangeburg, describes the cat-and-mouse antics of Greene's continental army and Rawdon's troops, and concludes with the drawing up of a plan of action to harass the English communication lines between Orangeburg and Charleston. *Eutaw* describes the execution of this plan and reaches its climax with the battle of Eutaw Springs. *Woodcraft* opens as the British evacuate Charleston and portrays the lawlessness of the country just after the war.

From even so brief a sketch as this it is apparent that Simms's interest was in events occurring in the Low Country or directly and seriously affecting that region. During the time of action of *Mellichampe*, the American victories at Cowpens and Kings Mountain occurred, but they are barely mentioned. Apparently Simms omitted them in the belief that, although they were important in the chain of events leading to Yorktown, they had little immediate effect on the conflict in the Low Country. It would be an error, however, to attribute this narrow interest to an intense provincialism. Actually Simms took an active part in the movements for a national and for a distinctively southern literature between 1830 and 1860,[27] and believed that "to be *national* in literature, one must needs be *sectional*.... He who shall depict *one section* faithfully, has made his proper and sufficient contribution to the great work of *national* literature."[28] This view is almost identical with the present-day one that values regional literature.

Most of Simms's historical material is presented as exposition, with no attempt made to dramatize it. For example, although Marion is the hero of the actions which the books describe, he never becomes a character in the novels. He is always an historical personage, frozen in the postures of formal record and judgment. He is described, his actions are recounted, his speeches are given, and yet he comes into no dramatic relationship with any of the actors of the fictional drama. Formal history is consistently handled in this manner, and it serves principally as an accurate background for the fictional narrative.

This careful use of material is accounted for in part by the reverence in which Simms held the facts of recorded history, but more significantly it is explainable by his desire to treat truthfully the impact of events upon individual men. He declared, "History . . . is quite too apt to overlook the best essentials of society . . . in order to dilate on great events . . . which a more veracious . . . mode of writing would distribute over states and communities, and the humblest walks of life."[29] He believed that "it is the true purpose of fiction to supply [history's] deficiencies, and to correct her judgments."[30]

In seeking to portray this aspect of the past, he naturally subordinated the mass occurrences of recorded history and turned to the traditions of his section as sources for characters and incidents in the novels. He said, "I summon to my aid the muse of local History—the traditions of our own home—the chronicles of our own section—the deeds of our native heroes—the recollections of our own noble ancestry."[31] Of *Woodcraft* he boasted, "The humorists of 'Glen Eberley' [the main characters of the novel] were well-known personages of preceding generations, here thinly disguised under false names and fanciful localities."[32]

For Simms perhaps the greatest source of such traditions was Mrs. Gates, the maternal grandmother who had raised him. She had been a child in Charleston during the Revolution and had lived through the days of British blockade, British occupation, and American victory. She supplemented her vivid memories with a vast store of traditions about Patriot heroism and Tory depravity and poured forth her flood of recollections into the willing ears of the young boy.[33] He wrote of the store of traditional history:

He [Simms] had his lessons at the knees of those who were young spectators in the grand panorama of our Revolution. . . . This was their favourite topic. . . . There was scarcely a personage, British or American, Whig or Loyalist—scarcely an event, mournful or glorious—scarcely a deed, grand or savage—occurring in the history of the low country of South-Carolina, which has not been conned, for his benefit, at the writer's fireside, by venerable friends and loving kinswomen, now voiceless in the dust. . . . [The Revolution] was made life-like to his imagination by personal histories, which appealed to his nearest affections and fondest sympathies.[34]

The Roots of Southern Writing

In *Mellichampe* he wrote of "the unquestionable records of history, and —in the regard of the novelist—the scarcely less credible testimonies of that venerable and moss-mantled Druid, Tradition."[35] And he lamented the failure to record these traditions, saying, "The work must not be delayed. Old memories are rapidly failing us."[36] Much of the "tradition" which Simms employed might have become formal history had a careful historian been working in the field at the time.[37]

The aspect of this tradition in which Simms appears to have been most interested had to do with the civil struggle that went on concurrently with the more formal pattern of military action. As he saw it, while the struggle between Cornwallis and Gates and later Rawdon and Greene was deciding the battle for political independence and while the crest of English control was slowly retreating from the Up Country to Charleston, the equally dramatic struggle for life and its bare necessities occupied the inhabitants of the state. The British army withdrew, leaving the dormant blood feud between Tory and Patriot free to flare up in unrestrained robbery and butchery. This conflict was the unwritten history of the Revolution in his state, and it was this conflict which he attempted principally to illustrate in his novels.

To present that story truthfully meant to picture the everyday life of people on all levels of society, rather than to describe the heroic deeds of soldiers on formal battlefields. For such a presentation Sir Walter Scott had prepared the way. Scott evolved a formula for fiction which produced the first true historical novels. This formula employed an accurate historical background representing a period of sharp conflict between two or more classes of people and used actual historical personages as actors in the story; however, the central interest rested upon imaginary characters caught in the vast tug of these historical events. The central fictional figures were young aristocrats engaging in a romantic love adventure; they were not, however, of sufficient prominence to determine the course of history. This formal and hackneyed plot was fleshed out with realistically drawn pictures of low-life characters done with a careful eye to actuality. The result was an imperfect but enjoyable fusion of historical event, romantic love story, and realistic portrayal of life.[38] The situation which the Revolution presented in South Carolina was startlingly similar to that which Scott had utilized in *The Heart of Midlothian*, *Redgauntlet*, and *Woodstock*. And Sir Walter Scott was Simms's acknowledged model as a novelist. He considered *Ivanhoe* "one of the most perfect specimens of the romance that we possess,"[39] and he had the highest praise for its author.[40] Although he recognized that Scott was not perfect, he said, "Scott is, nevertheless, more perfect, more complete and admirable, than any writer of his age."[41]

Simms's Picture of the Revolution

To present his picture of the Revolution, Simms adapted the formula of his master, employing the historical framework, attempting to achieve a unified plot through a hackneyed story of thwarted young aristocratic lovers, and filling this framework with minor characters from the lower walks of life. It was usually through the adventures of these minor characters that he attempted to present events typical of the history and traditions of the times. Occasionally he stopped to point out this quality of typicalness; for example, of an incident in *The Partisan* he wrote, "It was in such little adventures that the partisan warfare of Carolina had its origin."[42] And in *Eutaw* he wrote, "We have rather sought, by the exhibition of a few instances, to give a general idea of their [the Partisans'] spirit, enterprise, and vigilance, than to furnish a perfect chronicle of their doings."[43]

Valuable as the Scott formula was to Simms's purposes, however, it betrayed him into an apparent oversimplification about the nature of the civil struggle which he was portraying; and it is necessary in examining his picture of that conflict to keep in mind the fact that he was employing a literary model which exaggerated the extremes of the social system it portrayed—the aristocrat and the low-life character.

He saw the Revolution in South Carolina as a civil war, a class struggle, a conflict in which issues of objective right and wrong were usually submerged in hatred, revenge, and cupidity. He saw it as a struggle marked by hideous atrocities and excesses on both sides, and he expended a large portion of his energies in presenting the horrible and merciless aspects of a conflict fought from mixed and frequently ignoble motives. He declared, "We shall be compelled to display, along with its [Partisan warfare's] virtues of courage, patriotism, and endurance, some of its crimes and horrors!"[44] Jack Bannister, the titular figure in *The Scout*, describes the uncertain family-against-family aspect of the war when he says: " 'Ah, Lord, there's mighty few of us got brothers in these times in Carolina. A man's best brother now-a-days is the thing he fights with. His best friend is his rifle. You may call his jack-knife a first-cousin, and his two pistols his eldest sons; and even then, there's no telling which of them all is going to fail him first, or whether any one among 'em will stick by him till the scratch is over.' "[45] The hero of *The Forayers*, speaking of a murderous outlaw, says, " 'It would be useless to inquire after the birthplace of such a monster. The earth always breeds such in seasons of civil war.' "[46] Talking about an outlaw who had served with both the British and the American forces, he says, " 'The right side with him . . . is that which promises most plunder. . . . Courage and endurance are no doubt admirable virtues in a soldier, but they are such as we are just as apt to find in the bosom of a sturdy ruffian.' "[47] In

The Roots of Southern Writing

Eutaw Simms wrote of "the wretched condition of the country; the summary judgments usually executed by those having the mere power, irrespective of the laws or of society; the universal recklessness of human life which naturally follows a condition of civil war."[48] In another place he wrote: "To burn in wantonness, and to murder in cold blood, and by the cruellest tortures, were the familiar achievements of the time.... South Carolina, at the period of our narrative, presented the terrible spectacle of an entire people in arms, and hourly engaging in the most sanguinary conflicts.... Despair seems to have blinded the one party as effectually to the atrocity of their deeds, as that drunkenness of heart, which follows upon long-continued success, had made insensible the other."[49] Such statements as these are valuable for the clarity with which they represent Simms's belief that not all who fought with Marion and Thomas Sumter were heroes or patriots and that the "summary judgments" and "recklessness of human life" were by no means confined to the British and Tory warriors.[50]

Such a view of the nature of the Revolution in the South Carolina Low Country is not confined to isolated statements like those which have been quoted. It is a part of the basic design of the books. Character after character and incident after incident show the same attitude consistently held. In *The Partisan* Christian Huck's raiders maltreat Frampton's pregnant wife; she dies and he goes mad, taking to the swamps and horribly murdering British and Tories with a bloodthirsty zeal that shocks even the hardened Partisans. In *Katharine Walton* when Partisan forces under Colonel Walton capture General Andrew Williamson, it is almost impossible to secure a fair trial for him, despite Walton's best efforts; for the Americans insist on hanging Williamson without trial or ceremony. In *The Forayers* and *Eutaw* Hell-Fire Dick and his gang of marauders, deserters from the Loyalist army, rob and murder both Whigs and Tories when neither army is in the area; and a band of Florida refugees—American Loyalists who had fled to Florida at the beginning of the Revolution and had returned to the colony when the British gained control—were joined to no army but raided indiscriminately, stealing and killing. These are but a few of numerous such instances throughout the novels. As Parrington has pointed out: "Now and then in his [Simms's] pages war flashes out in romantic or heroic episodes, but for the most part it is mean and degrading, a thing to be hated. Simms loved action too keenly not to make the most of the countless onsets and forays, the ambushing of Hessians and the cutting off of wagon trains; he found in them material for many a brisk page and stirring adventure; but in the end it is the brutality of it all, the unhappy loosing of evil passions, that gives him most concern."[51]

Simms declared, "I am persuaded that vulgarity and crime must always preponderate—dreadfully preponderate—in the great majority during a period of war,"[52] and he referred to the Revolutionary War as "the fierce civil warfare of the South, when neighbors were arrayed against one another."[53] There is little of the romantic glow of noble action in such a conception of war. In these novels, despite their romantic love plots, war is treacherous, evil, and brutal; and each side has its share of the fateful darkness. The excitement of the stories depends, not on panoplied conflict, but upon the stark thrill of frantic action.

Simms believed that the issues which thus tragically affected the lives of the South Carolinians were not political to any great extent and had relatively little to do with the struggle for national independence. At no place in the novels does he discuss the basic issues of the war in a national sense. "It does not need that we should inquire, at this late day, what were the causes that led to this division among a people," he declared.[54] He believed that "the revolutionary war, in South Carolina, did not so much divide the people, because of the tendencies to loyalty, or liberty, on either hand, as because of social and other influences—personal and sectional feuds."[55] He seems to have doubted whether most of the inhabitants of South Carolina understood the issues at stake in the Revolution; for he said: "The subject of controversy was not very intelligible to our simple farmers [in the Orangeburg district], many of whom were foreigners, speaking no other language than the German.... For that matter, when parties rage, the true points at issue are rarely understood by the people—are rarely *made* before the people by their politicians—and, perhaps, are scarcely necessary to be made."[56] When Supple Jack Bannister, in *The Scout*, is attempting to convert Muggs to the Patriot cause, he discusses the tax issue; but the scene is intended to be humorous, and it is. Jack says: " 'It made the gall bile up in me to see a man that I had never said a hard word to in all my life, come here, over the water, a matter, maybe, of a thousand miles, to force me at the p'int of the bagnet, to drink stamped tea. I never did drink the tea, no how.... But, 'twas the freedom of the thing I was argying for.' "[57]

Apparently Simms considered the South Carolinian in the Revolution to be faced with alternate evil choices in a world that was neither soft nor easy. As Jack Bannister expresses it, " 'A man oughtn't to be too soft about the heart, in a world like this, so full of rascals that need the knockings of a hard and heavy hand.' "[58] Mother Ford, a simple and good woman of whom Simms expresses his approval, states a viewpoint that Simms suggests as his own over and over in the novels when she says: " 'Every man in Carolina, that's able, has to go out, and lend a hand

The Roots of Southern Writing

to the work, one side or the other, as you see; and when that's the case, the safe rule, and the right reason, is to stand up for the sile [soil] that gives you bread.... I'd give a good deal ef I could make Mat break off from the flurrida riffigees [Tory outlaws], and j'ine himself to one of our parties ... and make himself a free white man again, having the right understanding that freedom means the right to stand up agin the world, in defence of one's own sile.' "[59] Seemingly the issue at stake in the Revolution appeared to Simms to be a defense of the soil, of the native land. Other issues were finally of small importance to him.

One of the important causes for the adoption of the Loyalist side in the struggle, Simms believed, was the unwise and intolerant treatment that the Whigs had given those not actively supporting them in the early days of the Revolution when they had control of the colony. Barsfield, the villain of *Mellichampe*, became a Loyalist for this reason. Through Barsfield's words, as he explains why he murdered Colonel Max Mellichampe, Simms presented a passionate statement of this viewpoint:

"When this cruel and unnatural war commenced in South Carolina, I had taken no part on either side. The violence of the whigs around me ... toward all those not thinking with themselves, revolted my feelings and my pride, if it did not offend my principles. I was indignant that, while insisting upon all the rights of free judgment for themselves, they should at the same time deny a like liberty to others.... I dared to disagree—I dared to think differently, and to speak my opinions aloud, though I lifted no weapon, as yet to sustain them....

"My neighbors came to me at midnight—not as neighbors, but armed, and painted, and howling—at midnight. They broke into my dwelling —a small exercise of their newly-gotten liberty; they tore me from the bed where I was sleeping; they dragged me into the highway, amid a crowd of my brethren—my countrymen—all cheering, and most of them assisting in the work of punishment....

"They bound me to a tree—fast—immovable.... The lash, the scourge, rods from the neighboring woods were brought, and I suffered until I fainted under their blows....

"I came to life to suffer new tortures. They poured the seething tar over me.... Then, hurrying me to the neighborhood river ... they plunged me into its bosom, and more than once, more merciful than the waters, which did not ingulf me, they thrust me back into their depths, when with feeble struggles I had gained the banks....

"Hence it is, that I lift the sword, unsparingly to the last, against the wretches who taught me in that night of terror, of blistering agony, of manhood's shame, and a suffering worse infinitely than death, of what nature was that boon of liberty which they promised, and which it was in the power of such monsters to bestow."[60]

Simms's Picture of the Revolution

Simms said that this story bore "a close resemblance to the recorded history of the notorious [Loyalist] Colonel [Thomas] Brown, of Augusta ... one who is said to have become so [a vindictive Loyalist] solely from the illegal and unjustifiable means which were employed by the patriots to make him otherwise."[61] Of the episode he wrote, "It shows strikingly the evils to a whole nation ... of a single act of popular injustice. ... The excesses of patriotism, when attaining power, have been too frequently productive of a tyranny more dangerous in its exercise, and more lasting in its effects, than the despotism which it was invoked to overthrow."[62] Lieutenant Stockton, a British officer commanding a marauding Loyalist band, says: " 'Nothing, indeed, has secured them [his troops] to the king's side but the foolish violence of the rebels, which wouldn't suffer a thing to work its own way; and began tarring and feathering and flogging at the beginning of the squabble. Had they left it to time, there wouldn't have been one old Muggs [a Loyalist] from Cape Fear to St. Catharine's.' "[63]

But it seemed to Simms that the basic reason for the civil division rested on social and economic inequalities and the dissatisfaction and hatred which they engendered. He appears to have recognized that in South Carolina, contrary to the case in many of the northern colonies, the party of revolution against England was not a "rabble in arms," but the conservative party, the party of social and economic status quo, the party of the aristocratic merchant-planter class. He saw that, great leveler though the Revolution was, it preserved the southern social system against the agents of social revolt who, in large measure, embraced the British cause in the colony.

Simms's idea of class division seems to have been this: During the struggle for independence the Low Country of South Carolina had three major class divisions, exclusive of the Negro slaves. The upper class, virtually constituting an aristocracy, was made up of the merchants and planters, men who had controlled the economic interests of the colony under British rule and who were to control them under independent government. At the other extreme was a class of people, now known as poor whites, barely eking out an existence in the face of hopeless economic difficulties and steadily dropping further down the social and moral scale as their economic possibilities decreased from small to infinitesimal. In the middle was a class that was fluid and difficult to delimit. It was made up of the small landholders and the artisans. This class was constantly striving to advance itself into the aristocracy and at the same time to resist the economic pressure that tended to force it into a lower social order. Caught between the twin arms of a vise made

The Roots of Southern Writing

of aristocratic control and wageless slave labor that was often highly skilled, the man without wealth or slaves was in a fluid and often precarious position. That such was not the social order in the Up Country, Simms probably realized;[64] but in the Low Country at that time the middle class was highly mobile. As Rosser H. Taylor says, "The whites in the Low-Country tended to drift more and more into two classes— the gentry and the poor whites."[65]

That Simms was aware of the middle class and the struggle in which it was caught is obvious from several of the fictional characters whom he created. The Travises, in *The Forayers* and *Eutaw*, owners of an estate and holders of a few slaves, represent the upper limits of the middle class. Travis, a worker in the British commissariat, is attempting to raise himself to full planter status. The Framptons and the Griffins, in *The Partisan*, and Mother Ford and Widow Avinger, in *The Forayers* and *Eutaw*, although holders of land, are being steadily pushed down into the class of abject poverty. M'Kewn, in *Woodcraft*, is attempting by financial robbery to elevate himself into the aristocracy; and Inglehardt, a Loyalist captain in *The Forayers* and *Eutaw*, is attempting to rise from the lowest middle-class status—he is the son of an overseer— to the ruling class.[66] But despite these examples of Simms's awareness of an amorphous middle group, the fact remains that we complete the novels with a feeling that the middle class as we know it today hardly exists in Simms's portrait of the section. A partial explanation rests in the actual social condition; another probable cause is the literary model which he chose to follow, a model which emphasized the extremes of aristocracy and low-life characters. Probably Simms's novels, in their day, contributed a significant bit to the conception "of society in the Old South as one composed essentially of great planters, poor whites, and Negro slaves."[67]

Simms believed that it was from the poor whites and the lower middle class that the Loyalists drew much of their support, for by fighting with the British these groups were struggling to produce a social and economic anarchy which would give them greater opportunity to rise.

Within this social pattern Simms created 98 fictional characters who play parts of some importance in these seven novels.[68] Most of these figures are created, not as individuals, but as representatives of their classes and positions in society. Thirty are members of the upper class; 10 are British officers or officials; 46 are whites who are not members of the patrician class, ranging from poor white "squatters" to upper middle-class figures; and 12 are Negro slaves. Only 7 of the 30 patrician characters are Tories, while 25 of the 46 lower-class characters support the

British cause. Only 1 of the 12 Negroes performs pro-British actions. This classification becomes increasingly significant when the nonpatrician characters are further divided into groups by occupation or economic standing. Of the 6 tavernkeepers and members of tavernkeepers' families, 4 are Whigs. Of 10 characters in the class of small landholders, 8 are Whigs. The only nonpatrician physician introduced is a Whig. The 2 overseers—a borderline group in social and economic standing—are evenly divided in their allegiance. Four of the 6 scouts are Whigs. The scout, as Simms portrays him, is never a landholder, but he shows an independence and self-reliance too great to allow him to be classified with the poor whites, a group to which he almost belongs on economic grounds. Of the 21 members of the class that is known today as the poor whites,[69] only 3 are Whigs. Thus 13 of the 21 nonpatrician Whigs are in the middle-class landholders, tavernkeepers, and physicians—while 21 of the 25 nonpatrician Tories are in the lower class—poor whites, scouts, and overseers. This division, although not conclusive in itself,[70] is significant in terms of Simms's implication throughout the novels that the upper classes in large measure supported the American cause, and the Loyalists recruited their greatest numbers from the disaffected lowest class.

In his *History of South Carolina* Simms wrote, "The common appeal of the loyalist leaders was to the vulgar prejudices against rank and wealth, the haughty assumptions of the citizens and planters of the seaboard, and their free expenditure of the public money."[71] That he considered this prejudice to have a basis in fact is shown in two of his portraits of the patricians. Old Colonel Sinclair, in *The Forayers* and *Eutaw*, he portrays as "one of the despots of the old school . . . who expected that you should understand his condescension, and feel his generosity . . . [and who was unwilling] to acknowledge the claims of that fungus multitude [those not of his class], which it needed another hundred years to raise, in any degree, to a fairly human position."[72] In *Eutaw* Simms was openly critical of the conventional code governing the patrician class. Writing of Sherrod Nelson, a young aristocrat, he said: "He had lived in a conventional world—one of fashion. . . . With all his real virtues, affections, and natural strength, he could never brave that voice of vulgar fashionable opinion. Lose caste! no! no! . . . that conventional realm in which he had been trained . . . needs every now and then, some terrible event to shock it back into humanity."[73]

But perhaps more important than such arrogance on the part of the ruling classes was the lowly economic position of the poor. Robert Singleton, talking to the wealthy but lukewarm patriot Colonel Walton, says:

"You are wealthy, and avail yourself of your good fortune to buy yourself out of a danger to which the poor man must submit. By what right would you escape from and evade your duties, when he, as a citizen, having the same, must submit to their performance! His conscience, like your own, teaches him that to fight for his country and against her invaders is his first duty. You evade your duty by the help of your better fortune, and leave him, as in the present instance, either to perish hopelessly in unequal contest—unequal through your defection—or to take up arms in a battle to which his principles are foreign." [74]

This statement, typical of an attitude Simms several times expressed, shows his awareness that the poor man in South Carolina during the Revolution often fought from necessity, not from choice, and that under such circumstances he frequently took up arms for the Crown.

However, Simms stated the case in clearer and more emphatic language. Hell-Fire Dick, a Loyalist deserter and the leader of a gang of cutthroats, combines hatred for the patricians, revolt against economic oppression, and desire for personal improvement. He tells old Colonel Sinclair:

"Look you, old Sinkler, I knows you well, and all your kidney. You're one of them bloody, proud, heathen harrystocrats, that look upon a poor man, without edication, as no better than a sort of two-legged dog, that you kin lay the lash on whenever you see him lying in the doorway. And your son is jest another sich a tyrant heathen! And you've had a long swing between you, living on the fat of the land, and riding rough-shod over poor men's backs. But thar's a great change, thanks to the king's marcies! and the good time for the poor man's come at last!—and, now, we've got a-top of the wheel! We've got the chaince at the good things of this life; and we kin pay off old scores, wagon-whip and hickory, agin your nice gould-headed [gold-headed] cane!" [75]

This is not mere bluster from Hell-Fire Dick, but a deep-seated conviction. Later, when he is talking seriously with his gang of outlaws, he broods over the differences between himself and the powerful:

"It's worried me to think how it is, that working, and riding, and fighting as we does, thyar's no gitting on—no putting up—no comforting sitivations, where a man could lie down and be sure of good quarters, and enough to eat for a week ahead. . . . Now, what makes the difference twixt us and all these rich people. How's it, that whatever we does turns out nothing, and they seem to git at every turning in the road. We works more than they, and we has all the resks, and trouble, and danger; yet nothing comes from it, and by blazes, I'm jest as poor a critter this day, as the day I begun, and something poorer." [76]

This sense of wrong, of economic and social oppression, of envious hatred of those in power is apparent in dozens of the poor in these novels. Mother Blonay and her blear-eyed Indian half-breed son in *The Partisan* feel that everyone is their enemy and have a passionate hatred of every living thing. Inglehardt, the Loyalist captain and villain of *The Forayers* and *Eutaw*, is using the upheaval of the Revolution to rise above his origins as a poor white's son. M'Kewn in *Woodcraft* is amassing a fortune by foreclosing mortgages on estates during the war and raising himself to the status of plantation owner. Sam Bostwick, the squatter in *Woodcraft*, steals, lies, and kills for gold guineas. These characters, and many others like them in the novels, show how keenly Simms was aware that the civil strife in South Carolina was at least partly the result of economic and social inequality.

Yet spirited though his portraits of the poor were and detailed though his presentations of their frequently honest dissent from the Patriot cause were, Simms never treated the Loyalists with either sympathy or admiration. Clearly he would have considered a triumph of their cause a catastrophe. In *Eutaw*, speaking of Griffith's tavern, a place of Loyalist recruiting, he said, "Here, in brief, was the rendezvous of Motley, with all her tribes—the vagrant, vicious, worthless, selfish, scoundrelly, savage, and merely mischievous, who love to follow in her train."[77] Further recognition and disapproval of the basis of real and imagined grievances that had led hundreds into Loyalist ranks is apparent in Simms's statement that "many were beguiled by false counsellors—many had been driven by injustice into the ranks of the enemy."[78]

These books are filled with a multitude of characters and incidents; yet they serve in large measure to elaborate upon and emphasize the fundamental picture of the nature of the Revolution in South Carolina indicated by the examples that have been cited. The value of this picture is enhanced by other qualities in the works. Shields McIlwaine has pointed out that Simms was the first important portrayer of the southern poor white and that in his pages "for the first time in fiction, one can know an early Southern squatter intimately; how he feels, eats, walks, and talks."[79] Ima H. Herron says that the series of Revolutionary War novels "contains pictures of town life deserving far more than passing notice," that in Simms's pages "an exciting, but long-vanished, social regime comes to life," and that "because of his numerous interpretations of widely varied phases of community life and his courage to portray with marked realism, during a period given to romance, many individualized types of the common run of small town people Simms ranks high among the few able pioneer delineators of the small town in the South."[80] J. H. Nelson has pointed out that Simms was the first novelist consistently to

The Roots of Southern Writing

assign Negroes parts of importance in his books;[81] and Stirling Brown says, "In numbers, and a certain rudimentary realism, the Negro characters in Simms's many novels go beyond those of any other early nineteenth century novelist."[82] The findings of these scholars indicate that in his novels on the Revolution Simms was carefully reconstructing in fictional form the social life of a past age. Apparently he applied to his own work with seriousness his dictum that "The business of the [novelist] is 'to hold the mirror up to nature,'—and whether the reflection be terrible or pleasing, is no part of his concern. Is the picture *true*? If true, the author has succeeded."[83]

Within these seven novels Simms accomplished his primary object of illustrating the Revolutionary War in South Carolina and the social conditions of the time. Although the books reveal many shortcomings when judged by belletristic standards, he succeeded admirably in presenting "probable truth under intenser conditions,"[84] a phrase which formed his definition of fiction. Within these books is preserved a wealth of local tradition about the Revolution available nowhere else, and the mixed motives, the ambiguous situations, the horrible atrocities, the fundamental brutality and evil of warfare in South Carolina between 1780 and 1783 find vivid and valuable expression. The student who goes to these novels will find a clear and realistic picture of social conditions during the period and a record in detail of some of the attitudes that the antebellum South took toward the struggle for independence.

The Influence of Scott
and Cooper on Simms

William Gilmore Simms's historical novels have usually been classified as frank imitations of those by James Fenimore Cooper.[1] Most of those who have questioned this view have gone to the other extreme of asserting that Simms was a picaresque realist with no debt whatsoever to Cooper, except in *The Yemassee*.[2] Although a few have seen in Simms's historical novels a combined influence of Cooper and Sir Walter Scott,[3] no one has examined the nature of these influences. The result has been a tendency either to ignore or to oversimplify the effect upon Simms's novels of his predecessors in the historical romance. Although Scott and Cooper were not the only writers who influenced Simms,[4] in this essay I will examine the ways in which their works affected Simms's seven loosely connected Revolutionary romances.[5] Long before this series of novels was complete, Simms recognized that it formed a distinct unit of his work,[6] and almost all critics have acknowledged that it represents his finest efforts.[7]

There is almost universal acceptance of the fact that Scott first successfully fused fiction and history into the historical novel and that the sudden flowering of the form in America and on the Continent as well as in England was the result of the application of Scott's pattern.[8] Both Cooper and Simms wrote in the tradition Scott established. What has been often overlooked is that both modified the Scott pattern to fit their needs and talents and that their modifications turned their work in opposing directions.

[I]

The pattern Scott evolved for the historical novel has several distinctive features, of all of which Simms was keenly aware and most of which he praised.

The essence of the Scott novel is an actual historical event of great dramatic interest. In the introductions to the Waverley Novels, Scott discussed his reasons for choosing the particular portion of history which serves as the basis of his plot. For example, in *The Fortunes of Nigel*, he wrote, "The reign of James I . . . gave unbounded scope to invention in the fable, while at the same time it afforded greater variety and discrimination of character than could, with historical consistency, have

The Roots of Southern Writing

been introduced, if the scene had been laid a century earlier."[9] The problem of telling a good story within this framework of "historical consistency" Scott solved by shifting interest from actual to fictional personages, Saintsbury, after studying the Waverley Novels, concluded, "The first law of the historical novel [is] that the nominal hero and heroine, the ostensibly central interest and story shall not be or concern historical persons...."[10] These imaginary characters are caught in a vast tug of war between great issues and personalities, and their reactions to the pressures of social, political, and military events make up the story itself and give a dramatic continuity to history. Everything is seen through the eyes of fictional characters, free of the bondage of record, and the story leaves a vivid impression of what the times and events did to people caught within them. It is much the same impression that Simms intended to convey, according to the aim he stated in *Mellichampe*: "My object usually has been to adhere, as closely as possible, to the features and the attributes of real life, as it is to be found in the precise scenes, and under the governing circumstances" (p. 6).

The fictional characters, however, become active though helpless participants in occurrences beyond their control; and Scott's stories of battles, intrigues, treacheries, and politics are finally shaped by the iron mould of history. This control of event and character by historical fact led Louis Reynaud to write, "Walter Scott, en dépit de son apparent idéalisme, part d'une conception de l'homme sourdement *déterministe* et *sensualiste*. Ses personnages ne sont pas libres."[11] Simms was keenly aware of this quality in Scott's novels. He wrote, "We have no respect for heroes placed always in subordinate positions—sent hither and thither —baffled by every breath of circumstance—creatures without will, and constantly governed by the caprices of other persons. This was the enfeebling characteristic in Scott's heroes."[12] He was at least partially conscious of the cause of the weakness, for he said, "Genius dare not take liberties with a history ... well known, and approaches her task with a cautious apprehensiveness which is inconsistent with her noblest executions."[13]

The employment of this method results in a highly complex story of the impact upon imaginary characters of the events of history. As the thread to hold this material together Scott used a central plot of hackneyed young lovers' adventures, of which he declared, in the Introductory Epistle to *The Fortunes of Nigel,* "What the devil does the plot signify, except to bring in fine things?" The attitude approaching contempt in which he held his heroes is shown by his calling Waverley "a very insipid sort of young man."[14]

To Simms Sir Walter Scott was the greatest of all novelists. Although he knew the works of G. P. R. James and Bulwer-Lytton, whose popularity in the South rivaled that of Scott,[15] Simms was critical of their craftsmanship in his reviews of their novels.[16] He recognized flaws in Scott's novels—the weakness of his heroes, the "stupidity" of his humorous "bores,"[17] his lack of metaphysical insight and psychological analysis of character[18]—but he regarded *Ivanhoe* as "one of the most perfect specimens of the romance that we possess,"[19] and praised it at the expense of Richardson and Fielding.[20] Scott he believed to be the perfect example of an ideal romancer. He wrote, "Scott, perhaps, of all [writers], has shown himself the most catholic; combining the peculiar powers of the *raconteur* with those of the poet, painter, and the analyst of events and character."[21] And he called him "more perfect, more complete and admirable, than any writer of his age."[22]

[II]

That Cooper felt the impact of Scott's work and employed his pattern for fiction is almost a literary truism; but in using the Scott formula Cooper made significant variations in it—variations which Simms recognized but of which he did not approve. Cooper freed the Scott novel from historical event, except in his single experiment in *Lionel Lincoln;* he simplified the plot; and he centered attention on a single great figure outside both history and the love story. He made serious efforts to recapture the spirit of a past age and frequently used one or two historical personages, but he usually set them outside the bondage of historical fact. *The Deerslayer*, for example, is laid in a period of warfare; but, as Gregory L. Paine has pointed out, it is free of historical incident.[23] *The Spy* portrays the effect upon fictional characters of being caught between great opposing forces, but the story itself is the purest fiction. A single historical figure, Washington, moves through the plot, but in an unhistoric role. One actual event, the execution of André, helps to shape the plot, but it has already occurred when the book opens. "An authentic account of the activities of the Cow-Boys and, more particularly, of the Skinners"[24] is given, but actual deeds from their ignoble annals are not used. The American Revolution is not a determinant of the action of *The Spy*, but a backdrop against which the incidents of the story work themselves out. As John Erskine has said, "None of it is historical in the same sense as the great episodes in *Kenilworth* or *The Abbot.*"[25]

At one time Cooper planned a series of thirteen historically exact novels on the Revolution in each of the colonies. He completed only the first, *Lionel Lincoln.* For it he did a thorough job of historical research, studying histories, state papers, and official documents;[26] but the book itself, although it is "remarkably successful in the handling of the purely historical material [is] a dismal failure as a whole."[27] Simms called *Lionel Lincoln* a failure,[28] and thus would hardly have used the only novel in which Cooper dealt seriously with historical event in the Scott manner as a model for his own work.

Simms recognized that an almost conscious shying away from formal history is, except in *Lionel Lincoln*, characteristic of Cooper, and he was willing to justify it, even though he did not follow it in his own practice. He said, "Possessed of the requisite resources of imagination, [Cooper] needs but a slender skein of raw material—a solitary item—a fragmentary fact—a word—an action,—and his mind instantly conceives the plan and purpose."[29] He was aware that *The Spy* is the story not of historical events, but of a single character. He wrote, "A large portion of it depended entirely on Harvey Birch, and, to so great a degree was this disparity carried, in the use of his *dramatis personae*, that, in some of the scenes between the Spy and Henry Wharton, the latter almost sinks into contempt."[30]

Where Scott turned over the control of his fictional story to his young lovers, Cooper, although retaining the love story, gave the focus of interest to complex characters relatively independent of both the young lover plot and the historical situation. Simms considered this characteristic in Cooper's work a flaw. "To manage the progress of one leading personage, and to concentrate in his portraiture his whole powers, has been," he declared, "the invariable secret of Mr. Cooper's success."[31] Figures like Harvey Birch, the Pilot, and Hawkeye so definitely control the stories in which they appear that they take command of our imaginations. Simms believed that these massive figures were always essentially the same person: "Hawkeye, the land sailor of Mr. Cooper, is, with certain suitable modifications, the same personage [as the Pilot].... It would not be difficult to trace Mr. Cooper's one ideal through all his novels. Even in the Bravo ... we find the Pilot and Natty Bumppo, where we should least look for them, in the person of Jacopo, the assassin of Venice."[32]

These major figures differ from Scott's in another important respect. Where Sir Walter's actors are, in Simms's phrase, "baffled by every breath of circumstance," Cooper's are masters of their destiny who, as Grossman has noted, "will not be encumbered with the ordinary obligations of life and for whom freedom is the absence of permanent involvement."[33] Simms commented at length on this characteristic: "With the self-reliance which is only found in true genius, he [any Cooper hero] goes forward into the wilderness, whether of land or ocean; and the vicissitudes of either region, acting upon the natural resources of one man's mind, furnish the whole material of his work-shop.... In the hour of danger ... it is inevitable, most usually, that such a man will save them, if they are to be saved."[34]

Cooper reduced the complexity of plot which appears in Scott novels into what Parrington has called "the uncomplicated problem of flight and pursuit."[35] Simms condemned the resulting simplicity of Cooper's work. Of *The Spy* he wrote: "The defect of the story was rather in its action than its characters. This is the usual and grand defect in all Mr. Cooper's stories. In truth, there is very little story. He seems to exercise none of his genius in the invention of his fable. There is none of that careful grouping of means to ends, and all, to the one end of the dénouëment, which so remarkably distinguished the genius of Scott.... Mr. Cooper surrenders himself to the progress of events. He leaves to one to beget and occasion the other."[36] In all Cooper's work he finds this characteristic flaw: "The plots were generally simple, not always coherent, and proving either an incapacity for, or an indifference to the exercise of much invention."[37] He contrasted what he considered to be Cooper's structural weaknesses with Scott's plots to the great discredit of the American novelist. Scott's, he wrote, "is the harmonious achievement. It is a tolerably easy thing to write a spirited sketch.... But the perfecting of the wondrous whole—the admirable adaptation of means to ends ... the fine architectural proportions of the fabric,—these are the essentials which determine the claim of the writer to be the BUILDER!—by whose standard other artists are to model,—by whose labours other labourers are to learn."[38]

Scott's novels are complex studies of manners laid in a past age, carefully done pictures of the effects of social and political forces upon men. In contrast, Cooper's adventure novels, except for the late "land rents" trilogy, are, as Grossman has pointed out, "relatively free of social complication.... [Almost] everything happens for the sake of the excitement of the action."[39] Simms deplored this characteristic. He said that "the mind of Mr. Cooper is limited in its grasp. It is too individual in its aims and agencies.... In Indian life and sailor life, he was almost uniformly successful—for the simple reason, that such stories called simply for the display of individual character."[40] In his own novels Simms set himself a task at variance with what he thought Cooper's to be, the task of "show[ing] the fluctuations of the contest, the spirit with which it was carried on and ... embody[ing] certain events of great individual interest ... and their influence upon the general history."[41] In short he set himself the task of writing fictionized social history.

The Roots of Southern Writing

Simms was a sound analyst both of the Scott pattern and of the significant variations which Cooper made in it, and he uniformly deplored the northern novelist's modifications. Yet he also made variations in Scott's pattern in his own historical novels. They were, however, modifications that carried his work further away from rather than closer to that of Cooper. *The Yemassee* is imitation Cooper; however, as Parrington has said, "The best of Simms is not in *The Yemassee*, but in those stirring tales of Marion's men.... The ghost of Cooper does not haunt their pages to challenge comparison."[42]

Simms's Revolutionary Romances consist of three disparate elements: formal history presented in nondramatic exposition; stiff and hackneyed central plots; and living and vividly presented portraits of common people. Their characters fall into three corresponding groups: historical figures, who are handled with chilling restraint; papier-mâché aristocrats, who seem to belong to a world of Froissart and Malory and who remain puppets; and minor figures, who are pictured with skill and verve and are believable human beings. This same basic trichotomy exists in Scott's novels, but Sir Walter acquired a kind of unstable unity by subordinating history to his plots and establishing believable relationships between his major and his minor characters. It is in Simms's failure to achieve a similar fusion that his modifications of Scott's pattern are most apparent.

Where Cooper modified the Scott novel by dispensing in large measure with actual history, Simms moved in an opposite direction, incorporating large blocks of straight history into his romances. From the beginning of the series, as he states in *The Partisan*, Simms planned works "devoted to the illustration of the war of the Revolution in South Carolina" (p. v). He viewed the seven novels as panels in one large historical picture, and he declared of the series, "I have endeavored to maintain a proper historical connection among these stories, corresponding with the several transitional periods of the Revolutionary War in South Carolina" (*The Forayers*, p. 3). They deal accurately and in detail with almost every event of historical importance and almost every historical actor in the South Carolina Low Country from the fall of Charleston on May 12, 1780, through its evacuation by the British in December 1782.[43] Simms the historian[44] is clearly seen at work in these romances, following his belief that "it is the true purpose of fiction to supply [history's] deficiencies, and to correct her judgments."[45] However, he believed that "the privileges of the romancer only begin where those of the historian cease,"[46] and he approached the formal history which shaped the structure and determined the events of these novels with a stubborn accuracy and respect. In *Mellichampe* he wrote, "The events made use of are all historical; and scarcely a page of the work, certainly not a chapter of it, is wanting in the evidence which must support the assertion" (p. 2). In these works he used the material resources of history without violating them.

His respect for history was too great. In *The Partisan* he said, "The evidence is closed—the testimony now irrefutable—and imagination, however audacious in her own province, only ventures to embody and model those features of the Past, which sober History has left indistinct" (p. ix). He obeyed this self-imposed injunction to an extent that would have seemed incredible to Scott, whose books are loaded with notes explaining the conscious liberties that he took with recorded fact. Here the historian came in conflict with the novelist who quite properly believed that fiction should be presented in action and dialogue, not in description and narration;[47] and unfortunately the antiquarian won over the artist. With a very few exceptions the historical personages in the novels are described, estimated, viewed from a distance, but allowed to take no active part in the stories. Francis Marion, the leader of the Partisan revolt in the area in which six of the seven novels are laid (*The Scout* takes place in territory where Sumter was the leader), is the hero of the historical actions which the books describe, but he never becomes a character in the novels. He remains an historical figure, larger than life and strangely impersonal, stiffly holding the postures of formal record. He is described; his acts are recounted; his speeches are quoted; but he assumes no dramatic relation to any of the actors of the fictional drama. Placed beside the Elizabeth or Mary Queen of the Scots or James I or Louis XI of Sir Walter Scott, the figure of Marion reveals how completely Simms felt the restraint of history.

Simms employed as the framework within which each of the stories is cast a fairly complete picture of military events in South Carolina between 1780 and 1783. Each novel in the series, except *Woodcraft* and *Eutaw*, opens with an historical summary; and paragraphs, sections, and chapters explaining conditions, events, and past experiences of historical figures frequently interrupt the narrative. Pure historical exposition is used in the chapters describing major battles.[48] No attempt is made to dramatize, much less fictionalize, these masses of history.

Thus in large measure actual historical personages and events are not presented dramatically. We do not see the historical action through the eyes of the characters and do not experience it vicariously. Its appeal is almost solely to our intellect, rather than to our emotions, and we view it with the attitude with which we usually view a painting, not with the emotional response with which we witness a play. This is in sharp contrast to Scott's method of reporting history through the eyes and feelings of fictional characters. Simms declared that "it is to fiction that we must chiefly look for those living and breathing creations which history quite too unfrequently deigns to summon to her service. The warm atmosphere of present emotions, and present purposes, belongs to the *dramatis personae* of art."[49] But where Scott used history to create this art, Simms feared to breathe into it that "warm atmosphere of present emotions" so essential to the novel.

When we compare the historical accuracy of the Revolutionary Romances with the haziness of *Ivanhoe* or the historical freedom of *Kenilworth* and *Quentin Durward* or the lengthy footnotes in which Scott paid the lip service of correction to the history whose confidence he had violated, we see that where Scott used history for the purposes of romance, Simms used the romance for the purposes of social history. And if the cold mass of accurate historical fact in Simms's novels is compared with the absence of formal history in *The Spy* or *The Deerslayer*, one becomes acutely aware that in their use of history Cooper and Simms were each closer to Scott than either was to the other.

In the general structure of the Revolutionary Romances Simms followed Scott's pattern closely. From the Waverley Novels he borrowed the stock hero and heroine and their conventional love story, and like Scott he dutifully put his young aristocrats through their paces and used them as the only unifying threads in the novels. With the exception of *Woodcraft* each of the romances is centered on love situations. *The Partisan* and *Katharine Walton* together recount the love story of Robert Singleton, a Partisan officer, and Katherine Walton, the daughter of a plantation owner. A British officer who attempts to force Katharine to marry him is the villain. In *The Scout* both Clarence Conway, the patriot hero, and Edward, his half-brother and the Tory villain, are in love with Flora Middleton. In *Mellichampe* Ernest Mellichampe, the hero and a Partisan officer, is in love with Janet Berkeley, the daughter of a Loyalist. The Tory villain attempts to force Janet to marry him. In *The Forayers* and *Eutaw* Willie Sinclair, a Partisan officer but the son of a Loyalist, is in love with Bertha Travis, the daughter of a Tory. The Tory villain attempts to use force to gain Bertha's hand in marriage. Only in *Woodcraft* did Simms deviate from this hackneyed central plot. In that novel he centered his story on his comic character Porgy.

For this central situation Simms's debt is to Scott rather than to Cooper. Cooper, although he employed a story of young lovers in most of his novels, centered interest in some character who has only peripheral relationships to the love story. Although many critics have pointed out the weakness that resulted from Simms's failure to follow Cooper in this respect,[50] they seem to have overlooked the possibility that Simms, in failing to produce such a character, was not unsuccessfully copying Cooper but was rather going back to Scott's method and eschewing a characteristic of Cooper's work which Simms considered to be a flaw.

Simms's criticism of Cooper's novels makes it clear that he did not approve of the simple plots which the northern writer used and that he regarded Scott's more complex stories as superior to them. In his Revolutionary Romances he put this judgment into practice. Exclusive of historical figures and fictional creations who play minor roles, Simms created ninety-eight characters for these seven novels. He crowded the books with subplots, incidents, and characters only loosely related to the central love story and, though related to actual events, playing no historical parts. The tendency to subordinate the main plot to the activities of minor characters is present in *The Partisan* and is accentuated in later books of the series, until in *The Forayers* and *Eutaw* the love story is abandoned for such long intervals that the reader has difficulty in picking it up again when Simms returns to it.

This prodigal mass of loosely connected incident would tempt one to agree with Parrington that the pattern of the romances is picaresque,[51] if many of Scott's novels did not have a similar construction. In each of these romances there is, as Parrington said of *The Yemassee*, enough material "to serve Cooper for half a dozen tales."[52]

It is in the dozens of minor characters realistically drawn from low life and in the hundreds of incidents in which they act that the Revolutionary Romances appear to us to have their greatest value both as literature and as accurate pictures of the social conditions of the age they describe. In characters like Hurricane Nell, Hell-Fire Dick, the Blonays, the Blodgits, Thumbscrew, Jack Bannister, and Sam Bostwick, Simms gave believable and realistic sketches of the lowest levels of life during the Revolution. It is sometimes implied in modern criticism that in characters such as these and in the robust incidents in which they act, Simms was satisfying a "strong instinct for reality," which was unfortunately almost smothered by the romantic taste of the world in which he lived and which he attempted to please.[53] Actually, in the use of such characters and incidents, Simms was doing almost exactly what Scott had done. For as Samuel C. Chew has said, "[Scott's] greatest creations usually have but a small part in the conventional plot of the story or are altogether independent of it."[54] And Scott declared of himself, "I am a bad hand at depicting a hero ... and have an unfortunate propensity for the dubious characters of Borderers, buccaneers, Highland robbers, and all others of a Robin Hood description."[55]

The Roots of Southern Writing

Much of present-day criticism of Scott's novels is similar to the praise given Simms's "realism." Hugh Walpole has called Scott "a realist working in a romantic world."[56] Jacques Barzun believes that Scott's central figures are put in "to help out the management of the main business" and that "he was mainly a realist."[57] These views are typical of much present-day criticism of the Waverley Novels.[58] That criticism of Simms should have such a parallel to that of Scott is not surprising, since Simms followed Scott in crowding his pages with honestly observed and accurately portrayed people from the lower walks of life in the belief—which both men held—that meaningful historical fiction is primarily a study of manners and social conditions.

Thus it appears that Simms modified Scott's method significantly in placing greater emphasis on historical accuracy and in treating history in expository rather than dramatic style, but he owed a debt, implicitly acknowledged, to Scott for the central structure of his Revolutionary Romances, for his stiffly starched aristocrats, and for the wealth of richly realized incidents and low-life characters which give his works their principal literary value. Those qualities which have led some critics to call Simms's novels picaresque and to regard him as a nascent realist stifled by an overly romantic environment—his accurate pictures of common life and his realistic portrayal of common people—were also present in the work of his acknowledged literary master Scott, whom he called "the BUILDER!—by whose standard other artists are to model,—by whose labours other labourers are to learn."

There are no simple and final answers to the problem of Scott's and Cooper's influences on Simms's Revolutionary Romances. Certainly little can be gained by attempting to find parallels to individual characters and incidents in Simms's work in that of the other writers, for all three share a large area of common material and method. For example, Dr. Oakenburg, in *The Partisan* and *Woodcraft*, is a loquacious physician and a bore who seems to have marked similarities to Dr. Sitgreaves in *The Spy;* yet similar bores appear frequently in Scott's work, and Simms himself pointed out the similarity of such characters in Cooper's books to those in the Waverley Novels.[59] Hurricane Nell, in *Eutaw*, a half-mad girl with the gift of second sight, has similarities to Hetty Hunter in *The Deerslayer*, to Meg Merrilies in *Guy Mannering*, and to Norma of the Fitful Head in *The Pirate*.

Certainly Simms was indebted to Cooper. In the sense that he attempted to do for his region what Cooper had done for his, the judgment that he was a "southern Cooper" is true. He declared, "To Mr. Cooper the merit is due, of having first awakened us to this self-reference—to this consciousness of mental resources.... The Americanism of Mr.

Cooper would move us to forgive him all his faults, were they twice as many."[60] Simms followed a trail blazed by the northern novelist, a trail he might have been unable to follow without the courage he gained from the large footprints of Hawkeye and Harvey Birch. He credited Cooper with "having struck the vein [of a national literature], and convinced the people, not only that there was gold in the land, but that the gold of the land was good."[61]

Yet his criticism of Cooper and Scott shows that Simms recognized that Cooper had modified the Scott pattern and that he did not approve of the modifications. For him Scott was the admitted master. It is entirely possible that Simms set out consciously to do for the South what Cooper had done for his section, but the model he followed was that of Sir Walter Scott. The result is that he eschewed Cooper's variations and that almost everything present in the Revolutionary Romances has a recognizable parallel in method in the Waverley Novels, except for the chilling restraint with which Simms handled history. His structural debts are to the Scottish master.

It is in a sense ironic that Simms's greatest weaknesses are in those places where he is least like Cooper. Had he imitated the northern novelist in shifting interest away from the aristocratic lovers to more robust central figures, the individual books would have had far greater unity and interest. Had he created a figure like Natty Bumppo to serve as a focal point for the panoramic picture which he paints, he might have fused the seven separate novels into an impressive prose epic. Had he been willing to free himself from the harsh bondage of historical fact and been content to do almost exclusively what he did best—picture the social conditions of the Revolution through fictional characters—the books would not suffer so greatly from unevenness of dramatic tone and impact. In several important respects Simms's Revolutionary Romances suffered, not because he imitated Cooper, but because he did not.

Simms and the British Dramatists

That the works of William Godwin, Sir Walter Scott, and James Fenimore Cooper contributed significantly to the patterns, structures, and
plots of William Gilmore Simms's novels has been generally accepted. It
has not been pointed out, however, that one of the shaping influences on
his handling of character and situation within the framework these
writers contributed was the drama of the English Renaissance and Restoration. Its influence on his diction and on the uninhibited gusto of his
writing has been noted,[1] and the assumption that his greatest comic
character, Porgy, was a direct imitation of Shakespeare's Falstaff has
been made frequently.[2] But an examination of Simms's methods of
characterization in his seven connected Revolutionary Romances[3]—his
most serious and ambitious novelistic project—reveals that the British
dramatists were his tutors in more than diction and that Porgy, rather
than being an exception to Simms's usual practice in characterization, is
actually in keeping with his method and has but superficial similarities
to Falstaff.

That Simms knew the English dramatists well is clear. He was a student of Shakespeare, wrote articles on him, and annotated some of his
plays.[4] He edited a collection of Shakespeare apocrypha,[5] and in its general introduction and the introductions to the individual plays he demonstrated a thorough and loving acquaintance with the drama of Shakespeare's age, even though he lacked the scholarly equipment needed for
the task he had set himself in the volume. He wrote two five-act blank
verse dramas, *Norman Maurice* (1851) and *Michael Bonham* (1852);
and at the request of his friend Edwin Forrest, the actor, he adapted
Timon of Athens for the nineteenth-century stage.[6] During Simms's
adult life the Charleston theaters presented plays by many of the British
dramatists of the Renaissance, Restoration, and eighteenth century.
Among the playwrights whose works were presented were Addison,
Beaumont and Fletcher, Cibber, the Colemans, Cumberland, Farquhar,
Fielding, Garrick, Nathaniel Lee, Lillo, Massinger, Murphy, Otway,
Phillips, Rowe, Shakespeare (twenty-three plays), Sheridan, and Thomson. The plays of many of these dramatists were repeated frequently
throughout the antebellum period.[7] Simms's intimate friends Timrod
and Hayne were well read in Elizabethan drama, and Timrod more
than once complained that Simms was attributing a Dekker passage to
Middleton.[8]

Grace W. Whaley, after examining the quotations and allusions in eighteen volumes of Simms's fiction, concluded, "The comparatively large numbers of quotations from Elizabethan dramatists is striking."[9] Of 306 quotations she found that 180, or almost fifty-nine percent, were from Shakespeare, Beaumont and Fletcher, Jonson, Shirley, Massinger, Middleton, Webster, Heywood, Chapman, Marlowe, Dekker, Greene, and Brome. Simms listed Shakespeare, Marlowe, Beaumont and Fletcher, Peele, Greene, Dekker, and Jonson as being among the world's immortal story-tellers.[10] Of Porgy, a character of whom Trent wrote, "I have it on good authority that he intended Porgy to be a reproduction of himself in certain moods,"[11] Simms said in *Woodcraft* (p. 369), "Porgy, before entering the army, was well read in Shakspere, Milton, Dryden, and the best of the then current English writers. It must be admitted, we fear, that he had also drank [*sic*] freely of fountains less undefiled; had dipped largely into the subsequent pages of the Wycherlys, the Vanbrughs, the Congreves, the Wilmots, Etsereges, and Rochesters."

It is equally clear that Simms did not regard the methods of the dramatist as distinct from those of the novelists. He believed that the historical romance was "the substitute of modern times for the epic or the drama. ... The differences between them depend on the material employed, rather than upon the particular mode in which it is used."[12] In writing novels on American history, Simms employed Scott's structure, but naturally turned for technique to the plays of the English Renaissance, which he called "the great period in the literary history of Great Britain." In fact he admonished fellow historical novelists: "English history, from the time of the Eighth Henry to the First Stuart, will be best read in the records of the courts, and in the dramatic literature of the same period. They should be studied by him who seeks to turn to account our first American period in history."[13]

The drama which he knew and loved had created great characters and revealed complex motives through action, dialogue, and soliloquy; and these were the methods which Simms employed to create many of the figures in his Revolutionary Romances. Except for sections of exposition on a character's background and passages dealing with actual history, which he treated with an historian's formal and nondramatic reserve, there are few places in these novels where the reader learns more about a character than he would from witnessing the action and overhearing the speech of an actor on the stage.

Simms seldom attempts to enter a character's mind by the use of the author's omniscience. In fact he frequently disclaims knowledge of a character's thoughts or motives except as they can be inferred from action and speech. A passage in *The Forayers* illustrates this method of characterization clearly. Bertha Travis's brother Henry has brought her to the bank of a small stream where she is to meet her lover, Willie Sinclair. Sinclair has fallen asleep while awaiting her:

> Bertha walked around her lover, looked down upon him, stole nearer, looked out to see if Henry's eyes could watch her as well as the wood, and, *seemingly* satisfied of the impossibility of his doing the feat, she suffered herself to sink down near the head of our sleeping dragoon.
>
> Sinclair slept profoundly, breathing easily and gently, as if no load lay upon his chest or conscience. Bertha watched the noble ingenuous face as it lay revealed beneath the starlight, and she thought—*ah! that is beyond us—we really know not what she thought. But unquestionably thought was busy in her little brain, and feeling in her heart.* The picture made her think. The feminine mind thinks through pictures, precisely as does that of genius. . . .
>
> *We have no right to pry into Bertha's thoughts, but we may watch her conduct.* She gazed, for long, upon the face of the sleeper, *seeming* never weary of the gaze[;] after awhile her hands lifted his hair—he had made a pillow of his cap—and drew out the long masses, which had grown in the busy excitement of war . . . and, playing with his hair, and looking in his face—Bertha finally—slept also!—her head being quietly suffered to rest beside her lover's—while one of her arms—of course without her consciousness—stretched over and rested upon his bosom. (pp. 359–360; italics mine)

This scene, unusual only in the author's insistence in disclaiming knowledge of his character's thoughts, is clearly an example of a sequence visualized and reproduced by description of action. Simms apparently was so pleased with what he was doing that he stopped to congratulate himself: "The feminine mind thinks though pictures, precisely as does that of genius."

Another effective use of description of action to convey thought and emotion occurs in *The Partisan* when the illegitimate Ned Blonay forces his white mother to tell him the truth about his Indian father:

> She did so, passively as it were, and in a low tone, broken only by her own pauses and his occasional exclamations, she poured into his ear a dark, foul narrative of criminal intercourse, provoked on her part by a diseased appetite, resulting, as it would seem, in punishment, in the birth of a monster like himself. Yet he listened to it, if not passively at least without any show of emotion or indignation; and as she finished, and hurrying away from him threw herself into her old seat, and covered her skinny face with her hands, he simply thrust his fingers into the long straight black hair depending over his eyes, which seemed to carry confirmatory evidence enough for the support of the story to which he had listened. He made no other movement, but appeared, for a while, busy

in reflection. She every now and then looked towards him doubtfully, and with an aspect which had in it something of apprehension. At length, rising, though with an air of effort, from the couch, he took a paper from his pocket which he studied a little while by the blaze in the chimney, then approaching her, he spoke in language utterly unaffected by what he had heard—

"Hark ye, mother; I shall now go back to the camp. . . ." (p. 198)

These scenes are typical of Simms's methods of presenting characters' thoughts and reactions through a description of "stage business." But there are situations and emotions which do not yield themselves readily to such treatment. The dramatists whom Simms loved had found a solution to such problems in the soliloquy, and he often adopted their method in his novels. In *The Forayers* there occurs this passage reminiscent of Iago or Richard iii:

And when he had gone, the eyes of Inglehardt darkened into a scowl— and he muttered [to himself]:—

"I have him under my heel—have her at my mercy, or *will* have her— and we shall soon see who shall be the scorned and who the scorner? [*sic*] He can not elude me—can not escape—and he knows it! He will and must use the arguments I put into his mouth, and she must submit. Ha! ha! She shall to the altar, or he to the halter!" (p. 134)

Bombastically melodramatic though this soliloquy is, the distorted voice of a Shakespearean villain can be faintly heard behind it, even in the semipun with which it ends.

A clearer—although less amusing—example of Simms's use of the soliloquy occurs in *Eutaw*. Hurricane Nell Floyd, who has often been told that she is insane, is riding alone:

Even as she rides now . . . she asks, communing only with herself:—

"It is true? Am I crazed? Is there insanity in my blood and brain, as all these people tell me? Are my actions ordered by no reason? Do I not think as other women, feel as other women, understand as quickly, and compare and act as justly? I know not—I know not! My poor head! If I am not already crazed, they will make me so, if I keep with them any longer. I must break away from them altogether. . . ." [A page of this self-examination follows.]

And as she rode, at a smart canter, she continued to soliloquize after the same fashion. . . . They [her soliloquies] will probably afford us some clues to her own history as well as character:—

"Is it because I have been schooled differently from my people—that I have read many books—that I have heard the speech of those who were rich. . . ." [A soliloquy on her past history continues for about a page.]

Of these glimpses of her past, which she gives us in this rambling manner, we know nothing more. Of the Lady Nelson—in that day in America, it was customary to call the wives of very wealthy and distinguished persons by this title—of Bettie, and Sherrod Nelson, we hear from her lips for the first time. But we can follow these clues sufficiently to form some idea of the peculiar education of the orphan-girl, in the hands of a liberal, wealthy, and enlightened patronage. (pp. 69–72)

The echoes of Shylock in the first part of this quotation seem almost too obvious to require being pointed out.

That Simms conceived these soliloquies as being parts of dramatic scenes becomes apparent in the following sequence from *The Partisan:* Robert Singleton is approaching his lover-cousin's estate alone by night:

A passionate phase of thought broke forth in his half-muttered soliloquy:—

"How I remember as I look; it is not only the woods and the grounds— the river and the spot—but the very skies are here.... [He is brooding aloud on the scenes of earlier lovers' quarrels.]

"...And yet, none love her as I do; I must love on in spite of pride, and scorn, and indifference—I cannot choose but love her."

It is evident that Major Singleton is by no means sure of his ground, as a lover. His doubts are, perhaps, natural enough, and, up to a certain period, must be shared by all who love. His musings, *as we may conjecture*, had for their object his fair cousin, the beautiful Kate Walton. ...Meanwhile, the return of Humphries from his scouting expedition *arrests our farther speculations on this topic, along with the soliloquy of our companion.* (pp. 130–131; italics mine)

These examples of his use of action for character revelation and of soliloquy for presentation of motive and attitude indicate that Simms borrowed at least a part of his method for presenting his characters from the drama; and his frequent comments on his method indicate that his use of it was self-conscious.

But Simms's debt to English drama did not consist solely in his use of dramatic means for the presentation of character; it is also apparent in his use of the "humours" character, as it was evolved by Ben Jonson and employed by the Jacobean and Restoration playwrights. Jonson explains this character formula thus:

Some one peculiar quality
Doth so possess a man, that it doth draw
All his affects, his spirits, and his powers,
In their confluctions, all to run one way.[14]

This exhibition of predominating passion Simms declared to be an effective means of characterization.[15] The method is unusually effective for creating type characters, and it lends itself readily to comic situations. A number of figures in the Revolutionary Romances are plainly humours characters. In *The Scout* Supple Jack Bannister's garrulity is emphasized sufficiently to be called a humour. In *The Forayers* and *Eutaw* the greed for gold that drives Mother Blodgit to recommend murder and the most horrible cruelties represents the humour employed for gothic effects rather than for comedy; and Nell Floyd's obsession that her brother must be saved from the hanging which she foresees for him drives her to almost every action she performs before his death. In the same novels Jim Ballou becomes a more interesting and a more amusing character because of his infinite thirst for Jamaica rum and his oath to touch it no more. In *The Partisan* Dr. Oakenburg has a passion for snakes which leads him to seek them constantly, although he is a physical coward. These are characters whose most interesting and dominant traits represent the exaggeration of a single passion or appetite or quality until it controls almost all that person's actions. It is not an unusual method of characterization, and it might be dismissed as not indicative of such an influence as I am suggesting were it not that several characters in these novels seem to have been modeled, at least in part, on personages in British plays.

In *The Scout* Surgeon Hillhouse, whom Lord Rawdon leaves at the Middleton estate to treat the wounded leader of the Black Riders, is a fop straight from the pages of the Restoration comedy of manners. A brave enough man when fighting must be done and a good surgeon, Hillhouse becomes a veritable Sir Fopling Flutter[16] when he is off duty. Hillhouse, who is actually a very ugly person, "when he considered how hopeless it was, in one man, to attempt to render all [women] happy ... deplored the fate which had made him irresistible, and regretted that but a single life was allowed to execute all the desires even of universal genius" (p. 296). He detests everything in America, which he considers a crude and unmannered country, although he wants to win Flora Middleton, an American of true culture, and take her back to England as a beautiful savage princess, what he calls *"la belle sauvage* ... like Powkerhorontas" (p. 395). But his great affectation is his dress. "He had his purple and his violet, his green and his ombre, the one was for the day of his valor, the other for his sentiment, the third for his love-sadness, and the fourth for his feeling of universal melancholy" (p. 305). When he is about to propose to Flora, he declares (p. 366) : " 'I wish to put on a dove-colored suit. The dress which I now wear, does not suit the day, the circumstances, nor my present feelings.... I have always striven to make my costume correspond with the particular feeling that affects me. My feelings are classed under different heads and orders, which have their subdivisions in turn ... for all of which I have been long provided with a suitable color and costume.' " When the house is about to be attacked by the Black Riders, he attires himself in his finest full-dress crimson regimentals and explains: " 'The idea of this extreme danger, alone, sir, prompted me to this display.... In the conviction, sir that I might be called upon this day, to make my last public appearance, I have been at special pains to prepare my person to the best advantage, for the inspection of the fortunate persons who will make the final disposition of it ...' " (p. 438).

In *Katharine Walton* two British officers, Major Barry and Captain M'Mahon, are also twins of Sir Benjamin Backbite and Crabtree in Sheridan's *The School for Scandal*. Both are dandies, delighting in ladies' company; both have malicious tongues; and Barry composes extempore verses that M'Mahon insists on reading. At a social gathering a group is discussing, in true scandal school fashion, Colonel Balfour's deserting Moll Harvey for Katherine Walton. M'Mahon says:

"Ah, my friend Major Barry always discriminates the point most admirably. You must let me repeat his impromptu, made this morning as we left the hairdresser's on this very subject."

"Nay, now, M'Mahon, my dear fellow, honor bright!" and the deft and tidy little major affected to be horror-stricken at the threatened exposure, while his little eyes twinkled with his anticipated triumph.

"Oh, but I must repeat, Barry."

[The crowd insists that M'Mahon must read the verses.]

"If my friend, Major Barry, will only consent," said M'Mahon.

"I won't stay to listen, M'Mahon," cried Barry, trotting out of the circle, but immediately passing to its rear, where his short person might remain unsuspected; his ears, meanwhile, drinking in the precious streams of his own inspiration....

M'Mahon recites—

"When bounteous Fate decreed our Harvey's birth,
We felt that heaven might yet be found on earth;
But when the Walton to our eyes was given,
We knew that man might yet be raised to heaven.
Indulgent Fates, one blessing more bestow—
Give me with Harvey long to dwell below;
And when, at last, ye summon me above,
Then let the Walton be my heavenly love!"

"Bravo! bravo! Harry Barry for ever and his friend M'Mahon!" cried Major Stock, and the circle echoed the applause.

"And he did it, my friend Barry," said M'Mahon, with the sweetest simplicity of manner—"he did it in the twinkling of an eye, just as we left the hairdresser's. I was determined that it shouldn't be lost, and went back and wrote it down."[17]

In *Woodcraft* Sergeant Millhouse is another character who shows the influence of the early drama. His peculiar quality is an exaggeration of "practicality" until it becomes a "humour." He comes back with the Epicurean Captain Porgy to the dilapidated Glen-Eberley estate and becomes self-appointed overseer of the plantation. He institutes a regimen of hard work and no pleasure for all the hands and for his fun-loving and improvident captain. The plantation horses are not to be taken from the fields for hunting; no holidays are to be observed; when Porgy makes a gift to little Dory Bostwick, who desperately needs the money, he is censured for being extravagant. The sergeant finally decides that Porgy should not marry the poor widow in whom he is interested but the wealthy Mrs. Eveleigh, and sets about arranging the match to the great embarrassment of both parties. For Millhouse everything finally boils down to a question of whether it will make or save money. He tells Porgy (pp. 290–291):

> "You see your ixperience is jest none at all in the way of business. You don't know what's useful in the world. You only know what's pleasant, and amusing, and ridickilous, and what belongs to music, and poetry, and the soul; and not about the wisdom that makes crops grow, and drives a keen bargain, and swells the money-box, and keeps the kiver down. Now, I reckon, you'd always git the worst of it at a horse-swap. You'd be cheated with a blind horse, or a spavin'd, and you'd go off on three legs though you come on four. Now, ef there's wisdom in this world—that is *raal* wisdom—it is in making a crop, driving a bargain, gitting the whip hand in a trade, and always falling, like a cat, on one's legs. As for music and po'try and them things, it's all flummery. They don't make the pot bile...."

Certainly this character owes a debt, either direct or indirect, to Ben Jonson and the theory of humours.

Thus we see that Simms frequently employed dramatic devices for the presentation of character through action and soliloquy and often used characters who in their conception seem to bear a marked kinship to the humours creations of the English drama.

It is, perhaps, because this frequent method of characterization has gone unnoticed that most critics have been so sharply aware of the Elizabethan quality of Lieutenant (later Captain) Porgy, the character who was Simms's most successful creation, with the result that they have interpreted certain superficial qualities which he has in common with Falstaff as indicating Simms's conscious imitation of the fat knight of Eastcheap.

Porgy, owner of Glen-Eberley, a plantation on the Ashepoo River, and a member of Marion's troops, is introduced in *The Partisan* and reappears in each of the Revolutionary Romances except *The Scout*. He has a bulging belly, spindle shanks, an affinity for low characters, a great love for fine food and cooking, a delight in practical jokes, an elaborate conversational style, salty wit, and a convincing zest for living. A member of the patrician class, he has squandered his substance in riotous living, and his plantation is badly dilapidated and heavily mortgaged. It is upon this somewhat convincing accumulation of qualities that the belief that Simms modeled Porgy on Shakespeare's Falstaff rests.[18]

In *The Partisan* Simms wrote two long discussions of Porgy's character:

At a glance you saw that he was a jovial philosopher—one who enjoyed his bottle with his humours, and did not suffer the one to be soured by the other. It was clear that he loved all the good things of this life, and some possibly that we may not call good with sufficient reason. His abdomen and brains seemed to work together. He thought of eating perpetually, and, while he ate, still thought. But he was not a mere eater. He rather amused himself with a hobby when he made food his topic, as Falstaff discoursed of his own cowardice without feeling it. He was a wag, and exercised his wit with whomsoever he travelled. . . .

. . . Porgy was a good looking fellow, spite of his mammoth dimensions. He had a fine fresh manly face, clear complexion, and light blue eye, the archness of which was greatly heightened by its comparative littleness. (pp. 110–111)

. . . Porgy had taste. In the affairs of the cuisine, Porgy claimed to have a genius. Now, it will not do to misconceive Lieutenant Porgy. If we have said or shown anything calculated to lessen his dignity in the eyes of any of our readers, remorse must follow. Porgy might *play* the buffoon, if he pleased; but in the mean time, let it be understood, that he was born to wealth, and had received the education of a gentleman. He had wasted his substance, perhaps, but this matter does not much concern us now. It is only important that he should not be supposed to waste himself. He had been a planter—was, in some measure, a planter still, with broken fortunes, upon the Ashepoo. "He had had losses," but he bore them like a philosopher. He was a sort of laughing philosopher, who, as if in anticipation of the free speech of others, dealt with himself as little mercifully as his nearest friends might have done. He had established for himself a sort of reputation as a humourist, and was one of that class which we may call conventional. His humour belonged to sophistication. It was the fruit of an artificial nature. He jested with his own tastes, his own bulk of body, his own poverty, and thus baffled the more serious jests of the ill-tempered by anticipating them. We may mention here, that while making the greatest fuss, always about his feeding, he was one of the most temperate eaters in the world. (pp. 358–359)

The author's statements about his character, of which the two just given are unusual only in their length, show plainly that the theory of humours was in his mind when he conceived Porgy, but they indicate also an attitude toward the captain that casts suspicion on the idea that he is a copy of Falstaff.

Hampton M. Jarrell summarizes the evidence that Porgy is a copy of Falstaff thus: Simms was acquainted with Shakespeare's work; he mentions Falstaff in connection with Porgy once (in the first of the above quotations); Porgy himself refers to Falstaff once (in *Eutaw*, p. 351, he says: "Do you remember how the fat knight of Eastcheap conquered Sir Coleville of the Dale. We felt on taking our raw Irishman as Falstaff did in that conquest, and said to them—almost in his language—'Like kind fellows ye gave yourselves away, and I thank ye for yourselves.'"); Falstaff and Porgy both like strong drink; both employ casuistry and euphuism in speaking; both have enormous bellies and spindle shanks; both give comic relief amid scenes of war but have no serious connections with the plots; after the war both are the center of plots in which they court two widows, Porgy in *Woodcraft* and Falstaff in *The Merry Wives of Windsor*. Jarrell concludes, "It seems to me that we are safe in saying that Simms did use Falstaff as a 'sort of painter's model.'"

However, several of the similarities that Jarrell points out can be explained quite easily without taking the view that Falstaff was "a sort of painter's model" for Porgy. On the same page on which Simms mentions Falstaff in connection with Porgy (p. 110), he refers to the Carolinian as being like Sancho in Cervantes' *Don Quixote*. Although Porgy refers to Falstaff once, he is given to quotations and paraphrases from Shakespeare, and the comparison which he makes of himself with the fat knight of Eastcheap implies similarity of action rather than of character. Porgy's love for food and drink are largely affectation, "the fruit of an artificial nature," and he is actually very temperate. That Porgy employs casuistry and euphuism in speaking does not set him off from many of Simms's other characters; Elizabethan diction was characteristic of Simms's work.[19] The similarity of the situations in *Woodcraft* and *The Merry Wives of Windsor* has been exaggerated, for they have only the faintest echoes in common. By far the greatest portion of *Woodcraft* is concerned with action arising out of Porgy's destitute condition and the villanies of Bostwick and M'Kewn. The idea that Porgy should marry Mrs. Eveleigh is Sergeant Millhouse's, and the sergeant's attempts to carry out a courtship for Porgy against his wishes form some of the best incidents in the novel. The comedy of the situation, quite different from that of *The Merry Wives*, arises from Porgy's unwilling courtship of the wealthy widow, rather than from his pursuit of her. After the major plot has ended in Porgy's financial security, he finally goes to Mrs. Eveleigh with a proposal of marriage because Sergeant Millhouse has convinced him that the widow is frantically in love with him; and it is with obvious relief, rather than chagrin, that he receives her rejection (*Woodcraft*, p. 513). Porgy's liking for Mrs. Griffin, the other widow in the novel, began in an earlier book, *Katharine Walton;* his turning to her after his rejection by Mrs. Eveleigh represents no last-minute shift of affections. That she was already engaged to another man when Porgy came to propose, however, causes him pain and embarrassment, but saves him for the proposed but unwritten sequel, *The Humors of Glen Eberly*.[20] In *Woodcraft* there are no Mistress Fords, no Mistress Pages, no Mistress Quicklys, no disguises, no escapes in buck-baskets with soiled linen or in the disguise of the witch of Brainford, and no characters or incidents reminiscent of these people and happenings.

The similarities between Porgy and Falstaff are finally reduced to physical appearance, delight in low companions, a convincing zest for life, and the role of comic relief in time of war. Porgy is brave, kind, and generous, truthful and honest, given to horseplay, but a lover of poetry and music.[21] Most of his "Falstaffian" characteristics are worn as affectations to protect him from an insensitive world. One would be rash indeed to attempt to summarize a character who has meant so many things to so many people as Falstaff has; but certainly the qualities listed for Porgy are hardly applicable, at least in their majority, to the fat knight. Jarrell thinks that Simms was attempting to capture "the roguish charm of Falstaff" in a character containing "all the qualities necessary to the Southern gentleman" (p. 209). But an examination of Porgy's character reveals that he was in no sense a rogue, unless squandering wealth makes one roguish. Those qualities which seem most essentially to be Falstaff's appear as surface artificialities in Porgy; those qualities which seem most essentially to be Porgy's appear not at all in Falstaff.

Simms himself is responsible for one statement which should cause one to look with suspicion on the effort to press to any great extent a similarity between the two characters. In his introduction to the play *Sir John Oldcastle* he wrote:

Sir John Wrotham, who is meant to be a Falstaff, with the additional virtue of courage, might have been successful, but that Falstaff stood in his way. Whether drawn by Shakspeare or another, the character of Sir John of Wrotham fails only as it reminds us that we have known Falstaff. It was this knowledge that paralyzed the effort to repaint the character under another name, and with additional attributes. Our "sweet Jack Falstaff," "kind Jack Falstaff," "true Jack Falstaff," "valiant and plump Jack Falstaff," is already sufficiently perfect; and an accumulation of more virtues in his character might only withdraw him in some degree from our sympathies. Sir John of Wrotham is a failure; but we see what he might have been, but for the overwhelming excellence of his predecessor. (*Supplement to Shakspeare's Plays*, p. 89)

This opinion was published in 1848. At that time Porgy had appeared in *The Partisan* and *Mellichampe*. After 1848 the fat captain of Partisans appeared in minor roles in three novels and played the hero in *Woodcraft*. Simms would have been flying in the face of inevitable defeat, according to his own judgment, if he actually had intended his fat captain as a American "sweet Jack Falstaff." Simms regularly avoided in his own work what he believed to be errors in the work of others.[22]

Not all critics have seen the frequently urged similarity between Porgy and Falstaff. Poe, upon Porgy's first appearance, found the fat Partisan "a most insufferable bore ... a back woods imitation of Sir Somebody Guloseton, the epicure, in one of the Pelham novels."[23] John Erskine thought that "Porgy's boastfulness and his love of good eating might well be set up as claims to further kinship with Parolles and Friar Tuck; in the method by which his humor is developed—monologue assisted by timely questions—he might derive from, or anticipate, negro minstrelsy."[24] Yvor Winters added another possible literary ancestor for Porgy in Polwarth, from Cooper's *Lionel Lincoln*, who, he believes, "must beyond any question be the prototype of W. G. Simms' Porgy."[25]

But the strongest and most convincing statements on the subject of Porgy's literary ancestry are by Simms himself and by his biographer. In his dedicatory letter to Joseph Johnson, M.D., which prefaces *Woodcraft*, Simms wrote: "The humorists of Glen Eberley were well-known personages of preceding generations, here thinly disguised under false names and fanciful localities, which, I am inclined to think will prove no disguise to you" (p. 3). William P. Trent wrote: "Simms said that Porgy was a transcript from real life, and I have it on good authority that he intended Porgy to be a reproduction of himself in certain moods. Porgy is in many respects a typical Southerner, brave, high talking, careless, fond of good living, and last, but not least, too frequently inclined to take his own commonplaces as the utterances of inspired wisdom"

The Roots of Southern Writing

(*Simms*, p. 109). Trent had available so much manuscript material now lost to students of Simms and had talked with so many of Simms's contemporaries and friends that it is difficult to argue with so definite a statement as this without having strong external evidence to set against it.

Fundamentally, then, Porgy is an improvident and life-loving member of the planter-gentlemen class, possessed of great wit, the ability to view himself with amusement, and a passion for material good things, which has become what the author has frankly labeled an "affectation." No character in the Revolutionary Romances, including Surgeon Hillhouse, is more completely a humours character in the Jonsonian sense than Porgy, and the method which Simms employed for building the humours character finds its best expression in the fat captain. That aspects of Falstaff may have been borrowed for the portrait—his belly and spindle shanks—does not make Porgy an attempt at an American Falstaff. Certainly with critics finding a kinship to such dissimilar characters as Bulwer-Lytton's Guloseton, Shakespeare's Parolles, Cooper's Polwarth, Friar Tuck, and Falstaff, and with scenes in the novels at least faintly reminiscent of *Don Quixote*, one may be justified in accepting the idea that Porgy is an original creation compounded of a person Simms had known and his idea of himself in certain moods, and that he is developed by the dramatic methods and with the Elizabethan overtones which Simms frequently used. Parrington is correct in saying, "The Elizabethan influence comes out strikingly in the character of Lieutenant Porgy" (p. 131); Falstaff is an important part of that influence, but he is not all of it. There is no sound basis for believing that Simms ignored his own judgment that Falstaff is "already sufficiently perfect" and that a character modeled after him will fail "as it reminds us that we have known Falstaff."

In the midst of the paper-mâché heroes and heroines of his romances, Simms introduced a group of living people who played lesser roles in the stories but upon whose vitality the books are most likely to rest their claim to continuing existence. In fashioning these figures he seems to have taken the raw materials of life and to have formulated them into characters by methods similar to those of the English drama which he knew and loved. The description of character through action and soliloquy, the conception of character in terms of the humours theory, and the borrowing of attributes and attitudes from drama constitute demonstrable proof of his indebtedness to the English playwrights. To recognize this persistent indebtedness as characteristic of Simms gives a basis for judging a character like Porgy who seems thoroughly Elizabethan in attitudes and attributes, but who bears only slight and surface similarities to his alleged prototype, Falstaff. That Simms should take himself

Simms and the British Dramatists

"in certain moods," a "well-known personage" of a preceding generation, the Jonsonian humour character, and a few physical characteristics that parallel those of Falstaff and create a new and living person is the obvious end-product of his method at its best. That he did this, rather than use Falstaff as a "painter's model," seems to be fairly obvious.

William Gilmore Simms
and the "American Renaissance"

In 1941 F. O. Matthiessen published his monumental account of American letters in the mid-nineteenth century, *American Renaissance: Art and Expression in the Age of Emerson and Whitman*. He centered his study on the half-decade of 1850 to 1855, and declared that his work grew out of his "realization of how great a number of our past masterpieces were produced in one extraordinarily concentrated moment of expression." He argued his case with such cogent persuasiveness that American literary historians have come to view the first half of the sixth decade of the nineteenth century as being the "American Renaissance"; and thereby they have accepted both Matthiessen's view of its centrality to our cultural history and his use of the term "renaissance" to describe it, as he says, "not as a re-birth of values that had existed previously in America, but as America's way of producing a renaissance, by coming to its first maturity and affirming its rightful heritage in the whole expanse of art and culture."

Matthiessen found space in his book for extensive treatments of Emerson, Thoreau, Hawthorne, Melville, and Whitman; and he was able even to give a passing nod to those ladies who dominated the book stalls and the best-seller lists of the period, and whom an irritated Hawthorne called "a damned mob of scribbling women": Susan Warner, Maria Cummins, and Mrs. E. D. E. N. Southworth. But if one turns to *American Renaissance* for accounts of southern writing, he turns its pages in vain. George Washington Harris, with his "Sut Lovingood" yarns, is there in five pages that mark his rediscovery for American literary history. But there is no mention of William Gilmore Simms or John Pendleton Kennedy, of Augustus Baldwin Longstreet, of Joseph Glover Baldwin, of John Esten Cooke or Henry Timrod. Such omissions are at first startling. Is it possible, one is inclined to ask, that Matthiessen is following in the path of Barrett Wendell, whose *Literary History of America* was once called, with only slight exaggeration, "The Literary Activities of Graduates of Harvard College, with occasional reference to other writers"? But this is not true. Matthiessen's *American Renaissance* is, I believe, the most important and the best single work of American literary history, a judgment seemingly shared by the 250 professors of English in the United States whose ballots helped shape Lewis Leary's *Contemporary Literary Scholarship* and who rank it among the top five works on

English or American literature. (It is the only one of the five which deals with American literature.)

Actually the omission of southern writers from a study of the maturing of American letters is less surprising than the inclusion of "Sut Lovingood," about whose ungrammatical sadism I happen to share Edmund Wilson's misgivings. As a southerner I regret that Matthiessen is right, but as a student of literary history I must concede that he is. This paper is an attempt to determine a few of the many reasons why southern letters, which in the 1830s had been challengingly alive, could in the 1850s add nothing to the "American Renaissance," through an examination of what William Gilmore Simms, the antebellum South's most prolific and most representative writer, was doing between 1850 and 1855.

If the calendar is moved back twenty years from Matthiessen's renaissance, the South becomes an important segment of the American literary picture. The *annus mirabilis* of southern literature was 1835. In that year Augustus Baldwin Longstreet published the book-length collection of his sketches of frontier low-life known as *Georgia Scenes;* John Pendleton Kennedy published his popular romance of the Revolution, *Horse-Shoe Robinson*, and further enhanced the glittering reputation he had made with *Swallow Barn;* Edgar Allan Poe published some of his early short stories and assumed the editorship of the *Southern Literary Messenger;* and William Gilmore Simms published in April his romance of Indian warfare in the colonial South, *The Yemassee*, and in December the first of his seven loosely connected romances of the American Revolution, *The Partisan*. Never again was one twelve-month period to represent the Old South so impressively in the literary market place, which had already established itself along an axis represented by the stagecoach route linking Philadelphia and New York City.

That year also carried Gilmore Simms to a height he was never again to attain, although the steady and diversified flow of words from his pen would make him indisputably the representative man of letters of the Old South. The 1835 novels by Simms—following as they did upon the spectacular success in 1834 of *Guy Rivers*, his romance of raw life on the Georgia frontier—quickly elevated him to a position second only to that of James Fenimore Cooper among American novelists, and made him a member of that select group which contained America's eminent literary spokesmen of the 1830s, Irving, Bryant, and Cooper. The reviewers hailed *The Yemassee* as a glorious fulfillment of the earnest Simms had given in *Guy Rivers*. On April 2 the *New York Commercial Advertiser* said, "As a story of Indian warfare, and extinction, there is none in the whole range of American fiction, that is superior to it." On April 16 the *New York Times* declared itself "much pleased, to find our warmest expectations far exceeded by the reality of his performance." Park Benjamin, in the *New-England Magazine*, in June, joined the issue clearly with a comparison that was to persist to the present, when he wrote, "The Yemassee is superior, in plot, style, and execution, to the Last of the Mohicans."

Yet it was the half-decade between 1850 and 1855 which was the greatest flowering of Simms's various talents and the realization, in some form or other, of many of his fondest dreams. The youthful exuberance and creative energy of the 1830s was sobered and tempered by the passage of time. He had acquired an ease of style and manner that he lacked two decades before. His skill in the smooth conduct of a narrative had improved. His ability to fashion what the critics of our century call "round characters"—notably Captain Porgy, in the Revolutionary Romances, and Hell-Fire Dick, in *Eutaw*—had increased. His attention to the details of common life had been sharpened. In *Woodcraft* he wrote a comedy of middle age in which the parts were fitted more harmoniously than in any other of his novels. His dream of a collected edition of his poetry was realized; at last the Charleston Theatre brought before its applauding audience one of his blank verse plays; a major publisher began issuing his collected works, with illustrations by F.O.C. Darley, the most popular illustrator of the time. His ambition of giving the South a true and important voice through a major review journal was realized through his editorship from 1849 to 1855 of the *Southern Quarterly Review;* his friends pushed him for the presidency of his state university, an honor for which he declined to be considered. And he stood alone as the representative of the literature of the South. Poe was dead; Kennedy had given over the writing of novels for politics; Judge Longstreet, now president of the University of Mississippi, was trying to forget that he had written *Georgia Scenes*, a work which in the 1850s seemed to him a youthful indiscretion. The new southern voices, the portents of the generation that was to be shattered by the Civil War, were Simms's disciples and admirers. Henry Timrod and Paul Hamilton Hayne, the poets of his native South Carolina, gathered around him as "Father Abbot" when business or pleasure brought Simms from his Barnwell District plantation to Russell's Bookshop in Charleston. And in Virginia, the youthful and talented John Esten Cooke, whose *Leather Stocking and Silk*, published in 1854, was followed the same year by his historical romance of eighteenth-century Williamsburg, *The Virginia Comedians*, was a willing, proud, and self-acknowledged follower in Simms's footsteps. In 1849 the venerable Beverley Tucker, professor of law at the College of William and Mary from 1834 to 1851, novelist, and elder statesman of the cause of secession, became his correspondent and friend, honoring him with confidences and placing upon his shoulders the burden of his hopes for a southern confederacy. It is little wonder that one of the derisive jokes about the Savannah Convention on Southern Literature, held in 1856—an apocryphal joke, it is true—was that the Convention concluded with a Resolution: "That there be a Southern Literature" and "That William Gilmore Simms, LL.D. be requested to write this literature."

Yet during this period Simms virtually lost the stature which he had once had as a national literary figure. At no point during the half-decade did he strike a note, conceive a series of actions, or create a group of characters which caught the national public fancy or spoke directly and forcefully to a large segment of the American reading public. In *The Yemassee* in 1835, despite its tendency to present slavery as an ideal institution, Simms was dealing with an aspect of the southern experience that was harmonious with the broad pattern of the national experience, with one of the great matters of American tragic romance, the conflict of Indian and white cultures, the pain and injustice with which civilization hacks its path into the American wilderness, the suffering and the tragic grandeur of being one of a fated folk overwhelmed by the onrushing wave of history. It is in this moment of his extinction that the Indian has made his greatest claim upon our literary interests. It is that fated, admirable, almost-Hemingwayesque pitting of honor, courage, and pride upon the conscious, desperate, and last battle which may be said to epitomize a recurring aspect of our national past and our character. With all its flaws of imitation, of carelessness, of haste, of infelicity of style, of strained coincidence and huddled action, *The Yemassee* achieved its author's expressed purpose of creating an American epic and speaking truthfully and powerfully to a resonant chord in the American spirit. But in the 1850s Simms seemed able no longer to speak forcefully to his readers as fellow Americans.

The half-decade opened auspiciously for Simms. In January 1850 he returned to the publication of full-length, major novels with the serialization in *Godey's Lady's Book* of *Katharine Walton*, his romance of Revolutionary Charleston during the British occupation. This novel was Simms's first long work since he had completed *Beauchampe* in 1842. The hiatus in his novel-writing career was in no sense unusual; indeed a similar hiatus struck almost every writer and publisher of serious fiction in the nation in the 1840s. This publishing hiatus resulted from three distinct but complementary causes. The effect of the Panic of 1837 was a long range depression extending into the mid-forties, and the book trade was an early victim of the financial collapse. It was in 1838 that Poe published his first—and only—novel, *The Narrative of Arthur Gor-*

The Roots of Southern Writing

don Pym; it would have been difficult for him to have found a less auspicious time for the launching of a career as a novelist, and he died before the native novel again found a profitable market. In 1838 Kennedy published his third novel, *Rob of the Bowl;* yet, despite the enormous success of *Horse-Shoe Robinson* in 1835, his publishers gave Kennedy only $1850 for the copyright to the new work; this low payment was certainly not the sole reason for his abandoning fiction, but it contributed to a decision which cost the South one of its most promising writers. A second reason for bad publishing conditions was the extensive pirating of the works of such popular English authors as Scott, Bulwer, Disraeli, Thackeray, and Dickens—works of proved appeal, which could be produced in cheap editions without the payment of royalties to their authors. A third cause of the depression in native fiction was the advent of the "mammoth weeklies" such as those published by Park Benjamin and George Roberts, whose Boston *Notion* proudly advertised "104 square feet of reading matter." Park Benjamin's *New World* not only published a complete novel in a single issue, but also issued an extensive series of "Extra Numbers," the most famous single one of which was a temperance novel *Franklin Evans* by Walter Whitman.

It was to Benjamin that Simms in 1845 sold *Count Julian,* a Spanish romance which he had written in 1838 and which had been lost in the mail and recently recovered. He tried once to get a contract to write serials for Roberts's *Notion,* to which he sold a few poems and shorter pieces of fiction, although he declared, "Nothing but the necessities of our literature, in these painful ... times, of pressure, could reconcile me to this form of publication." However, he insisted on anonymous publication, and Roberts, who was buying his name more than his work, backed down on this point. H. W. Boynton, in his *Annals of American Bookselling,* says: "Matters went from bad to worse for the American writer and for all but a few American publishers, so far as the publication of original imaginative writing was concerned. In 1840 and 1841 Cooper succeeded in 'coming back' with two more 'Leatherstocking Tales': but that was the end for him." In this period some of Cooper's novels were rebound in paper to be sold at twenty-five cents a volume. During the 1840s Simms had turned to magazine writing, to biography, and to other sources than the novel for income. By the 1850s publishing novels was again profitable, and the worst hiatus in the history of American fiction was over.

Seldom has an historical event marked a division between literary movements with as much precision as that interruption in the publication of novels marked a break in the course of American fiction. The historical novel, modeled after the work of Sir Walter Scott, was the dominant mode in fiction in America in the 1830s, and it commanded the best efforts of the finest literary practitioners. When novel writing was resumed around 1850 other modes engaged the finest fictional talents and other objectives than those of Scott and Bulwer-Lytton commanded the attention of American writers. Hawthorne, who had revered Scott in the 1820s and 1830s, by 1845 had discarded the historical romance as inadequate and external. Somehow, between 1840 and 1850 American fiction came of age, and it spoke in the half-decade of the renaissance with an authority, an earnestness, a seriousness, and a passionate skill foreign to its earlier modes. In 1850 Hawthorne and Simms both published novels; both novels were laid in the past; both novels rested on serious and thoughtful research; both novels have been praised for their historical accuracy. Simms's novel was *Katharine Walton;* Hawthorne's was *The Scarlet Letter*.

Simms published a blank verse tragedy laid in contemporary times and dealing with contemporary political issues, *Norman Maurice*, in 1851. The effort to make a tragedy of the materials of contemporary life is admirable and daring; the effort to use the outmoded form of Shakespearean blank verse resulted in such absurdities as these allegedly pentameter lines:

> Another action,
> The insurance case of Fergusson and Brooks,
> Secures him handsome profits.

In 1852 he published another blank verse drama, *Michael Bonham*, this time dealing with Texas and including such historical figures as Davy Crockett. This play was produced by the Charleston Theatre on March 26 and 27, 1855. To the present day reader it seems largely fustian bombast.

In 1852 he wrote *The Sword and the Distaff*, a comedy of the days immediately after the Revolution, later published under the title *Woodcraft*. The next year saw the publication of his two-volume collected poems, the beginning of the publication of the Uniform Edition of his *Works*, and the publication of *Vasconselos*, a historical romance of the Spanish settlement in America, much of which he had actually written in the 1830s. In 1854 he collected some of his previously uncollected short stories, tried to weave them into a pattern of conversations among people on a boat from New York to Charleston—conversations that tended to defend the South and its peculiar causes with heat and passion—and published them as *Southward, Ho!* In 1855 he published *The Forayers*, a Revolutionary Romance, which reached full-volume length before reaching a satisfactory conclusion and which actually extended itself on into *Eutaw*, its conclusion, published as its sequel in 1856.

The four Revolutionary Romances which Simms published between 1850 and 1856 deserve considerable praise. They give an accurate and vivid picture of a violent and significant period of history in South Carolina. Furthermore they bring to a conclusion the series of romances on the American Revolution which began with *The Partisan* in 1835 and continued with *Mellichampe* in 1836 and *The Scout* in 1841. They certainly represent that passion for Scott and the Scott-type historical novel which lingered on in the South long after it had died in the North. Harper & Brothers, for example, was shipping sets of Scott's works to the South in freightcar lots in the 1850s, when the North had largely given up reading him. Yet I would hesitate to link this continuing interest in the historical novel too readily and easily with the South's well-known and well-documented interest in the past. For one of Simms's chief motives in returning to the Revolution as the subject matter for his major romances during this period was not a passion for the past but was the defensive desire to set the world straight about South Carolina and her part in the War for Independence.

It is a well-established fact of history that the Revolution in the South was essentially a Civil War, fought between Loyalists and Rebels, which drenched the region in fraternally shed blood. The civil nature of the struggle for independence in South Carolina had been one of the subjects of *The Partisan*, had been a dominant theme in Simms's *Mellichampe*, and had been the issue between the two brothers who were hero and villain of Simms's *The Scout*. John Pendleton Kennedy's novel of the Revolution in South Carolina *Horse-Shoe Robinson* bore the subtitle "A Tale of the Tory Ascendency."

In the growing antagonism of North and South, however, this aspect of the Revolution in the South became increasingly a bone of contention. Heated northern debaters were likely to point to the South's part in the Revolution as being too small to entitle the region to claim a full share in the winning of independence. Simms, a serious student of the Revolution throughout much of his adult life, took very strong exception to this view. The first really vigorous defense of the South's part in the Revolution he made in a Fourth of July address at Aiken, South Carolina, in 1844. "The Sources of American Independence" is an oration which defends the South as being not only essential to the success of the struggle for independence but as having won for America, after they had been lost in the North, those blessings of freedom of which it boasts. When in 1847 Lorenzo Sabine published his serious and well-documented history, *The American Loyalists*, Simms felt that its portrayal of the nature and extent of the Loyalist sentiment in the South was erroneous and insulting, and he attacked the work with bitterness and anger. In 1848 Simms, in two long articles in the *Southern Quarterly Review* entitled "South Carolina in the Revolutionary War," argued powerfully against the northern historian. In 1853 the two articles were issued as a pamphlet. Simms greeted the publication of a revised edition of *Horse-Shoe Robinson* in 1852 with an eighteen-page review in the *Southern Quarterly Review* (XII, July 1852) in which he took heated exception to Kennedy's picture of the Loyalists' sentiment in South Carolina, denying that the colony took a lukewarm attitude toward independence, as northern critics charged, and asserting that the British were so incensed by the ingratitude of a favorite colony of the crown that they sent their ablest generals to the section. In 1835 he had admired *Horse-Shoe Robinson* very much.

Certainly Simms in attacking this issue of the southern contributions to the War of Independence—one, by the way, which was at stake in the famed "Crime Against Kansas" speech by Charles Sumner that resulted in his being caned by the South Carolinian Preston Brooks in the Senate in 1856—felt that he was defending his beloved state against evil oppression from without. In a letter to Beverley Tucker on May 6, 1849, Simms wrote. "Have you seen the number [of the *Southern Quarterly Review*] for July last containing an article entitled 'South Carolina in the Revolution'? I could wish you to read that. You will see how much of a Southron I am, & how little of a Yankee. You probably are not aware that I am a proverbial object of hate and denunciation in New England. You will see the reason for it when you read my books."

It was the fictional portrayal of this view of his region in which Simms was engaged in the Revolutionary Romances of 1850s. The war for independence was actually won in South Carolina largely by the Partisan warriors under men like Sumter and Marion, guerilla fighters who raided British outposts, attacked scouting parties, and played havoc with British lines of communication. It was won in part by General Greene's Fabian tactics, but in chief measure by the hundreds of minor engagements, most of them between Patriot and Loyalist bands. Cornwallis, a brilliant military strategist, declared that he had little fear of the rebel army itself, but that the activities of the guerrillas behind the British lines kept the country in constant alarm and made necessary the presence in South Carolina of British regulars that were desperately needed elsewhere. The individual and bloody struggles of a citizenry at war with itself measured the final price that South Carolina paid for independence. That story, told with vigor and force and presented as the essential steps that led to American victory, was Simms's answer to those who criticized his state's contribution to the Continental army.

In *Katharine Walton*, in *The Forayers*, and in *Eutaw* he tries to show how completely the chain of American victories that led to Yorktown rested on the citizen armies under the Partisan leaders rather than upon the Continental army under Greene. And in *Woodcraft* he opens with a bitter picture of the men of Francis Marion's army being insulted and ignored by the Continental army and its leaders in the moment of the triumph which Marion and his men had won. From this grim picture he goes on to show a citizen army returning to a "Soldier's Pay" of betrayal, duplicity, and fraud. This intense defensive anger can and often does vitalize the pages of these novels; Simms's skill with low-life characters finds in their pages a full and rewarding play; his ability to sketch violent action with great excitement and power is often well employed. Yet the ultimate purport and the final impact of these works is obviously and unmistakably local, defensive, and finally trivial. The author of *The Yemassee* was a young man with something compelling to say to his nation, with a vision of the nature of its reduplicating experience to communicate, and with a generous admiration for courage and integrity in friend and foe alike. In that novel he wrote of Carolina history as an American; in the Revolutionary Romances of the 1850s he wrote of American history as a Carolinian.

James Fenimore Cooper, who had started earlier on literary paths in which Simms walked all his life, came in the last decade and a half of his career, like a shaggy and uncouth behemoth among gazelles in a jungle to try novels of depth and meaning: *The Monikins, The Crater, Home As Found*, the trilogy called *The Littlepage Manuscripts*. His purpose was superior to his skills, but his growing mind in his changing world demanded of his art new attitudes and new methods and he labored to create them. The writer whom Vernon L. Parrington, with forgivable enthusiasm, could call "a rich and prodigal nature, vigorous, spontaneous, creative...the most richly endowed of any son [Charleston] ever gave birth to," could also have been expected to grow with his world and his time. The author of *The Yemassee*, flawed by the errors and redeemed by the exuberance of youth, should have found what Cooper sought and Hawthorne sought and found, "a more earnest purpose, a deeper moral, a closer and homelier truth."

That he did not is, in one sense at least, simply a measure of his grave limitations as a writer. For in the world of literature, as in all the other worlds we know, the will to do is as much a part of ability as the aptitude and skill to do. So Simms cannot be forgiven his failures because we are able to understand them. Yet understanding them may help us guard against similar failures ourselves.

Parrington believed that Simms's great talent produced no great art because "he lived in a world of unreality, of social and economic romanticism, that was forever benumbing his strong instinct for reality" and that he was the victim of his adulation for an ungrateful and snobbish Charleston. I doubt the attractive but simple thesis. His biographer William Peterfield Trent believed that Simms's failure to accomplish great things with a great talent was because nothing permanently enduring can come out of a slave society, and this thesis, too, I question. Rightness of social and economic theory are not essential to great art. A man may believe in monarchy and still be Shakespeare; writers can and have flourished in social, ideational, economic, political, and religious environments utterly foreign to the beliefs of readers who have found them to be profound and stimulating artists.

I believe that the Simms of the 1830s as a writer promised more than the mature Simms delivered, but it was the Simms of the 1830s who wrote the essay on slavery that began in 1837 as a review of Harriet Martineau's *Travels in America*, that was reprinted as a pamphlet in 1838, and that finally became one of the four essays in the infamous *Pro-Slavery Argument* volume of 1853. (The other essays were by Thomas R. Dew, president of the College of William and Mary; James H. Hammond, later U. S. Senator from South Carolina; and William Harper, chancellor of the University of South Carolina.) *The Yemassee*, in episode after episode, argues dramatically for slavery as a desirable institution, and Simms's position on this matter did not change. Furthermore Simms was active in the "Young America" group of literary critics in the 1840s, who, under the guidance of Evert A. Duyckinck and his literary magazine, the *Literary World*, attacked the *Knickerbocker Magazine* and argued vigorously for a national literature. He was never a conscious sectionalist in a narrow sense in literary theory, although in practice he often proved to be. In politics in the 1840s he was a Loco-foco Democrat. It was not his social, political, or economic beliefs that betrayed his art. Great authors have been more grievously wrong than was Gilmore Simms in these respects.

The answer to Simms's failure to grow, to the increasing insularity of his subject matter and the increasing triviality of his purposes in art, to his failure to mature as a serious artist during that period when American art was reaching its first maturity is both simpler and more compelling than most of the critics have thought. The erstwhile Loco-foco Democrat of the New York literary wars became more and more deeply embroiled in the essentially one-party but many-factioned South Caro-

The Roots of Southern Writing

lina political conflict. Calhoun's efforts to unite the factions of the state behind his banner of unrelenting opposition to the growingly vocal abolition movement had so completely succeeded, even with men like Simms who disliked and distrusted Calhoun, that the slavery issue was not subject to debate, that the concept of federated sovereign states was not subject to question, and that the presenting of a common front to the North was superior to all other things. This process, which proceeded with unusual force in South Carolina, Clement Eaton has seen as the decline of "government by discussion and the repression of independent thought" which he believes "forms the central problem in the social and intellectual history of the South." Beginning in the 1830s and accelerating rapidly in the 40s and 50s the South came more and more to take a Manichaean view of the world, in which North—and particulary New England—was evil and South was good. And to dream of that day of conflict when Right should prevail. As Mr. Eaton expresses it in *Freedom of Thought in the Old South:* "Only an atmosphere of good will and understanding could have led to an interchange of ideas and fruitful reforms between the radical North and the conservative South.... But the bitter feeling of sectionalism continued to grow, exacerbated by politicians, fire-eaters, and antislavery crusaders, until an intellectual blockade was set up by the South not only against abolitionism, but also against many associated isms that were destined to triumph in the future."

The steady narrowing of interests, the centering of attention in South Carolina, the passionate defense of a position and an attitude, the involvement with the region and its peculiarities, and the belief that the outer world was somehow a menace that did not understand and was to be feared and fought—these things resulted in a closing of the mind, in a self-imposed restriction of thought. It was not so much that Simms and his region were wrong as that they closed their minds to the possibility that any position other than their own could be right. A closed mind does not grow, and its product is the self-absorptive triviality into which Simms's talent tended to fall, for he was a victim of the intellectual blockade, the *cordon intellectuale* by which the South guarded its endangered pride. For that blockade shut out from him, by centering his attention on other things, that growth of mind and interest that might have made him properly a part of Matthiessen's renaissance.

The result was that one of the brightest talents of the 1830s found itself, in a time when Hawthorne and Melville were creating America's first great novels, spending his mature years proving how right Hawthorne had been when he said in 1846 in a review of Simms's *View and Reviews:* "The themes suggested by him, viewed as he views them, would produce nothing but historical novels, cast in the same worn-out mould that had been in use these thirty years, and which it is time to break up and fling away."

The Novel in the South

The South is more distinctively a region than any other section of the United States is. Far more important than its geographical boundaries—than Mason and Dixon's line and the Mississippi River—are the boundaries of experience and tradition which have given it a unique identity in the nation. These experiences have taught it attitudes sharply at variance with some of the standard American beliefs. Among these attitudes are the sense of failure, which comes from being the only group of Americans who have known military defeat, military occupation, and seemingly unconquerable poverty; the sense of guilt, which comes from having been a part of America's classic symbol of injustice—the enslavement and then the segregation of the Negro; and the sense of frustration, which comes from the consistent inadequacy of the means at hand to wrestle with the problems to be faced, whether they be poverty, racial intolerance, or the preservation of a historical past rich in tradition.

If the characteristic American attitude is "know how," in the South "make do" has had to be substituted for it. It is idle to point out that each of these attitudes is the product of postures struck willingly by the South and maintained with intractable stubbornness. The fact remains that "Dixie" is a state of mind, and a southern state of mind haunted by the imperfection, the guilt, and the tragedy of human experience as no other American's mind is. Out of such a view of experience the southern novelists in our time have fashioned a serious and often tragic literature.

In the years just after the Civil War the southerner attempted to deny these things by the simple, but ultimately ineffectual, process of ignoring them. The southern local-color writers concentrated on the quaint, the eccentric, and the remote; and the creators of the "plantation tradition" idealized the past. Each created a synthetic South for export purposes. One was a papier-mâché world of quaint, whimsical, charming folks in mountain coves and Latin Quarters, on bayous and plantations. The other was a world over which hung, like a gossamer sheen, an idealized past crowded with happy, banjo-strumming darkies grouped about a vast mansion from between whose tall, white columns rode out "the last of the cavaliers." Both tended to convert the tragic center of southern history—the Civil War—into something as remote and glamorous as a page from Froissart.

Thus a region obsessed with the past, as no other portion of America has been, so sentimentalized that past that it became the materials of empty romance, a kind of antiseptic Disneyland, filled with idealized figures. This literary fantasy has been realized today in the guided tours, the reconstructed towns, the outdoor pageants of the tourist's South.

Against this sentimental view the first two voices that were strongly raised were those of Ellen Glasgow and James Branch Cabell, Virginians who, in their differing ways, defined the patterns which twentieth-century southern fiction was to take when it became serious and fell into the hands of that group of writers of talent who have practiced it in this century. Miss Glasgow turned upon the sentimental myth of her section the realism and irony which were her special tools. In the record of Virginia's immediate past she saw little that was comforting and nothing that was optimistic. She declared that she could not recall a time when "the pattern of society as well as the scheme of things in general, had not seemed to [her] false and even malignant." She stated that the doctrine of her best-known novel, *Barren Ground*, was that "one may learn to live, one may even learn to live gallantly, without delight."

History was, for Miss Glasgow, a tragic fable of man's lot in a hostile world, in which defeat was inevitable, but "tragedy lies, not in defeat, but in surrender." She devoted much of her career to a series of novels which collectively present a panoramic history of Virginia from the Civil War to the 1940s. Using the realistic method of Howells and Henry James, she sketched with irony and anger the social history of a doomed race of aristocrats and a democratized state wherein a sense of duty—her famed "vein of iron"—could give dignity to lives rendered unhappy by the exigencies of destiny. In the best of these novels—*The Miller of Old Church*, *Barren Ground*, and *Vein of Iron*—she achieved the somber tragic sense of Thomas Hardy, whom she admired greatly. In four novels laid in the city of Richmond she employed the comedy of manners to subject Virginia assumptions to the analysis of the ironic method. Although in certain respects—command of narrative techniques and consistency of style—she fell short of the goal she set herself, Miss Glasgow saw her region in terms of its history, saw that history as a tragic fable, and imprisoned her vision in a vast and ambitiously planned group of books.

James Branch Cabell, who was nurtured on the sentimental version of Virginia history, learned early a love for the dignity, the beauty, the gallantry which it worshiped. In his maturity, however, he brought the witty cynicism of Oscar Wilde and Anatole France to bear upon a tradition which he could laugh at without ceasing to love. Where his friend Ellen Glasgow had tried to rewrite the history of her region more in accord with the facts and to give it a tragic pattern, Cabell turned from it completely and in a vastly ambitious collection of novels, *The Biography of the Life of Manuel*, explored in the history of imaginary Poictesme, between 1234 and 1750, the successive manifestations of chivalry, gallantry, and poetry. Finally he brought these qualities over the Atlantic and examined them in Virginia in such works as *The Rivet in Grandfather's Neck* and the ironic *The Cream of the Jest.* The tendency to reshape the world into something new and freshly meaningful and to represent that reshaping in a vast novelistic scheme which asserts that truth is found in men's dreams of beauty and not in their imperfect actualities is present in Cabell's work, although his basic seriousness is perhaps permanently spoiled by archness, slyness, and an uncomfortable tendency to snicker.

When a group of talented young writers in the 1920s and 1930s addressed themselves to the representation of the world through the image of their region, they followed—sometimes afar off—the paths blazed by Miss Glasgow and Cabell. These writers not only were southern but they were also the products of the same social and cultural forces that were shaping the work of other American writers. One of the most obvious characteristics of the period is that it was an age of protest against certain aspects of the American present which seemed to many to violate the American ideal. The realistic movement produced a host of social critics who busily protested against their world; they might, like Sinclair Lewis, spring from the middle-western small towns and be in passionate revolt against the "village virus"; they might, like James T. Farrell, grow up on the dingy pavements of American cities and attack the poverty of spirit which they found there. In other movements than realism the revolt against the present and past went forward, notably in Gertrude Stein's experiments with language and in the expatriates' espousal of continental art forms. In political terms, particularly during the depth of the depression, collectivist writers like John Dos Passos attacked the capitalistic system under which they had grown up and which suddenly seemed to fail them. All these writers measured the present against the American dream and found it lacking, and they relentlessly pointed out to their fellow citizens the flaws they found.

The southern writer responded to these same impulses. The group of young poets and critics who published the *Fugitive* magazine in Nashville, Tennessee, in 1922–1925, declared that they "fled from nothing faster than the Brahmins of the Old South," and the editor of the New Orleans little magazine the *Double Dealer* declared that it was time to end the treacly sentimentality of southern writing. Both were joining hands across the sea with Hemingway and Fitzgerald, with Gertrude Stein and Sherwood Anderson. But when the southern revolt against the American present was uttered, it was a call to an agrarian order. True to his traditions, the middle-western writer called for social reform and pleaded for a utopia of the future, but his southern cousin, bound by the past, looked backward for his answers. Midwesterners went east and from Greenwich Village and New Haven chided the Middle West for its failings. Easterners went to Paris and Rome and there purified their art forms. Southerners, by and large, stayed home and sought to correct rather than to destroy their heritage.

The southern writers sought to revitalize for the modern world a view of man that the South had held since Thomas Jefferson. This view saw man as best in his relation to the soil, particularly as that relationship existed in the pre–Civil War South. This myth of a good order in the past, southern writers generally used as a weapon of attack against the bad order of modern industrialism.

They tended to seek in the past a pattern, to evolve a meaning out of large sweeps of history, converting the pattern of event into myth, and uniting the sense of tragic dignity with the irony of comedy. Some, like T. S. Stribling and Hamilton Basso, have tried to construct great connected records of social change; others, like Erskine Caldwell in his early novels, have fashioned laughter into a social weapon; still others, like Katherine Ann Porter and Eudora Welty, have used highly refined and almost poetic, brief art forms to state their visions of experience. But out of the welter of fictional accomplishment that came in the 1930s, when the southern renascence was at its height, emerge most impressively the names of Thomas Wolfe, William Faulkner, and Robert Penn Warren.

Thomas Wolfe was a man of great sensitivity and of Gargantuan appetite. He was possessed by a passionate desire to embrace all human activity, to experience all emotions, and to express through his self and the impact of the world upon that self the totality of life. Coupled with this desire to express himself was the egalitarian belief that the self whose attributes he could state was not only Thomas Wolfe but also generic man, that the world he could know and imprison on paper was America. Once he declared: "I have at last discovered my own America. . . . And I shall wreak out my vision of this life, this way, this world and this America, to the top of my bent, to the height of my ability, but with an unswerving devotion, integrity and purity of purpose."

Wolfe's "epic impulse" to define the American character and typify the American experience makes him in some respects much like Walt Whitman, but there are also notable differences. Where Whitman's self exists in an endless upward spiral of achievement—"I am the acme of things accomplished, the encloser of things to be"—Wolfe's self is trapped in the coils of time. Wolfe's characteristic feeling is not the joy of comradeship but the melancholy ache of loneliness. Man seeks everywhere, he declared, "the great forgotten language, the lost lane-end into heaven."

The Roots of Southern Writing

And in this search for what he called "a stone, a leaf, an unfound door," time and the past played a strange and treacherous role, a threefold controlling function in human life, the adequate representation of which became for Wolfe the great structural problem of his novels.

The first and most obvious element of Wolfe's Time was the simple present—what he called "clock time"—the sequential flow of clock ticks, seconds, events. The second element was past time—what he called "the accumulated impact of man's experience," which makes the present and determines the moment's actions, conditioning every instance of our existence and sometimes making the unpremeditated action of an insignificant person two-hundred years ago more important to our actions than the immediate sights and sounds that surround them. The third element was "time immutable, the time of rivers, mountains, oceans, and the earth; a kind of eternal and unchanging universe of time against which would be projected the transience of man's life, the bitter briefness of his day." History and memory by whose action history can be made real to the individual become for Wolfe, therefore, not casual by-products of experience as they have tended to be for many American writers, but essential elements of life.

In trying to "wreak out" this vision, Wolfe turned to many literary models—notably James Joyce, Dickens, Dostoevski, Proust, and Sinclair Lewis—and he employed the complex methods of their varying kinds of art, using physical symbols, interior monologues, objects and phrases as leitmotif, an evocation of the multiple sensory response to the physical world as directly presented as any American writer has ever achieved, and finally—apparently not trusting symbol, leitmotif, and lyric evocation to do their jobs alone—the rhetorical assertion of his meaning in dithyrambic prose poems.

In an almost pure form Wolfe represents the struggle of the novelist to record his personal experience and to find cosmic meaning in it. In short stories and short novels like *A Portrait of Bascom Hawke* and *The Web of Earth*, as well as in individual chapters of sections of his long novels, such as "The Party at Jack's" and "I Have a Thing to Tell You" in *You Can't Go Home Again*, Wolfe demonstrated that he had artistic control and the ability to realize characters and actions in compelling scenes. However, he never solved the riddle of the longer form, and his four long books—*Look Homeward, Angel, Of Time and the River, The Web and the Rock*, and *You Can't Go Home Again*—are made up of ambitious fragments giving in formless profusion a record of the novelist's own experience in his world. *Look Homeward, Angel*, an apprenticeship novel, has a form dictated by its account of growing up and is a richly evocative picture of the pains and joys of childhood and youth, but the later works lack what they most seriously need: a controlling narrative to tie their symbols together and to give them an objective reality and meaning.

In William Faulkner that controlling narrative is, at first glance, the most obvious element. For him, as it had been for Ellen Glasgow, southern history was the frame, a tragic fable of the human lot. In twenty-four volumes of short stories, short novels, and full-length novels, Faulkner has recorded the events of that history as he sees them impinging upon the denizens of imaginary Yoknapatawpha County in Mississippi. That county represents in its complex history and its varied citizens one of the great imaginative creations of the American mind.

As it had been for Wolfe, time is an entity in Faulkner's world. The past exists so compellingly in the present for his characters that it sometimes seems that only the past really exists for them. In *Absalom, Absalom!*, Quentin Compson, trying to understand himself and his region, seeks for an answer to the riddle of the South and the self in the past events of Thomas Sutpen's life. The past and the present coexist so completely in that novel that the order in which the segments of the narrative are told defies any normal sequential sense, and Faulkner has to supply a timetable in an appendix, so that the reader can straighten out the chronology of the story. Like Wolfe, too, Faulkner often explores the inner self, particularly in *The Sound and the Fury* and *As I Lay Dying*, both of which experiment with the interior-monologue technique. But in the lonely selves of his characters are no satisfactory answers; for such answers we must see the characters against the larger context of the history of Faulkner's imaginary country. For this reason Faulkner's work did not immediately receive the attention or the understanding that it deserves, because the large context has to be seen before the parts can be understood, and in Faulkner's case the parts came first.

That historical context is almost infinitely complex, and to simplify it to short statement is to do it the gravest violence; yet it is something like this: The South once knew an order and a tradition based on honor and personal integrity, but it was guilty of the exploitation of fellow human beings, the Indians and the Negroes. Because of this great guilt, the Civil War came like a flaming sword and ended the paradise of the noble but guilty past. After the war noble men for ignoble reasons submitted themselves to the moral duplicity and the mechanical efficiency of the mindless new world, and the region fell into the darkness of moral decay. If it is to win its way out again, it will do it through the reawakening moral vision of its youth and the prevailing strength of its Negroes. Such a reshaping of history into myth functions in Faulkner as a controlling shape for the characters whose individual actions some-

The Roots of Southern Writing

times seem to run counter to the general pattern. It is startlingly close to a cosmic view of history, a view that seeks with passionate intensity for meanings that transcend and explain facts and particularities.

And not content with this vast frame of reference, Faulkner uses a variety of devices to assert meaning in the smaller fragments of the vast work. One of the most persistent of these has been the retelling of the Christ narrative in various forms, as an account of guilt, vicarious suffering, and attempt at expiation. In some of the early stories, written in the beginning of his career and collected as *New Orleans Sketches*, Faulkner has used the Christ story as a means of investing the actions of his books with meaning. Echoes of the Christ narrative appear in *The Sound and the Fury*, in the actions of Quentin Compson. In *Light in August* the protagonist, Joe Christmas, believes he has a trace of Negro blood, a symbol of guilt which he must expiate; and Faulkner bolsters this suggestion with a long chain of parallels between Joe's actions and those of the Passion Week. In *A Fable* Faulkner moves all the way to allegory and uses the Christ story as a frame for a fable of a modern attempt to establish peace on earth.

Faulkner also employs images and symbols drawn from many sources, particularly from Freud, to strengthen and enrich his meanings, even to the extent in *The Sound and the Fury*, it has been suggested, of making the three leading male characters into personifications of the id, the ego, and the superego. Like Wolfe, too, Faulkner is not averse to rhetoric as a device for stating meaning. In fact Faulkner's power with words is one of his most important characteristics. In his later years he used it increasingly to state his meanings, perhaps because his creative powers were lessening, perhaps because the southern writer does not distrust rhetoric as other American writers tend to.

Faulkner also shares with Wolfe the quality of intensity. Everything in Wolfe's world is vast, every emotion is cosmic, every action gigantic. A similar intensity exists in Faulkner's world. The figures who act out the steps in their damnation on the streets and roads of Yoknapatawpha County are the creation of a nonrealistic imagination; they loom larger than life, immense in feeling and movement. Upon them sweep howling winds from the past. Their actions—even simple, homely actions—assume cosmic significance. They are illumined by lurid lights and they cast vast shadows. Although they are simple, earthy, natural folks, when the furies possess them—as the furies always do in Yoknapatawpha County—they become gods and demigods. They resemble most the grim and extravagant creatures of Webster, Ford, and Marston, for they belong in the dark tragedy of the English Jacobean stage. That these figures and their actions are often redeemed by earthy humor, comic speech, and simple verisimilitude should not blind us to their essentially un-earthly nature. They exist as phantasms in a cosmic dream of history, a dream that pictures the glory and the tragedy of man.

Wolfe's fury-driven and soul-searching protagonist, in his effort to state meaning, was often guilty of what seems to be empty bombast. In Faulkner through symbol, allegory, and rhetoric this fury-driven search is given objective dramatic existence. Each writer seeks not the portrayal of the world, but the discovery and enunciation of a cosmic truth.

In Robert Penn Warren's novels these tendencies and concerns are employed by a writer of great talent, great sophistication, and great intellect. The most notable characteristic of Warren's work is his serious concern with religious and philosophical ideas. He attempts to write the novel of ideas in which the essentially southern view of man is drama-tized through melodramatic actions involving southern characters.

For Warren the problems of man are the twin problems of finding identity and expiating guilt. In finding identity man moves, he believes, from nontime to time, from innocence to guilt; for guilt is an inevitable property of identity. Warren repeatedly tells the story of that guilt and that search in poetry, short stories, and novels, frequently laid in the historical past or involving legendary folk characters.

Warren's novels are uniformly technical tours de force, in which the normal demands of their apparent type of fiction are set aside in order to achieve meaning through the manipulation of action and the special use of witty, knowing, and metaphysical language which can express mean-ing in its complexity and ambiguity. Jack Burden, the stylized and speculative narrator in *All the King's Men*, becomes the chief explicator of the universal problems which Warren finds embedded in the am-biguous career of a political demagogue, Willie Stark, and ultimately the novel is about Burden's self-discovery through Willie Stark—and not about Willie Stark as a political figure.

In *World Enough and Time* Warren deserts the formal characteris-tics of the historical romance to write a novel that surrenders immediacy in order to brood over the Beauchamp-Sharp murder case, an early nineteenth-century Kentucky tragedy which had already engaged the attention of Poe, Hoffman, Simms, and others. He leaves the materials of the story essentially abstract and its characters symbolic, and Jeremiah Beaumont, who writes much of the book as a philosophic speculation, remains a symbol of man's search for the meaning of justice, death, and the end of man. In *Band of Angels* Warren writes what looks like an-other historical slave narrative, loaded with melodrama, about a sup-posedly white girl who proves to be a Negress and is sold into slavery. Yet the story, with its extravagant action and intense emotions, is actually an exploration of the nature of freedom. In *The Cave*, through a fine-tuned use of folk voices, each carefully keyed to its place in the narrative, Warren employs the events centering around a man trapped in a cave and the attempts to rescue him to explore a number of people's search for identity, a search which is defined as seeking original innocence through escaping out of time into nontime. Each man is seeking self-recognition, of which, in *Brother to Dragons*, Warren said:

> The recognition of complicity is the beginning of innocence.
> The recognition of necessity is the beginning of freedom.
> The recognition of the direction of fulfillment is the death of the self.
> And the death of the self is the beginning of selfhood.
> All else is surrogate of hope and destitute of spirit.

And he once said, "The story of every soul is the story of its self-definition for good or evil, salvation or damnation."

Warren is not friendly to Thomas Wolfe's fiction, as was Faulkner, who considered Wolfe one of the greatest American writers. In a telling comment on Wolfe's inability to objectify his vision of experience, Warren once reminded Wolfe that Shakespeare was content to write Hamlet: he did not have to *be* Hamlet. Yet Wolfe's central theme, which was the soul's search for surety, the endless seeking for communion, for meaning, "the search for the father," is remarkably close to Warren's. For Warren's characters seek in the ambiguity of a world of shadows, of intermingled good and evil, to know the nature of themselves and to understand the quality of identity.

In dramatizing this tragic view of man caught in his nature and the trap of time, southern novelists have returned to a vision of human experience that is sharply at variance with that of much of America, to a vision that is essentially romantic and idealistic. The southern novelist sees man as a tragic figure rather than a mechanical victim and relates his meaning to a large structure of event and history. Wolfe, Faulkner, and Warren each has created a kind of fiction out of the materials of his region and its past which can and does counterpoise the despairing view of man that naturalism and realism have taken in our time. In expressing their revolt against the modern world they have looked backward to a tradition and an order wherein meaning is to be sought and found, man has dignity, and history is a record of a purpose. Out of these materials they have formed a fictive world of great intensity, beauty, and worth.

The View from the Regency Hyatt

The interpretation of southern culture and southern literature has suffered from absolutism almost as much as it has from sentimental adulation and from vindictive enmity. Usually in the minds of each of its critics, whether of its life or its letters, there is a monolithic South, but early and late few of these monoliths have been very much like the others. Yet the fact that individual concepts of the region are remarkably varied does not alter the monistic tendency that calls them all into being. Let us review briefly some of the most obvious of these absolutist views.

There is the aristocratic South of broad lawns, great trees, tall, white columns, and happy banjo-strumming Negroes. This is the old South of Thomas Nelson Page of Virginia and, more recently, it is the South of Stark Young of Mississippi and, to a certain extent, of Margaret Mitchell of Atlanta. It managed to survive the destruction of war and the abolition of slavery without losing its good manners or its sense of honor and without soiling its damask linen—although that linen is growing increasingly threadbare.

There is also a South which became an apocalyptic vision in which one sees arrested forever beneath lurid skies a blasted Gothic landscape, wherein Simon Legree alternates between lusting after the slave girl Cassy and beating Uncle Tom to death. This is the South of the abolition societies, although it is actually not the South of Mrs. Stowe herself, despite the fact that she created its most enduring metaphors in *Uncle Tom's Cabin*. It is also the South of many of the modern reconstructionists and has been at least once, in *Band of Angels*, that of Robert Penn Warren.

There is a South of industrialization, liberalism, and all the middle-class democratic virtues, a South which is primarily viewed as a problem in the management of society, its natural resources, and its people. This South was announced by Henry Grady of Atlanta and documented by Howard Odum and his cohorts at Chapel Hill, and it is still a very lively ideal in both these places. There is also a South that represents a special and feverishly deceitful state of mind torn between dreams of past grandeur and a sense of guilt. This South was most clearly defined by W. J. Cash of Charlotte, but it has frequently been echoed since the publication of Cash's brilliant book, *The Mind of the South*, in 1941.

There is a South that is a degenerate, poverty-stricken world—a land of people ill-housed, ill-clothed, and ill-fed, wherein economic deprivation and cultural illiteracy combined with despair to produce utter hopelessness and violence. This South has remarkable similarities to many of the pictures that are currently being painted of the ghettos in our great cities, and it may be achieving a new relevance in our tormented world. It is the South of Mark Twain's river towns, of Franklin Delano Roosevelt's economic programs, of Erskine Caldwell's Georgia uplands, and of William Faulkner's Snopeses and Bundrens.

And there is also a South which is a lost paradise of order and stability, of honor and a religious view of man. This South is a challenge, an ideal, and a star by which to steer, even though the mariners themselves admit that it really is a light never seen on land or sea. This is the South of the Vanderbilt Agrarians, a South which has proved to be a powerfully dynamic symbol of agrarian opposition to capitalistic industrialism. It has been magnificently celebrated in some of the best poetry and fiction of the region as a repository of the finest traditions of the old South.

Each of these monistic concepts is true within its own limits, and each is false as a picture of the entire region. For each of these concepts has been an attempt to bind together a heterogeneous land and a varied people through the application of a Procrustean model made of monistic and simplistic—although often highly sophisticated—generalizations.

It seems to me that Walter Sullivan, has argued for still another monolithic approach to an aspect of Southern culture, when he cogently stated the case for what I believe to be a special aspect of the southern experience, an aspect peculiarly amenable to a highly sophisticated and self-conscious literary technique, basically that of James Joyce. To me his argument for the existence of his South and its special literary resurgence was convincing. The famed southern renascence would have been a lesser thing by far had the movement that Mr. Sullivan describes not occurred, and, indeed, had it not found expression in novels, such as his own and Louis D. Rubin's. Yet, as a pluralist and as one who believes that there are many Souths with many histories and many problems, I should like to suggest that there are other strings to the literary bow which sped the arrow of this renascence and that, though perhaps of coarser and less-enduring fiber than the one that Mr. Sullivan has described, they were of importance to the development of southern letters in the second third of this century and can be ignored in a serious examination of what southern literature has been like in the days of its glory and is likely to be tomorrow only at the peril of dangerous incompleteness.

The occurrence of genius, even of high talent, is always finally inexplicable. Who would have dreamed that Stratford would produce a Shakespeare and, yet, as Matthew Arnold has observed in "The Function of Criticism at the Present Time," the proper cultural and intellectual climate must exist if genius is to flourish and truly realize itself in significant art. Shakespeare did leave Stratford and did find among the dramatists and poets of the first Elizabeth's London a cultural and artistic environment conducive to the fruitful working of his genius. I think the South in our century has had many elements which have made it a promising field for the serious artist. For all its divergence within itself, for all the varied Souths, there is still a geographical region that has certain common and easily recognized qualities which set it apart from the rest of the nation. Among those qualities, I believe, these are of special importance: the presence of the Negro and the shame of his enslavement and his disenfranchisement; an agricultural economy; the historical experience of military defeat, military occupation, and reconstruction. The union of this body of experience as subject matter and a passionate concern in terms of the region with a great many men of marked literary talent produced a period rich in works of literary art.

But literary works have literary as well as social contexts, and they possess the miraculous ability to grow by feeding upon themselves. The existence of a substantial body of serious writing is a requisite—or at least a substantial encouragement—to any literary movement of importance. Such a burgeoning of writing—good, bad and mediocre—in poetry, in drama, in criticism, and particularly in fiction—began to occur in the 1920s. It had many sources. After the First World War, as Allen Tate has suggested, the South made a belated entry into the modern world.[1] Mr. Tate is impressed—and properly—with the backward look which the South cast at its own past in this moment of transition, and he sees that look as the central energy of the renascence. The tragic history of the South made it a vital metaphor for the war-torn and disillusioned twentieth century in which its crucial and frustrating experiences began to speak with remarkable directness to the entire nation which, except for the South, had been oblivious to the human potential for disaster and had believed itself immune to permanent defeat. In our time, as there was not for the rest of the nation in the nineteenth century, there is deep meaning in witnessing the symbolic act of biting the bullet. But more occurred than merely a looking backward into history; for this time the South also began looking around and looking at itself and no longer solely through the rose-colored glasses of sentiment or the defensive blinders of a lost cause, and the contemporary condition of the region could, and it still does, also speak with immediacy and authority to its artists.

This condition was in many parts of the South one of bone-gnawing poverty and endless defeat. It rested on depleted soil, deflated markets, dilapidated buildings, and debilitating malnutrition. It was a reflection of a vicious tenant-farming and sharecropping system, a most rudimentary educational system for the underprivileged, and an intense emotion-charged, pietistic, fundamentalist, nontheological religion that expressed itself in grotesqueries such as snake-handling and speaking with tongues. These conditions were as much a part of the subject matter of the southern renascence as were the history of the region or the humor of its retreating frontier or the dream of the days of its baronial glory. They also formed a subject which could deeply engage the moral and social conscience of the author. And southern writers who took this subject usually applied to it a socioliterary method which was essentially that of critical social realism, and this method should be added to—certainly not substituted for—the tradition which Mr. Sullivan has admirably described, and I should add parenthetically that his and mine together do not cover or exhaust the field of the South as a subject inspiring to writers of talent.

In the 1920s, 1930s, and the early 1940s the work of Sinclair Lewis as social critic and satirist, as the coruscating portrayer and diagnostician of a society lacking in values and the bases of a good life, was at least quantitatively as important to southern writing as that of James Joyce. Certainly the brash iconoclasm of H. L. Mencken was echoed fully as often as the Tory tones of T. S. Eliot. While many writers did seek in themselves the answers to their own riddles and to the riddles of their world, many others saw in the outside world a challenging subject for portrayal and criticism.

And one of the generating forces for the renascence was the energy of this social anger and regional criticism. It rose from a skeptical look at the legend of the Old South—as, indeed, the early Fugitive movement had—from a distaste for sentimentality—which characteristic was almost a hallmark of the renascence—and from a clear-eyed surveillance of the region in terms of its weaknesses and its suffering. Behind this analysis of the present was a sense of the past and a reverence for the dignity of man, but it expressed itself in anger and protest. Jeeter Lester, in *Tobacco Road*, is a shiftless, hopeless, and helpless man, but there echo in his vacant brain thoughts that rest on other days and other ways, and he abides by a faithfulness to the soil which, in his case, is both insane and self-serving but is also real. As Caldwell said, "They had so much faith in nature...that they could not understand how the earth could fail them. But it had failed them, and there they were waiting in another summer for an autumn harvest that would never come."[2] Such a response as Caldwell's was grounded in essentially economic concerns and was a response to a South that was real and could not be ignored.

I believe that this body of social criticism was and is an indispensable part of the southern renascence, that some of the greatest figures of the renascence participated, at least partly, in it, and that it must be weighed in the balances when we are defining the character of the remarkable literary resurgence that the South has known.

I should like to look briefly at some works by four writers of fiction who were committed in varying ways to such social criticism of sections of the South once notorious for their poor whites. These writers are T. S. Stribling, Thomas Wolfe, Erskine Caldwell, and Flannery O'Connor.

At first glance these writers may seem to be strangely grouped. Thomas Wolfe, an early apostle of James Joyce and a writer of the *Bildungs-roman*, would apparently not belong in such a group at all. Flannery O'Connor, with her deep involvement with theological issues within the framework of Catholic belief, seemed to have different objectives from those of the others. I am not intending to suggest that these four writers, each of them in his way representative of fairly widespread movements, did have a great deal in common except a concern with a common subject matter and an attitude that reflected a basic sense of deprivation in the lives of their characters. Certainly they wrote for different audiences, from different points of view, and for different motives. They shared, however, an interest in the twentieth-century Piedmont and mountain South and its people and their problems.

T. S. Stribling was an obvious disciple of Sinclair Lewis. In 1922 he published his first significant novel, *Birthright*, which is concerned with the hopeless struggle of an educated mulatto to return to a Tennessee town, and make his way in a world dominated by prejudice, narrow-mindedness, and misunderstandings at every point. The attack upon the small town by Sinclair Lewis's method is everywhere manifest in *Birthright*. In 1926, in *Teeftallow*, Stribling produced a bitterly realistic novel of a Tennessee mountain town, emphasizing its bigotry, its ignorance, its pietistic hypocrisy, and its crushing of those who do not conform. Certainly *Teeftallow* is discernibly similar to *Main Street* in subject and tone. It also draws a telling picture of a southern small town politician, Railroad Jones, who builds his way into dominance in the town and into riches for himself, all of this resting upon his playing upon the cupidity of his townsmen. In 1928 again Stribling attempted to penetrate the nature of the pietistically religious, superstitious small towns in their crassness, ugliness, materialism, and narrow suspicion of those from outside, in *Bright Metal*, the story of a sophisticated woman's marriage into a Tennessee mountain town and her adjustment to this environment. Stribling's major work came in the early thirties. It is a trilogy, *The Forge* (1931), *The Store* (1932), and *Unfinished Cathedral* (1934), dealing with the middle-class Vaiden family in and around Florence,

Alabama, its rise from its near poor-white status to its dominance as an important family in the region, its collapse after the Civil War into the poor-white class, the building of a fortune by Miltiades Vaiden, former leader of the Ku Klux Klan, who attempts by various means and ultimately by a major and unscrupulous theft to build a store upon which his fortune shall rest, and who finally, in the last novel of the trilogy, set in the days of Muscle Shoals, has achieved his local greatness, and tries to build a cathedral to be his monument to the future. He has a quadroon sister, who is the mother of his son for whose death he is responsible. He has a daughter whose liaison with a local boy during an attempted lynching results in her subsequent marriage to a schoolteacher attracted by her obvious charms. These books are realistic studies in a broadly satiric manner of the conditions of southern life, and they bring under continuous scrutiny the ideal of an aristocratic South and subject it to iconoclastic examination. The result is a picture of middle-class and poor-white life existing just above the level of poverty. Stribling's portrait of the South is devastating, and it is little wonder that the Agrarians turned upon him in rage and called him a "scalawag" writer. Donald Davidson, for example, in reviewing *Teeftallow* called it "the sort of realism that turns up stones in Tennessee pastures in order to display the slime and the crawling, hideous creatures underneath."[3]

Stribling's novels are seldom marked by a very high level of literary accomplishment. He writes with a crude and blunt directness, destroys his sometimes fascinating characters by making them more often the instruments of his satire than the subjects of his art, and has a certain juvenile quality that undercuts his obvious seriousness. There is no reason to revive his novels, although anyone seriously interested in the totality of literary experience in the South in the twentieth century can ignore *The Forge, The Store*, and *Unfinished Cathedral* only at the risk of being ignorant of many of the sources of far better works which came later. The significance of Stribling is that he recognized the subject matter of the middle-class and poor-white South existing in the Piedmont and mountain sections, and that he wrote a series of novels treating this material seriously as a commentary on one southern way of life. In so doing he established a manner and he foreshadowed with remarkable accuracy a great many of the themes which later were to be undertaken by better writers. Without intending to suggest for one moment that William Faulkner borrowed the energy, the art, or even the plots of his works from anyone other than his own private daemon, I think that it is worthy of note that Faulkner did purchase upon publication and preserve until his death copies of Stribling's trilogy,[4] and that the history of the Vaidens, their decline to the level of the shiftless white, and their rise through unscrupulous methods to the control of the bank and then the town parallels closely enough the saga of the Snopes clan and the history and the treatment of miscegenation parallel *Absalom, Absalom!* closely enough to suggest that in walking Frenchman's Bend and Sutpen's Hundred, Faulkner was following at however much higher a level of excellence the footsteps of an early trail blazer. It is Stribling as trail blazer upon whom I would center your attention. He discovered a lode of subject matter in the South and a method for mining that lode, and the example of his limited success in dealing with it must be measured against the far greater success of others who mined with higher skill the lodes which he had initially pointed out.

While Stribling was producing this work, Edith Summers Kelley in 1922 wrote *Weeds*, a grimly realistic picture of the life of the share-cropper's wife in Kentucky. *Weeds*, a book that deserves far broader circulation than it has received in recent years, establishes too a pattern which was to be followed for a long time and which added an edge of bitterness and willingness to discuss the ugly facts of life to the concern with "plain people" which Ellen Glasgow had been showing in her novels since the turn of the century.

Thomas Wolfe's South was the mountain world which, with only slight changes, Stribling had portrayed in *Bright Metal* and *Teeftallow*. Certainly his subject was primarily his own individual growth and his struggle toward identity. Yet it was a growth and a struggle that took place against a definite and sharply realized place. Even in his *Bildungs-roman, Look Homeward, Angel*, the people, customs, and beliefs of his home town are drawn in depth and with unflattering attention to warts and weaknesses. He declared that he had begun writing under the influence of James Joyce and that he had first written in a lyric mode. He came at last to seek "objectivity" and to attempt the portrayal of an outer world.[5] That world was often New York and Europe, but it was also—until the end—the South of middle-class small towns and cities, and upon it he turned a distinctly satiric touch. In *You Can't Go Home Again*, which is more nearly a collection of short novels and sketches than a unified work, three instances might be cited: "I Have a Thing to Tell You," a short novel attacking the German Third Reich and written with almost startling objectivity; "The House That Jack Built," a short novel describing through satiric portrait and recurrent symbol the injustice and insecurity of the rich in New York; and the last five chapters of Book One of the novel, much of which was originally written as a short novel "Boom Town," and portions of which were published in the *American Mercury* and the *New Masses*.[6] In all these sections Wolfe writes with directness, impersonality, and in a style which, when com-

The Roots of Southern Writing

pared to most of his work, is barren. Few more devastating attacks on crass materialism, impersonal capitalism, and surrender of moral values in a southern town have been drawn than those in the "Boom Town" section. It is Stribling's attitude presented by a novelist of great merit, much as Faulkner's Snopeses are Stribling's poor whites portrayed by a genius.

Thus Wolfe came back at the end of his life to a position which he had held as early as 1923 when he had written contemptuously of "people who shout 'Progress, Progress, Progress'—when what they mean is more Ford automobiles, more Rotary Clubs, more Baptist Ladies Social Unions.... What I shall try to get into their dusty, little pint-measure minds is that a full belly, a good automobile does not make them one whit better or finer,—that there is beauty in this world,—beauty even in this wilderness of ugliness and provincialism."[7] Now that is the brashness of youth mixed with the brashness of Lewis, but there is every reason to believe that Wolfe never deserted the position or changed his belief that it was a defensible—even a fine—subject for fictional treatment. Yet few writers have been more intensely of the South or—whatever you may think of the problem of form—are more essential to the southern renascence. One of the Agrarians once suggested that Wolfe went to the wrong college; I think he is wrong, for Wolfe was simply true to the impulse he felt to love and write of his region while subjecting it to serious criticism.

And I think that, at least in the beginning, this was also true of Erskine Caldwell. In his autobiography Caldwell says of *Tobacco Road:* "I felt that I would never be able to write successfully about other people in other places until first I had written the story of the landless and poverty-stricken families living on East Georgia sand hills and tobacco roads. ...I wanted to tell the story of the people I knew in the manner in which they actually lived their lives ... and to tell it without regard for fashions in writing and traditional plots. It seemed to me that the most authentic and enduring materials of fiction were the people themselves."[8] In *Tobacco Road* Caldwell wrote with great simplicity and force of style—a clean, hard, clear, and forceful prose—of the lives of people so stripped of economic and social hope that they become grotesques and parodies of human beings, twisted by the simplest hungers and lacking in dignity or integrity. The stage version has produced the view that this story is comic. Caldwell has expressed his distress at this view and has suggested that the desire to portray, the desire to define, and a substantial degree of social anger are behind his early efforts. "All I wanted to do," he has said, "was simply to describe to the best of my ability the aspirations and despair of the people I wrote about."[9]

He was to continue describing the people of his depleted South in many novels and stories. At least two other novels and a number of his short stories demand our consideration when we write of the renascence. *God's Little Acre* follows the people of the depleted countryside to a cotton mill village during a strike. *Trouble in July* is a powerful lynching novel. Perhaps the finest single piece of work of Caldwell's is the short novel "Kneel to the Rising Sun," a story of a sadistic white land-owner, a spineless tenant farmer, and a courageous but doomed Negro. Those who think of Caldwell exclusively in terms of the semipornographic paperbacks which in recent years have made him one of the best-selling novelists of all time, might well reread this grim tale of wanton cruelty, injustice, and cowardice. It has a controlled fury that lingers in the mind and heart, and it is written with an apparently artless simplicity which the artist can achieve only after many hours of seeking for clarity and grace.

Flannery O'Connor has taken what are essentially these same people and almost this same locale and has fashioned from them, their lives, and their frustrations a series of short stories and two novels rich in religious symbolisms that speak to the present world with great authority. Her characters and Caldwell's are remarkably similar and one has the feeling that they might move with relative ease from the books of one writer to the other and be at home. That this similarity is present should not be surprising, for both writers are dealing with the same region and its poor whites and Negroes, people to whom sex and religion are practically the only interludes in a world of ignorance and despair. The characters of each writer are truly grotesques—that is, distorted or twisted permanently out of the normal. I think that *A Good Man Is Hard To Find*, Miss O'Connor's first collection of short stories, is her best work—although her total production assays remarkably high—and of that group of tales I think the best is the final short novel, "The Displaced Person." There is not a character in "The Displaced Person" who would have trouble orienting himself in the world of *God's Little Acre*. Yet there is a tremendous difference between the approaches of Erskine Caldwell and Flannery O'Connor to their worlds.

Caldwell's people are twisted and misshapen by social and economic deprivation. Fertilize the soil, return the price of cotton to a subsistence level, supply them with opportunity, and hope will follow and in another generation something like the good life may return. It is the system that is wrong, and the system is remediable. Hence the social anger and the protest.

Not so with Flannery O'Connor. For her these people are made grotesque by their unsatisfied hunger for God, and around them she weaves

The Roots of Southern Writing

her religious, almost theological themes. The twisted lives which Erskine Caldwell saw and drew become in her hands telling metaphors for the restless soul's disquiet when it rejects the God it seeks. But the materials she uses are indigenous to her time and place. If the peacocks in "The Displaced Person" are epiphanies of God's love for man, they are also like the fowls that roosted in the trees around the O'Connor farmhouse outside Milledgeville. If Mr. Guizac, the displaced person, brings salvation to Mrs. McIntyre's farm, he does it by displaying the virtues of neatness, cleanliness, and mechanic skill, and we must wait for Mrs. McIntyre to say, "Christ was just another D.P."[10] before we can be certain that Miss O'Connor intends us to see this story as a parable of the rejection of Christ.

Miss O'Connor's succinct, witty, and very direct style is a far cry from Stribling's overwritten sentences or Wolfe's rhetoric, but it is applied with great success to picturing her segment of the South as a microcosm of the human lot. Like Hawthorne Miss O'Connor wanted to produce a work which had physical substance enough to stand alone and yet bodied forth some deep philosophic truth. Her truth was Catholic and universal, but her physical substance was distinctively southern and clearly related to a part of the South which was far removed from the historical heritage of aristocratic grace and chivalric dignity and honor.

I have tried to suggest that there is a body of southern material represented by Stribling, Wolfe, Caldwell, and O'Connor which is closer to the tradition of social realism rather than that of the Joycean aesthetics or the *Künstlerroman*. Lest you should have to take such a view on faith, I should like to suggest that it can be tested by a reading of Book One of *You Can't Go Home Again* as a portrayal of middle-class materialism in the manner of Sinclair Lewis; "Kneel to the Rising Sun," as a portrayal of hopelessness created by extreme poverty; and "The Displaced Person," as a portrayal of spiritual deprivation and denial. These works have certain characteristics in common which are worth noting. In the first place none of these stories is centered in the individual or the individual's growth or development. Each describes a social world outside the narrator and places its emphasis on the conduct of people in that social world. In other words each belongs, in its differing way, to the broad school of social fiction.

In the second place—and this is true even of the selection by Wolfe—the styles are remarkably uniform, not mixed;[11] that is, each writer in these selections maintains a single voice. Wolfe's is literary, edging toward rhetoric, but essentially geared to the satiric presentation of a slightly exaggerated transcript from life. Caldwell's is simple, direct, with underlying folk rhythms, resulting in part from repetition and in part from a folk vocabulary. Miss O'Connor's is clear, sharply focused, simple, sardonic and detached in tone but possessed of great energy.

In the third place all deal with distinctively southern subject matter, but with people and places outside the setting of the Tidewater or the deep South, and with characters who can accurately be called grotesque. Wolfe wrote scathingly of the ugliness of the life of the hill people— what he called the "mountain grills"—and certainly blind and syphilitic Judge Rumford Bland should rank high on any list of grotesques. Yet the characters of these three writers are really less literary grotesques than nonsouthern critics would have us believe. These authors have not made grotesques: they have pictured tormented, twisted, and diseased lives which most of us can recognize as actually existing and within our experience. As Miss O'Connor once said, "Any fiction that comes out of the South is going to be called grotesque by northern readers—unless it is really grotesque. Then—it is going to be called photographic realism." [12]

A fourth common characteristic that these works share is a consistent vision of the unrealized potential in the life of the section they describe. All of these works portray characters defeated and depleted by social forces and circumstances that impoverish their lives. Wolfe's characters are the victims of a false sense of values in a business world. Caldwell's are the victims of grinding economic depression. Miss O'Connor's are the victims of a religious environment that stifles the hunger for God. All, too, are looking forward not backward, outward not inward, and each in his own way is preaching change.

Yes, I think we must insist that social criticism was a legitimate and significant part of the southern renascence. But the social conditions which called this wave of criticism forth are passing or have passed. Caldwell's characters' children have moved to town; they buy a new car every two or three years; and their children are in high school and applying for fellowships to the University of Georgia. Wolfe's characters batten on affluence and their towns are now cities. Miss O'Connor's people are closer to our time, and, significantly, their problem is really not economic poverty.

The moment when Mr. Tate's backward look was fruitful has passed. The history it embraced is recognized as legend and manipulated as myth and it has lost its generative force. Is the same thing also true of the social criticism of the renascence? As tobacco roads give way to interstate highways, as country stores become shopping centers, as small towns become the suburban areas of booming cities, is the South as social subject any longer relevant? Can one take the glass-enclosed elevator to the twenty-second floor of the Regency Hyatt in Atlanta and look out upon a world distinctively different from what he might see in

New York, Chicago, or Los Angeles, even if he doesn't glance at the nationally televised game being played in the Falcons' and Braves' splendid new stadium, or listen to the homogenized accents of its announcer? The answer is that he can, if he looks closely enough at home. As Louis Rubin pointed out to me, within two blocks of the Regency Hyatt you can find street evangelists extolling their primitive religions in tone and manner that make you think Hazel Motes of *Wise Blood* has come back to life.

Now certainly the problems have changed, but I believe that the characteristics that distinguish the region from the rest of the nation are still distinctively here, and that they give a special southern aspect and a unique value to the artistic representation of life in the United States. These distinctive characteristics are, as you may recall that I asserted in the beginning, the presence of the Negro and the shame of his enslavement and second-class citizenship; the historical experience of military defeat, military occupation, and reconstruction; and a predominantly agricultural economy. Only one of these—the agricultural economy— seems likely to pass soon; and to the extent to which the southern renascence assumed such an agrarian way of life, that renascence ended with the Second World War. But the South remains a self-conscious region. Its hamlets may become towns, its towns cities; its accent may be flattened by television and radio; its passion for religious dimensions to life may take the form of studied ritual rather than primitive spontaneity; but so long as the Negro remains and history can speak with authority, the South will be a potent subject for serious art. That art will, I believe, continue to be interested both in the problems of social situations and in those of individual development and identity. I hope, and believe, that southern writers will continue to use these problems with high seriousness and great relevancy. After all, as Miss O'Connor once observed, "Southern writers are stuck with the South, and it's a very good thing to be stuck with."[13]

Ellen Glasgow: The Novelist
of Manners as Social Critic

Even her realm of phantasy was a small enclosed province, peopled
by skeletons of tradition and governed by a wooden theology.
—Ellen Glasgow.[1]

The oldest culture produced by English-speaking people in the Colonial
South was that of Tidewater Virginia, a region settled in large measure
as an economic enterprise by English adventurers who were financed by
large trading companies and who brought with them not only the
inclination to name their new lands in honor of their old monarchs—the
Virgin Queen and James and William—but also to create, so far as in
them lay, a social order as nearly like that of the British aristocracy as
they found to be possible. Perhaps only a few of these Tidewater explorers
and colonizers carried within their veins the blood of noble families, but
most of them carried within their brains the dream of noble orders; and
the Cavalier tradition in government, the Episcopal tradition in religion,
the pragmatic profit motive in philosophy, and the hedonistic aim in social customs helped to establish along the Atlantic seaboard a South of
hierarchical values and class and caste distinctions.

In the latter part of the century other Englishmen came to settle the
lands assigned by Charles II to the Lords Proprietors, and they created at
the confluence of the Cooper and Ashley Rivers a city called Charleston
and a culture which finally resulted from the mingling of several races—
among them the English, the Spanish Jews, the French Huguenots, and
the Irish immigrants. This society achieved a quality in Colonial times
that made South Carolinians aspire, as Henry Adams notes, "to a desire
to other distinctions than those which could be earned at the bar or on
the plantation." As Adams said in his monumental *History of the United
States During the Administrations of Jefferson and Madison,* "The small
society of rice and cotton planters at Charleston, with their cultivated
tastes and hospitable habits, delighted in whatever reminded them of
European civilization. They were travellers, readers, and scholars; the
society of Charleston compared well in refinement with that of any
city of its size in the world, and English visitors long thought it the
most agreeable in America."[2]

At the area around Williamsburg, Jamestown, and Richmond, there
early developed a society of the tobacco aristocrats whose plantations
stretched along the James and its tributaries and formed the basis for a

The Roots of Southern Writing

demanding but urbane agrarian culture. There, as it had been in South Carolina, the culture was established as a result of what Thomas J. Wertenbaker called the four great factors acting on Colonial society—foreign inheritance, local conditions, continued contact with Europe, and the melting pot. By the end of the eighteenth century, as Wertenbaker also points out, "the Boston merchant, the Virginia tobacco aristocrat, the rice millionaire of South Carolina . . . had the time and the inclination to turn from the counting room or the management of slaves or the disposing of crops to the higher things of life."[3]

At its noblest and best, in the vast rice plantations along the Ashley River, in estates like William Byrd's Westover, and in the genteel life antiseptically recreated in Mr. Rockefeller's Williamsburg, this Tidewater and Low Country culture was the closest thing to a society of fixed classes with an ideal of impeccable manners and gracious living that the North American hemisphere has ever known. That it was realized only in part, that it crested in colonial days and began its slow decline in the early years of the nineteenth century, and that it had more power as a dream and a faith than it did as a fact does not alter greatly—and, in fact, may enhance—its pervasive and continuing influence on America and Americans.

The attempt to create an actual order of social conduct, of manners, and of gracious living was unique among American societies. This order rested upon a caste system in society, upon an established religion, and upon a concept of honor which expressed itself primarily through manners. In this seaboard society there was little room for the skeptic, the cynic, the malcontent, or the criminal. The western frontier—and the "lubberland" of North Carolina—both welcomed and enticed these classes, so that those who remained had a remarkably large body of commonly held assumptions and ideals. Behind this relatively stable society was a way of life not far removed from the ideals of neoclassic England in the days of the country squire. Few Virginia or Carolina planters were American equivalents of Sir Roger de Coverley, but many of them knew the essays by Addison and Steele which made de Coverley a permanent part of the American as well as the British mind. This seaboard culture was perhaps as fruitful an area for the novel of manners as America has ever produced.

The term "novel of manners" describes a work in which the outer forms of a relatively closed society are stable, so that a character may be tested against them as against a fairly inflexible yardstick of conduct and belief. At few times in the history of the modern world have adequate conditions existed for such novels of manners in an absolute sense. Jane Austen, writing of the country gentry in English rural villages in the

days of the Napoleonic Wars, produced the most nearly absolute comedies of manners which the English language has known. Within her
rural villages change occurred very slowly, and the English squirearchy
defined a view of life being modified at a snail's pace; yet Jane Austen
wrote during two decades of British history which produced the most
radical changes in the structure of England which occurred before the
Second World War. She sat in country parsonages while Napoleon
dominated Europe and penned novels concerned essentially with marriage as a social institution; and while two brothers were in Nelson's
fleet at Trafalgar, she continued to portray not the world of war but the
same closed British society. Two years after her death, the Peterloo
Massacre occurred; and fifteen years later the first of the great Reform
Bills was passed by Parliament, so that Miss Austen's novels of manners
were essentially novels which tested men and women in a sharply arrested moment in human history. In a world of dynamic change—and
particularly in a democratic society—the novelist of manners must always
seek such arrested moments. The adequacy of the Tidewater culture for
such novels of manners has perhaps been approached in America only
by the society of Knickerbocker New York and certain portions of New
England. Thus it early attracted the attention of writers of fiction who
were interested in preserving a record of its structure.

In 1832 John Pendleton Kennedy in *Swallow Barn* attempted to define
the nature and the ideals of the Tidewater plantation society. His work
was, as even he insisted, not a novel but a collection of fictional sketches
describing life at Swallow Barn, "an aristocratical old edifice which sits,
like a brooding hen on the southern bank of the James River."[4] Behind
Kennedy's view of life on the plantation was the example of Washington
Irving's attempt in *Bracebridge Hall* to define the conventions, customs,
and eccentricities of the British squire. Kennedy's book has often been
regarded as the first fictional document in the creation of the concept of
a plantation tradition. It was followed by the work of many other writers,
and Virginia became the subject for a representation of a society with a
social structure resting upon a tradition of manners. This structure
found its expression in many different ways over the years of change.
Thomas Nelson Page, in *In Ole Virginia*, a collection of short stories,
and in the novel *Red Rock*, gave this society an idealized and sentimental
treatment through which he presented an apologia for the vanished
South. He once said that this South "partook of the philosophical tone
of the Grecian, of the dominant spirit of the Roman, and of the guardful-
ness of individual rights of the Saxon civilization. And over all brooded
a softness and beauty, the joint product of Chivalry and Christianity."[5]
It was thus, as Ellen Glasgow saw, that "the spirit of adventure had dis-

integrated into an evasive idealism, a philosophy of heroic defeat."[6]

James Branch Cabell attempted in a long series of novels under the collective title *The Biography of the Life of Manuel* to pick up the themes of such a society, to trace them through an imaginary European country, and finally to bring them to Virginia and in particular to Lichfield, a city very much like Richmond. The themes he chose were the chivalrous, the gallant, and the poetic; and in applying them to his imaginary world, he saw the chivalrous as a testing, the gallant as a toy, and the poetic as raw material. The finest of these novels dealing with Virginia were *The Cream of the Jest: A Comedy of Evasions*, *The Rivet in Grandfather's Neck: A Comedy of Limitations*, and *The Cords of Vanity: A Comedy of Shirking*. Cabell was consciously constructing through an art a world that was remote, ironically romantic, and, finally, strongly suggestive of an ideal. He believed that only in the effort to assert the impossible through a dream can we begin to approach making that dream in any sense real. Thus one of his novelist characters declares that he is writing "an apology for romance by a man who believes that romance is dead beyond resurrection"; and particularly in his Virginia novels Cabell presents in each book a protagonist who "after his allotted jaunt, with youth to incite him, into outlandish regions, accepts more or less willingly his allotted place in the social organisms of his own people and country."[7]

It was to this South that Ellen Glasgow looked in her long career as a novelist; and out of its structure of manners undergoing steady attrition through the rise of the middle class, she made both serious fiction and comic novels. In the world about her she thought she saw that "what distinguished the Southerner, and particularly the Virginian, from his severer neighbours to the north was his ineradicable belief that pleasure is worth more than toil, that it is worth more even than profit. Although the difference between the Virginian and the far Southerner was greater than the distance between Virginia and Massachusetts, a congenial hedonism had established in the gregarious South a confederacy of the spirit."[8] Thus the Tidewater South became for her "a living tradition decayed, with the passage of years, into a sentimental infirmity." She knew that by and large this old South did not exist, that it had "vanished from the world of fact to reappear in the permanent realm of fable.... What we are in danger of forgetting," she said, "is that few possessions are more precious than a fable that no longer can be compared with a fact."[9] It is out of that fable that she fashioned her best work; and the result is that the most obvious serious artistic use which has so far been made of Virginia as a subject for the novel of manners has been the work of Ellen Glasgow.

Ellen Glasgow as Social Critic

In the long series of novels which she published between 1897 and 1941 she attempted to produce a body of work which spanned the social history of Virginia from the Civil War to the present. She said, "I began a history of manners that would embrace those aspects of Southern life with which I was acquainted.... I planned to portray the different social orders, and especially, for this would constitute the major theme of my chronicle, the rise of the middle class as the dominant force in Southern democracy."[10] Whether this intention of Miss Glasgow's indeed existed clearly in her mind as early as 1897 and continued on until the 1940s is a matter of substantial debate. Her friend, James Branch Cabell, has declared that he suggested to Miss Glasgow that she arrange her work in this historical pattern in the late 1920s, and that she embraced the idea and made it retroactive. She has, of course, had gallant defenders against Mr. Cabell's unchivalrous remarks, and the truth seems to lie somewhere between.[11] Probably she did, with only partial consciousness, attempt to construct a fictional history of her state and then after the fact embraced the firm idea when Mr. Cabell pointed out to her the presence of many characteristics of social history in her fiction. She arranged into three groups the thirteen novels she valued most highly of the nineteen books of fiction which she produced. The first of these groups consists of six novels of the commonwealth, in which she sketches the history of Virginia from 1850 to 1912. The second group consists of three novels of the country, which span the period between 1898 and 1933 and which deal with the changing agrarian culture of rural Virginia with a substantial emphasis upon those people of good character, strong effort, and pietistic religion whom she called "plain people" and to whom she attributed the qualities of respectability and sound common sense. (She seems to have shared the belief of General Archbald in *The Sheltered Life* that they are people "who could be trusted in revolutions."[12]) The third group is made up of four novels of the city—three of them tragicomedies of manners; the fourth was a final and despairing farewell to an urban life in which beauty, dignity, and value can be found only in the enduring sacrifice of oppressed people.

She felt that she had written her best books after 1922. These books were *Barren Ground* (1925), a Hardyesque narrative of Dorinda Oakley who personified in the country "the spirit that fought with gallantry and gaiety, and that in defeat remained undefeated";[13] *The Romantic Comedians* (1926), a comedy of manners laid in Queenborough; *They Stooped to Folly* (1929), a Queenborough comedy of marriage; *The Sheltered Life* (1932), a tragicomedy laid in Queenborough; *Vein of Iron* (1935), a grim novel of the country; and *In This Our Life* (1941), a dark novel of the city. She regarded *The Sheltered Life* and *Barren Ground* as her two finest novels, and her judgment has been accepted by most of her critics.[14]

Ellen Glasgow was both the self-conscious spokesman for the seaboard southern culture and at the same time one of its sharpest critics. For her the tradition of manners and the pattern of conduct which the Tidewater South had produced served the function of making those tests of character and of custom upon which she wished to expend her energies. She was a part of the region of which she wrote and lived most of her life in Richmond. She was caught up herself in a pattern of behavior common to the patrician citizen of the post–Civil War world; and yet it was a world whose traditions seemed to her to have survived as empty forms long after the demise of the moral convictions and the ethical systems which originally had called them forth.

Her subject matter, as she herself defined it, was the "retreat of an agrarian culture before the conquests of an industrial revolution, and the slow and steady rise of the lower middle class."[15] From the beginning of her career irony was the device which she used to lay bare the inner nature of the social order which was her subject. The South's greatest needs, she declared, were "blood and irony." "Blood," she said, "because Southern culture had strained too far away from its roots in the earth"; and irony because she thought it to be "the safest antidote to sentimental decay."[16] That her society was one in which tradition had solidified into meaningless postures made it, she felt, a proper subject for comedies and tragicomedies of manners, for she saw everywhere about her what she called "a tone of manners [which] rang hollow [because] the foundations of the old aristocratic order ... had never safely settled back on their cornerstone of tradition."[17]

It is in the three comedies of manners, *The Romantic Comedians,* *They Stooped to Folly*, and *The Sheltered Life*, that she dealt most effectively with the manners and traditions of the Tidewater after they had reached a state of decay; and the representation of the impact of this stultifying tradition thus becomes the major subject of her novels of the city. This tradition creates a way of life at a price that is extremely high. At one point in *The Sheltered Life* she writes about "the code of perfect behaviour [which] supported her as firmly as if it had been a cross."[18] Most of her characters are, like Judge Gamaliel Honeywell in *The Romantic Comedians*, representations of Virginia society, "spritely in speech ... ceremonious in manner."[19] The judge had, she felt, been "Southern in sentiment, yet not provincial in thought, he had attached himself to the oppressed minority ... the urbane and unprejudiced South."[20] However, he was, she felt, "disposed to encourage liberty of thought as long as he was convinced that it did not lead to liberal views."[21] This kind of society ultimately shaped a conventional mind that was safe from the onslaught of reality. The people who made up her social world, Miss Glasgow felt, were like Mrs. Upchurch in *The Romantic Comedians*, who "had a small mind but knew it thoroughly," and they could "recite the Apostles' Creed so long as [they were] not required to practice the Sermon on the Mount, and could countenance Evolution until it threatened the image of its Maker."[22] She was, she declared, describing in these novels of manners "an epoch when faith and facts did not cultivate an acquaintance."[23]

She was a polished craftsman, and her effort to describe this society was one in which she exercised a very well developed and most effective literary artistry, and she was self-conscious about the extent to which the work she was doing differed from much fiction that was being written in her own time. She included many of her southern contemporaries in the class of those who wrote without learning their craft first, as a painter might do when he never learned how to make his brushstrokes. Faulkner's creations, for example, she regarded as "monstrous." In a querulous tone she said, "Pompous illiteracy, escaped from some Freudian cage, is in the saddle, and the voice of the amateur is the voice of authority.... To the poet, it is true, especially if he can arrange with destiny to die young, the glow of adolescence may impart an unfading magic. But the novel . . . requires more substantial ingredients than a little ignorance of life and a great yearning to tell everything one has ever known."[24]

In keeping with this view her novels of manners are well made and self-consciously written books. Behind almost every sentence can be heard the urbane voice of the novelist guiding the reader to consciousness of the final absurdity of lives surrendered to dead traditions. She said of *The Romantic Comedians* in one of her franker and less modest moments that she felt that as a comedy of manners it had never been surpassed in the novel form. Acknowledging that it was, she felt, "a slight novel," still she could maintain that within its limits it was nearly perfect.[25]

In her novels of manners Ellen Glasgow repeatedly shows us men and women of wisdom and perception who lack the moral courage to act upon their knowledge and hence are destroyed by societies whose fundamental weakness they recognize but to which they bring not anger or resistance but amusement and retreat. Nowhere is this characteristic more obvious than in her novel *The Sheltered Life* where her protagonist, she claims, is General Archbald. She regards the general as an example of "the civilized mind in a world where even the civilizations we make are uncivilized";[26] and yet despite that kind of praise General Archbald is finally a representative figure of his own world, a world that subscribes to a false idealism. At every crucial point he has lacked the quality of character which would have enabled him to make his civilized mind felt as an active force in his decaying civilization.

In *The Sheltered Life* Miss Glasgow was attempting to examine Queenborough society through two opposing points of view. One is that of youth, personified in Jenny Blair Archbald, whose innocence and adolescent ignorance ultimately become the instruments of destruction. The other is age represented by General Archbald, who views at the end of a long life the conflict of tradition with change and sees that the shelter which his fixed society has erected to protect its members against reality ultimately has failed despite the fact that from him it has elicited a cost that is far greater than any values it could have given in return. In his eighties he knows that "what he had wanted, he had never had; what he had wished to do, he had never done."[27] He had given up the woman whom he had loved because an accidental delay in a snowstorm had forced him to compromise another woman in the public view, although not in the private fact. She was a woman for whom he had much respect but no affection, yet he followed the demands of tradition and married the "compromised" woman. Looking back across his past, he could declare, "Few men at eighty-three were able to look back upon so firm and rich a past, upon so smooth and variegated a surface. A surface! Yes, that, he realized now, was the flaw in the structure. Except for that one defeated passion in his youth, he had lived entirely upon the shifting surface of facts. He had been a good citizen, a successful lawyer, a faithful husband, an indulgent father; he had been, indeed, everything but himself. Always he had fallen into the right pattern; but the centre of the pattern was missing."[28] Jenny Blair says of him, "Grandfather has very queer notions. Mamma told me he was so queer when he was young that everybody was surprised when he made a good living. I asked him about that, and he laughed and said that he made a good living by putting an end to himself."[29]

General Archbald and Jenny Blair, youth and age, viewing a system that is rapidly passing away, are the instruments by which Miss Glasgow defines a view which she expressed in a letter about *The Sheltered Life*: "The two overlapping themes are ... that we cannot put up a shelter against life and we kill what we love too much." By the term "sheltered life" Miss Glasgow meant, she said, "the whole civilization man has built to protect himself from reality";[30] and the harshest of the criticisms that she can level is implied in that statement, for it is the willing separation of her characters from reality which allows them finally to become the sources not of tragic power but of comic laughter.

In *They Stooped to Folly* Miss Glasgow was, by her own definition, attempting to embody "one of the immemorial women-myths in a modern comedy of manners."[31] In this case the myth was that of the "ruined woman" and the varying ways in which the tradition within which she lived expressed itself through its handling of her. *They Stooped to Folly* also demonstrates another of Miss Glasgow's methods of dissecting this society. In this novel she shows Mr. Littlepage and those who are around him as subservient to an imagined but sterile moral order. The title applies to three different instances in three succeeding generations of Oliver Goldsmith's lovely woman "who stoops to folly and finds too late that men betray." In three generations this "ruined woman" moves from the attic where the family imprisons her in their joint disgrace to the center of the social scene where her moral error is almost a social asset. That Mr. Littlepage has given his life in support of an ideal of no more finality and longevity than this would be tragic if Mr. Littlepage had the appropriate "magnitude" to meet Aristotle's definition. The fate of a great man can be tragic; the same fate earned by a pleasant fool can be amusing; and Miss Glasgow is a skilled (and sometimes malicious) painter of male fools.

Each of these novels is close to the novel of manners even though none of them succeeds in completely realizing the full novel of manners as a form. The English novel of manners is, as we have said, essentially a novel which tests men and women by accepted standards of conduct in a sharply arrested moment in history. Miss Glasgow had no such arrested moment with which to deal. For her, life itself and the lives of her characters were lived out at a time when order and tradition, if they survived at all, had to survive not as a meaningful or as a static ideal but through a vain defiance of the great realities of social change which made her world. Her comedies of manners, therefore, if we can apply the term to them, are significantly different from those of Jane Austen, for Miss Austen's world was a world of social conventions that adequately reflected its inner beliefs about the nature and interrelationship of men. Miss Glasgow's world was a world in which the conventions had outlived the beliefs which they once expressed. Hence she could and did use terms like "evasive idealism" and "sentimental decay" and use them with accuracy. Her characters are tested not by their conformity to a meaningful code but by their futile rebellion against a dead one. Yet the structure and nature of the society of the Tidewater is imprisoned in these books in what Miss Glasgow once called "a single luminous drop of experience."[32] And, although the "single luminous drop" has a brief life span, the Tidewater society is her subject, and she describes it out of knowledge and affection. Nevertheless the mode she has chosen and the style she has used become ultimately a thoroughgoing and quite unsentimental attack upon the positive values of the Tidewater South.

Miss Glasgow's ultimate position on this tradition and on other southern writers and their treatment of it is ambiguous, however. The "comfortable mediocrity" which constitutes for her the essence of "Americanism" she deeply distrusts. The rebellion of the twentieth century southern writer is for her a source for praise, even while she maintains serious reservations about the artistic and technical adequacy of the writers. "After breaking away from a petrified past overgrown by a funereal tradition," she says, "an impressive group of Southern writers recoiled from the uniform concrete surface of an industrialized South ... for the first time in its history, the South is producing, by some subtle process of aversion, a literature of revolt."[33] When she names some of the writers who are accomplishing this ideal, she includes Thomas Wolfe, William Faulkner, Allen Tate, and Caroline Gordon.

The Tidewater culture introduced into America the dream of the British aristocracy. It flourished in a dream of chivalric glory. The Tidewater and Low Country South gave order, leadership, and intellectual guidance to an agrarian culture. But, as Miss Glasgow demonstrates by personal example, by reiterated statement, and by dramatic presentation, it had reached the stage by the 1930s where its virtues were of the past, its strength in legends and not facts, and its structure honeycombed with the dry rot of time and custom. Not to love it was, for Miss Glasgow at least, impossible; and yet to fail to subject it to ironic analysis would be to succumb to its worst failings. Such a culture in such a state compellingly demanded to be treated in the novel of manners. Both it and we are fortunate that such a novelist was available as Ellen Glasgow.

The Dark, Ruined Helen of his Blood
Thomas Wolfe and the South

Thomas Wolfe was born and grew to young manhood in Asheville, North Carolina. When he went north after his graduation from the University of North Carolina, he went as a southerner, to write of southern subjects in George Pierce Baker's "47 Workshop" at Harvard University, and to compose his first novel out of the southern scenes of his childhood with an autobiographical candor and an accuracy shocking to the residents of his native city. Yet Thomas Wolfe never returned for long to the South, once he had left it—indeed, he declared that "you can't go home again"—and the portrait that he drew of his native region in his first novel elicited from his former Chapel Hill classmate Jonathan Daniels the charge that "in *Look Homeward, Angel*, North Carolina and the South are spat upon." Some critics have believed, as Maxwell Geismar suggested, that Wolfe "was born in the South, but he shared with it little except the accident of birth."[1]

Upon his native region he heaped a Gargantuan scorn in his sprawling, loosely constructed tales and novels, condemning what in *Look Homeward, Angel* he called the southerners' "hostile and murderous intrenchment against all new life . . . their cheap mythology, their legend of the charm of their lives, the quaint sweetness of their drawl." In *The Web and the Rock* he expresses his anger at "the old, stricken, wounded 'Southness' of cruelty and lust," at men who "have a starved, stricken leanness in the loins," and at the lynchings that end with castrations, betraying his mingled disgust and sense of shame. The southern intellectual fared little better in Wolfe's novels. He had contempt for the Agrarians whom he called in *The Web and the Rock* "the refined young gentlemen of the New Confederacy . . . [who] retired haughtily into the South, to the academic security of a teaching appointment at one of the universities, from which they could issue in quarterly installments very small and very precious magazines which celebrated the advantages of an agrarian society." And he wrote with feeling in the same novel of "the familiar rationalizing self-defense of Southern fear and Southern failure: its fear of conflict and of competition in the greater world; its inability to meet or to adjust itself to the conditions, strifes, and ardors of a modern life; its old, sick, Appomattoxlike retreat into the shades of folly and delusion, of prejudice and bigotry, of florid legend and defensive casuistry. . . ."

The Roots of Southern Writing

This South was feminine to him—what he called once "*the female principle*—the *earth* again...a home, fixity"—and in his thinking he opposed it to the father principle, which, in *The Story of a Novel*, he called "the image of a strength and wisdom external to his need and superior to his hunger, to which the belief and power of his own life could be united." From the maternal and subjective South, "the dark Helen of his blood," he turned to storm the male citadels of the North and to find in the "enfabled rock" of the northern city a defense against the web of the South. Yet this South beat in his brain and pounded in his veins. "Every young man from the South," he said in *The Web and the Rock*, "has felt this precise and formal geography of the spirit," in which South and North are sharply dichotomized autonomies; and these qualities in young southerners brought to the North "a warmth you lacked, a passion that God knows you needed, a belief and a devotion that was wanting in your life, an integrity of purpose that was rare in your own swarming hordes. They brought...some of the warmth, the depth, the richness of the secret and unfathomed South. They brought some of its depth and mystery.... They brought a warmth of earth, an exultant joy of youth, a burst of living laughter, a fullbodied warmth and living energy of humor." Wolfe could proudly boast in a letter to James Boyd, "I'm a Long Hunter from Bear Creek, and a rootin', tootin', shootin' son-of-a-gun from North Carolina"; and he could write Maxwell Perkins that "the people in North Carolina ... are rich, juicy, deliberate, full of pungent and sardonic humor and honesty, conservative and cautious on top, but at bottom wild, savage, and full of the murderous innocence of the earth and the wilderness." What he said of his character George Webber is true of Wolfe himself: "He was a Southerner, and he knew that there was something wounded in the South. He knew that there was something twisted, dark, and full of pain which Southerners have known all their lives—something rooted in their souls beyond all contradiction." But all his knowledge of her darkness and damnation could not stifle his love for the lost and ruined and burning Helen in his blood.

That his vision of his native region was both obsessive and ambiguous was not surprising. Wolfe was born to a northern father and a southern mother, and the division of life into male and female, North and South, wanderer and homebound, was a simple extension of what he saw daily as a boy. He grew up in a southern mountain town, but at a time when it was changing into a resort city, flourishing in the shadow of the baronial estate of the Vanderbilts, the pseudo-French chateau "Biltmore," and literally mad for money. He went to college at Chapel Hill, a southern state university, but at the time when that school was beginning the pattern of liberalism that made it the symbol of New South progressivism, completely opposite to the agrarianism of Vanderbilt University. Furthermore, at the feet of a locally famed teacher of philosophy, Horace Williams, he imbibed a form of Hegelian dialectic that made him see all life in terms of opposites and gave his work the fundamental structure of thesis and antithesis in sentence, paragraph, and scene as well as in its more obvious oppositions, such as South and North, female and male, Jew and gentile, mother and father, the web and the rock.

Ambiguous and contradictory though his views of his native region were, the South was a theme and a subject matter for much of Wolfe's work, and it existed for him in a sensuous, irrational emotional state of mutual attraction and repulsion. And this contradiction and ambiguity, this coexisting intense love and passionate hatred are characteristic not only of Wolfe's attitudes toward the South but also of his total work. His published writings consist of four novels (two of which appeared posthumously and were prepared for the printer by an editor), two volumes of short stories and sketches (one published posthumously), a play, and a few other items—plays and sketches in magazines—which are of minor importance. The six volumes of novels and short stories represent the significant corpus of his work, and they were carved out of a vast and complex outpouring of words.

The term most often applied to these works is "formless," for their structure is difficult, diffuse, uncertain. *Look Homeward, Angel* and *Of Time and the River* are the adventures of Eugene Gant in his growth from childhood to maturity, and Eugene Gant is an embarrassingly direct portrait of Wolfe himself. *The Web and the Rock* and *You Can't Go Home Again*, the posthumously published novels, trace the similar story of George Webber and carry it on through his love affair with Esther Jack and his success as a novelist. Webber is seemingly as autobiographical as Gant. The stories in *From Death to Morning* and *The Hills Beyond* were all—or almost all—written originally as episodes in the great "book," of which the four novels are parts. Here, in these millions of words, then, is the intensely felt experience of a single person, the author, presented almost entirely without benefit of formal plot or traditional structure. Subjectivity has seldom more totally dominated a major work, and it is difficult to read Wolfe without feeling the justice of Robert Penn Warren's wry comment: "It may be well to recollect that Shakespeare merely wrote *Hamlet;* he was *not* Hamlet."[2]

But imprisoned within this vast body of words are hundreds of sharply realized scenes, dozens of characters who have an authentic existence— W. O. Gant, Eliza Gant, Bascom Pentland, Helen Gant, Francis Starwick, Esther Jack, Judge Rumford Bland, Nebraska Crane—and literally thousands of descriptive passages of such lyric intensity and sensuous directness that they impinge upon the senses of the reader and achieve for a moment in his consciousness a concrete reality.

Few American novelists have projected more ambitious programs or had more demanding plans for their novels. The task Wolfe set himself was, he once wrote in a letter, the representation of "the whole consciousness of his people and nation ... every sight sound and memory of the people." In order to formulate this vast subject, he sought encompassing themes. He concocted a three-part theory of time, which he found inherent in his materials: actual present time, past time, and "time immutable," and saw in their simultaneous projection in a work of fiction a "tremendous problem." He attempted to express the essential loneliness and isolation of all human existence. He borrowed Greek myths, sketching characters to fill the roles of Antaeus, Heracles, Poseidon, Kronos, Gaea, Helen, Jason—seeking to find in the patterns of their lives a controlling myth or metaphor for the meanings he wanted to convey. His letters are filled with the outlines of vast projects before whose scope Balzac seems limited and Faulkner cautious. As he himself once wrote in a letter, "The book on which I have been working for the last two or three years is not a volume but a library."

The motive force of his works seems to have been his desire to express the elements of a universal experience, and this universal experience was for him closely tied up with the national, the American experience. To a remarkable degree Thomas Wolfe was using himself to describe and to define both this universal experience and his native land, to produce the American epic, to create the egalitarian and generic hero. In a letter to Perkins he once said, "My conviction is that a native has the whole consciousness of his people and nation in him; that he knows everything about it, every sight sound and memory of the people." Much of his career was a search for America, and he came to see fairly early that, as he expressed it in *The Story of a Novel*, "the way to find America was to find it in one's heart, one's memory, and one's spirit."

And thus he fell in with the powerful epic impulse that has motivated much American writing since the eighteenth century: the attempt to encompass in a fable or narrative the spirit and the nature of the land, to represent the soul of a people through a representative hero and archetypal actions. As Tocqueville suggested, over a century ago, in an egalitarian democracy the traditional heroes of the aristocratic plots and literary genres are forbidden to the artist, and somehow he must find in the common man the center of his patriotic art. Walt Whitman, feeling the demands of the epic impulse, attempted a solution by celebrating his own generic qualities:

> One's-self I sing, a simple separate person,
> Yet utter the word Democratic, the word En-Masse.[3]

This self of Whitman's became the spokesman of his nation by its ability to witness all things imaginatively and to participate vicariously in all actions.

For Wolfe the center of his art was in a similar view of the self, but the method was different. Like Whitman he believed that the writer "ought to see in what has happened to him the universal experience." All the people, events, images, and visions that crossed his experience became a part of him, and were to be transmuted into a "final coherent union" in which America was to be embodied. For Whitman this embodiment was expressed in chants. The embodiment would be for Wolfe, as he said, "a story of the artist as a man who derived out of the common family of earth and who knows all the anguish, error, and frustration that any man alive can know." To find an adequate experience, an effective language, and a unifying structure for this man became for Wolfe the obsessive task of the American artist. He said in *The Story of a Novel*:

> In the cultures of Europe and of the Orient the American artist can find no antecedent scheme, no structural plan, no body of tradition that can give his own work the validity and truth that it must have. It is not merely that he must make somehow a new tradition for himself, derived from his own life and from the enormous space and energy of American life, the structure of his own design; it is not merely that he is confronted by these problems; it is even more than this, that the labor of a complete and whole articulation, the discovery of an entire universe and of a complete language, is the task that lies before him.[4]

In his efforts to accomplish that tremendous task, to realize the self as generic American and make his personal pilgrimage the national odyssey, Wolfe functioned with uneven effectiveness. He magnificently realized individual scenes and sections of his mammoth work, especially in the form of short novels, but he only imperfectly formed the faint outlines of the larger task. That the elements which made up his all-encompassing effort were woven from the filaments of his self and that that self was both woven and torn by his southern heritage should be beyond dispute; but in the interest of illuminating a little of both Wolfe and the literature of his region it may be worth while to point to some of the southern qualities in his work.

The urge to represent America, to embody it in a work of art, although by no means unique to the region, has been persistent in southern literature. The southerners of the antebellum period often raised their voices in support of a native literature and stood with the "Young America" group of critics in their intensely nationalistic demands for art in the 1840s and 1850s, despite the serious political differences between them and the New York critics. They distrusted the "internationalism" of New Englanders like Longfellow and of New Yorkers like the editors of the *Knickerbocker* magazine. Yet these southerners were aware that the nation could better be represented by drawing its particularities than by picturing the whole. In 1856, for example, William Gilmore Simms, of South Carolina, had written, "To be *national* in literature, one must needs be *sectional*. No one mind can fully or fairly illustrate the characteristics of any great country; and he who shall depict *one section* faithfully, has made his proper and sufficient contribution to the great work of *national* literature."[5] This view is not far from Wolfe's own, when he insists upon the representation of his unique self as the proper subject for a national art. Wolfe was like Thoreau, who said, "I should not talk so much about myself if there were anybody else whom I knew as well. Unfortunately, I am confined to this theme by the narrowness of my experience." However, for Wolfe, the observation of his fellow men was a basic part of that experience, as it was not for Thoreau.

It is also typical of the southern writer that this epic portrayal of America should constitute a project of great magnitude and tremendous complexity. Wolfe's letters and *The Story of a Novel* carry the evidence of the vastness of scope and the complexity of design of the "work in progress" on which he expended his days and hours and which he left incomplete. It is startling to one who has accepted the standard view of Wolfe's work as the spontaneous and unpremeditated overflow of the author's powerful feeling, recollected in abnormal intensity, to find him writing to Maxwell E. Perkins, "I think you may be a little inclined to underestimate the importance of arrangement and presentation, and may feel that the stories can go in any way, and that the order doesn't matter much." In the light of his efforts to get on paper the theme, the argument, the structure of the large work as he labored on its parts, such a statement—although it does not redeem his novels from formlessness—makes poignant and telling Wolfe's protests against the publication of *Of Time and the River* in the form in which Perkins sent it to the press.

This large design would have traced the history of the Pentlands (or, later, the Joyners) from the Civil War to the present, emphasizing the southern roots of the generic hero. It would have included thousands of characters and episodes—the whole, Wolfe, said, to be "seen not by a *definite personality*, but haunted throughout by a consciousness of *personality*," and that personality was to be the perceptive "self" through whom the writer could know and express his America. Before a work of such magnitude as he projected, time became the great enemy. The scope of his ambitious plan—which was to be no less than the record of his nation and his people told through one representative man—merits in its magnitude comparison with the master projects of literary history, with Balzac and Zola and with Tolstoy. To embark upon such vast projects has also been typically, although by no means exclusively, southern, perhaps because the southerner tends to distrust abstraction and to doubt that one can see a "world in a grain of sand, /And a heaven in a wild flower." Whatever the reason, twentieth-century southern writers have tended to plan work of enormous scope, such as James Branch Cabell's many-volumed and incomplete record of Poictesme; Ellen Glasgow's fictional record in thirteen volumes of Virginia's social history from the Civil War to the 1940s (whether such a structure was her original intention or a design she imposed after a good portion of the fact); and William Faulkner's vast record of Yoknapatawpha County. Wolfe, like these other southerners, set himself a task that staggers the imagination and defies the reality of time. Little wonder that Faulkner considers him among the greatest of American writers because he dared the most!

Near the beginning of his first novel Wolfe wrote, "Each of us is all the sums he has not counted: subtract us into nakedness and night again, and you shall see begin in Crete four thousand years ago the love that ended yesterday in Texas. . . . Each moment is the fruit of forty thousand years." This concern with time grew more intense as his career developed. The artist's problem, he believed, is the resolution of a threefold consciousness of time into a single moment so that scenes can represent "characters as acting and as being acted upon by all the accumulated impact of man's experience so that each moment of their lives was conditioned not only by what they experienced in that moment, but by all that they had experienced up to that moment," and with these actions set somehow against a consciousness of "a kind of eternal and unchanging universe of time against which must be projected the transience of man's life, the bitter briefness of his day." Whether or not Wolfe is indebted to Proust and Bergson for these ideas, he certainly envisions his characters as set in a complex fabric of time, and their actions as having remote roots and immeasurable forward extensions. Louis D. Rubin, Jr., has noted that "the interplay of past and present, of the historical and the contemporaneous, causes all the modern southern writers to be unusually sensitive to the nature and workings of time."[6] This interplay is one of the basic materials of Wolfe's fiction.

Wolfe shares with many southern writers his concerns with the reality of the past in the present and with the nature of time. One can find examples of the southern writer's concern with time and belief that it is, not only fact or sequence, but, more important, a key to the nature of human experience in Robert Penn Warren, particularly in *The Ballad of Billie Potts* and *World Enough and Time;* in Ellen Glasgow; in William Faulkner, with his elaborate dislocations of time sequence in many of his narratives; in Allen Tate's *Ode to the Confederate Dead;* in William Styron's inverted structure in *Lie Down in Darkness;* and in many other places. It is not surprising that one of Wolfe's best-known short stories should be "Chickamauga" and that the novel fragment on which he was working at the time of his death, *The Hills Beyond*, deals with his southern ancestors in the nineteenth century. Among twentieth-century American novelists only the southerners have with any frequency treated the past outside the pattern of romance and adventure. William Faulkner, Robert Penn Warren, Ellen Glasgow, and James Branch Cabell have written extensively with a historical orientation.

The mixture of styles in which Wolfe wrote is also not uncommon in southern writing. On one level Wolfe illustrates with great effectivenss the concrete, the immediate, the sensuous. He accurately described himself when he wrote in *The Story of a Novel*, "The quality of my memory is characterized, I believe, in a more than ordinary degree by the intensity of its sense impressions, its power to evoke and bring back the odors, sounds, colors, shapes, and feel of things with concrete vividness." It is this quality in his work that gives many of his pages an intensity which almost approximates direct experience. This lyric aspect of his writing, in which the object is evoked with such power that it seems to be rubbed against the reader's exposed nerve ends, this ability to make "the world's body" vividly real, succeeds again and again in giving the reader new insights, in Wolfe's terms, in making "the utterly familiar, common thing ... suddenly be revealed ... with all the wonder with which we discover a thing which we have seen all our life and yet have never known before." A passage from *Of Time and the River* will illustrate the centrality of the concrete in Wolfe's writing. Eugene Gant is daydreaming and not worrying about where the money to fulfill his dreams is to come from.

> If he thought about it, it seemed to have no importance or reality whatever—he just dismissed it impatiently, or with a conviction that some old man would die and leave him a fortune, that he was going to pick up a purse containing hundreds of thousands of dollars while walking in the Fenway, and that the reward would be enough to keep him going, or that a beautiful and rich young widow, true-hearted, tender, loving, and voluptuous, who had carrot-colored hair, little freckles on her face, a snub nose and luminous gray-green eyes with something wicked yet loving and faithful in them, and one gold filling in her solid little teeth, was going to fall in love with him.[7]

Here, where he is mocking Eugene's stereotyped dreams, the rich young widow is made concrete and detailed; the lucky purse is found in a particular place. This use of the particular, this tendency to distrust the conceptual and abstract, is one of the most widely recognized characteristics of southern writing. As Robert Penn Warren has pointed out, the southerner lives in "the instinctive fear . . . that the massiveness of experience, the concreteness of life, will be violated . . . [in] the fear of abstraction."[8] Virginia Rock has noted that the southern poet feels "not only a rage for order but also a rage for the concrete, a rage against the abstract."[9] Even in criticism, southerners have concentrated their attention on particular works of art and have not formulated abstract systems. As Allen Tate put it, "There was no Southern criticism; merely a few Southern critics."[10]

Closely associated with this concern for the concrete is Wolfe's delight in folk speech, dialect, and speech mannerisms. His works are full of accurate transcriptions of vivid speech. His characters seem sometimes to talk endlessly, but they always talk with vigor and with great distinctiveness of diction, syntax, and idiom.

Yet the same writer who displays these startlingly effective qualities of lyric concreteness and speech accuracy is also guilty of excesses in both quantity and quality of rhetoric perhaps unequaled by any other American novelist. With the power to evoke a particular object, scene, or character with remarkable clarity he is unwilling to let these creations speak for themselves, but must try by the sheer force of rhetoric to give expression to the peculiar meanings that they suggest, to define ineffable feelings, to formulate the inchoate longings and the uncertain stirrings of spirit which he feels that all men share. These qualities are manifest in the following passage from *Of Time and the River*, where he is trying to define the "fury" that drives Gant toward the North and away from the South:

It is to have the old unquiet mind, the famished heart, the restless soul; it is to lose hope, heart, and all joy utterly, and then to have them wake again, to have the old feeling return with overwhelming force that he is about to find the thing for which his life obscurely and desperately is groping—for which all men on this earth have sought—one face out of the million faces, a wall, a door, a place of certitude and peace and wandering no more. For what is it that we Americans are seeking always on this earth? Why is it we have crossed the stormy seas so many times alone, lain in a thousand alien rooms at night hearing the sounds of time, dark time, and thought until heart, brain, flesh, and spirit are sick and weary with the thought of it; "Where shall I go now? What shall I do?" (p. 90)

Set beside some of the apostrophes from *Look Homeward, Angel*, like the one to Laura James at the end of Chapter 30, this passage seems restrained, yet it represents pretty clearly that rhetorical groping toward understanding and expression which is a very large element in Wolfe's work. He is fascinated by language, enchanted by words, carried away by rhetorical devices. A kind of primitive logomania is in him: if the word can be found and uttered, vast forces are unleashed and great truths miraculously uncovered. The artist's search, Wolfe declared in *The Story of a Novel*, is the search for a language, for an articulation. "I believe with all my heart, also, that each man for himself and in his own way, each man who ever hopes to make a living thing out of the substances of his one life, must find that way, that language, and that door—must find it for himself as I have tried to do."

The drift toward rhetoric is the aspect of Wolfe's work most frequently called southern. Alfred Kazin observed of Wolfe and Faulkner: "It is their rhetoric, a mountainous verbal splendor, that holds these writers together . . . the extravagant and ornamental tradition of Southern rhetoric."[11] Wilbur J. Cash believed that it was their use of the rhetorical tradition that tied Faulkner and Wolfe to earlier southern literary traditions, and Joseph Warren Beach felt that "Wolfe's inclination to extravagant and ornamental writing" should be associated with "something in the tradition of Southern culture."[12] As Floyd Watkins has asserted, "Wolfe must be viewed as a Southern rhetorician."[13] Certainly the passion for the sound of the word, the primitive desire to give the name, the sense of the power present in the magic of incantation, show up with alarming frequency in southern writing. The particular linguistic combination that Wolfe used—the combination of concrete detail, accurate speech, and incantatory rhetorical extravagance is also present to a marked degree in the works of Faulkner (particularly since 1932) and in the novels of Robert Penn Warren.

Wolfe likewise shares the southerner's willingness to accept and find delight in paradox. At the heart of the riddle of the South is a union of opposites, a condition of instability, a paradox: a love of individualism combined with a defense of slavery and segregation, a delight in polished manners and at the same time a ready recourse to violence, the liberalism of Thomas Jefferson coexisting with the conservatism of John C. Calhoun. Such paradoxes bother southerners less than they would bother their northern neighbors, for while they hunger for order and are moved by a rage for tradition, they can at the same time accept instability as a permanent aspect of human existence and the unresolved contradiction as a part of man's condition. Southern writers often value paradox as a primary element in art.

Wolfe saw his world and himself through an only semilogical application to life of the Hegelian dialectic. He seemed to need to define a thing's opposite before he could comprehend the thing, and to have a naive faith that somehow the meaning was manifest if the opposites were stated. Hence there is in his work on practically every level—sentence, paragraph, scene, theme, large project—a structure of paradox.

But all these attributes of Wolfe's work individually are essentially superficial qualities of his "southernness." So strong a combination of these attributes as he displays does not often occur in America outside the South; yet these qualities suggest rather than define a distinctively southern quality. In certain other respects, however, Wolfe seems definitively southern. One of these is his attitude toward capitalistic industrialism; another is his sense of the tragic implications of experience; and a third is his deep-seated sense of human guilt.

That Wolfe had little patience with the group of southern writers known as the Agrarians is obvious from what has already been quoted. He regarded their intellectualism as false, their devotion to the life of the soil as pretentious and unreal, and he heaped scorn on them more than once, calling them by the opprobrious name "New Confederates." Yet one has the feeling that much of his contempt rested on ignorance of what the Agrarians were advocating, and that he would have been pretty much of their party if he had known what the party really was. However, he belonged loosely to the New South school, which saw in industrial progress the key to a new and better life and believed that the South must emerge from its retreat into the reality of the modern world. In *The Web and the Rock* he wrote:

> There was an image in George Webber's mind that came to him in childhood and that resumed for him the whole dark picture of those decades of defeat and darkness. He saw an old house, set far back from the traveled highway, and many passed along that road, and the troops went by, the dust rose, and the war was over. And no one passed along that road again. He saw an old man go along the path, away from the road, into the house; and the path was overgrown with grass and weeds, with thorny tangle, and with underbrush until the path was lost. And no one ever used that path again. And the man who went into that house never came out of it again. And the house stayed on. It shone faintly through that tangled growth like its own ruined spectre, its doors and windows black as eyeless sockets. That was the South. That was the South for thirty years or more.
>
> That was the South, not of George Webber's life, nor of the lives of his contemporaries—that was the South they did not know but that all of them somehow remembered. It came to them from God knows where, upon the rustling of a leaf at night, in quiet voices on a Southern porch,

The Roots of Southern Writing

in a screen door slam and sudden silence, a whistle wailing down the midnight valleys to the East and the enchanted cities of the North, and Aunt Maw's droning voice and the memory of unheard voices, in the memory of the dark, ruined Helen in their blood, in something stricken, lost, and far, and long ago. They did not see it, the people of George's age and time, but they remembered it.

They had come out—another image now—into a kind of sunlight of another century. They had come out upon the road again. The road was being paved. More people came now. They cut a pathway to the door again. Some of the weeds were clear. Another house was built. They heard wheels coming and the world was *in*, yet they were not yet wholly of that world.[14]

Yet Wolfe was also keenly aware that industrial progress and the things associated with it could have damaging effects on American and southern culture. He defined the "essential tragedy of America" as "the magnificent, unrivaled, unequaled, unbeatable, unshrinkable, supercolossal, 99-and-44-one-hundredths-per-cent-pure, schoolgirl-complexion, covers-the-earth, I'd-walk-a-mile-for-it, four-out-of-five-have-it, his-master's-voice, ask-the-man-who-owns-one, blueplate-special home of advertising, salesmanship and special pleading in all its many catchy and beguiling forms." Certainly for him, capitalistic industrial progress had as little appeal as it did for the Agrarians; for him, as for the twelve southerners who wrote *I'll Take My Stand*, the modern industrial world had become a perversion of the American dream. The twelve southerners declared, "If a community, or a section, or a race, or an age, is groaning under industrialism, and well aware that it is an evil dispensation, it must find the way to throw it off. To think that this cannot be done is pusillanimous. And if the whole community, section, race, or age thinks it cannot be done, then it has simply lost its political genius and doomed itself to impotence."[15] George Webber shared these sentiments when he said, in *You Can't Go Home Again:*

"America went off the track somewhere—back around the time of the Civil War, or pretty soon afterwards. Instead of going ahead and developing along the line in which the country started out, it got shunted off in another direction—and now we look around and see we've gone places we didn't mean to go. Suddenly we realize that America has turned into something ugly—and vicious—and corroded at the heart of its power with easy wealth and graft and special privilege.... And the worst of it is the intellectual dishonesty which all this corruption has bred. People are *afraid* to think straight—*afraid* to face themselves—*afraid* to look at things and see them as they are. We've become like a nation of advertising men, all hiding behind catch phrases like 'prosperity' and 'rugged individualism' and 'the American way.' And the real things like freedom, and equal opportunity, and the integrity and worth of the individual—things that have belonged to the American dream since the beginning—they have become just words too. The substance has gone out of them—they're not real any more."[16]

Admittedly this sounds more like Sidney Lanier's condemnation of "trade" than Donald Davidson's advocacy of the agrarian way, yet the enemy that all three faced was an enemy well known to the South and commonly confronted by southerners.

Wolfe looked upon himself as a radical, even, as he once called himself, a "revolutionary," and he angrily expressed his hatred of the gross injustice and inhumanity that the depression produced. But to him the solution was never material; indeed the substitution of the material for the spiritual was the cause for his belief "that we are lost here in America," and only his confidence that ultimately America would put aside the material for the spiritual made it possible for him to add, "but I believe we shall be found."

Wolfe is peculiarly southern, too, in the degree to which he sees the darkness, pain, and evil in life, and yet does not succumb to the naturalistic answer of despair. "The enemy," he tells us in *You Can't Go Home Again*, "is old as Time, and evil as Hell, and he has been here with us from the beginning. I think he stole our earth from us, destroyed our wealth, and ravaged and despoiled our land. I think he took our people and enslaved them, that he polluted the fountains of our life, took unto himself the rarest treasures of our own possession, took our bread and left us with a crust."

Wolfe seemed to feel, as George Webber did, "the huge and nameless death that waits around the corner for all men, to break their backs and shatter instantly the blind and pitiful illusions of their hope." He was supremely the novelist of death in American literature, for the ending of life was an obsessive theme with him. All his characters come to face the fact of death; as he expressed it, "They knew that they would die and that the earth would last forever. And with the feeling of joy, wonder, and sorrow in their hearts, they knew that another day had gone, another day had come, and they knew how brief and lonely are man's days." And the end, at least in its physical sense, was ugly. In *Of Time and the River* he described it this way: "This was the sickening and abominable end of flesh, which infected time and all man's living memory of morning, youth, and magic with the death-putrescence of its cancerous taint, and made us doubt that we had ever lived, or had a father, known joy: this was the end, and the end was horrible in ugliness. At the end it was not well." In *The Story of a Novel* Wolfe is

explicit about this darkness and evil in life. "Everywhere around me
...I saw the evidence of an incalculable ruin and suffering," he said, and
enumerated the "suffering, violence, oppression, hunger, cold, and filth
and poverty" he saw, so that through "the suffering and labor of [his]
own life" he shared the experiences of people around him.

This sense of evil and suffering is more typical of southern writers
than of other Americans, for a variety of reasons: the South's distrust
of progress, its refusal to believe in perfectibility, its experience of compromise and paradox—all culminated in the defeat in the Civil War and
its long and bitter aftermath. As C. Vann Woodward has cogently argued, the South is the only American region where the principles of
progress and the concept of perfectibility are demonstrably false. "Nothing," he asserts, "about [its] history is conducive to the theory that the
South was the darling of divine providence."[17] This sense of defeat
could lead Ellen Glasgow to say that she could never recall a time when
"the pattern of society as well as the scheme of things in general, had not
seemed to [her] false and even malignant,"[18] and the same feeling found
expression in the dark damnation of Faulkner's world and the ambiguous calamities of Robert Penn Warren's.

When, however, the nation as a whole began to experience the cata-
clysms of the twentieth century and to react to scientific and philosophic
views of man that were less optimistic, the American artist outside the
South tended to turn to programs of Utopian reform or satiric correction or naturalistic despair. The southern writer on the other hand,
older in the experience of calamity and defeat, saw the tragic grandeur
of man, the magnificence of his will in the face of disaster, and the glory
with which he maintained the integrity of his spirit in a world of material defeat. Southern writers have often used their history to make a
tragic fable of man's lot in a hostile world, and to celebrate the triumph
of the human spirit when challenged by an idea or a responsibility. As
Ellen Glasgow asserts, "One may learn to live, one may even learn to
live gallantly, without delight." And as Ike McCaslin says in Faulkner's
Delta Autumn, "There are good men everywhere, at all times. Most men
are. Some are just unlucky, because most men are a little better than
their circumstances give them a chance to be." This view of man changes
defeat into tragic grandeur and touches the spectacle of suffering with
the transforming sense of human dignity.

Thomas Wolfe's view of man and life had this tragic sense. In *The
Story of a Novel* he expressed it very directly. "And from it all, there
has come as the final deposit, a burning memory, a certain evidence of
the fortitude of man, his ability to suffer and somehow to survive." At
the conclusion of Chapter 27 of *You Can't Go Home Again*, in what is

a too-obvious extension of a speech by Hamlet, Wolfe attempts to answer the question, "What is man?" and in his answer states as clearly as he ever did the extent to which his vision of experience had tragic magnitude. Man to him is "a foul, wretched, abominable creature . . . and it is impossible to say the worst of him . . . this moth of time, this dupe of brevity and numbered hours, this travesty of waste and sterile breath." Yet Wolfe stands in awe of man's accomplishments. "For there is one belief, one faith, that is man's glory, his triumph, his immortality—and that is his belief in life. . . . So this is man—the worst and best of him—this frail and petty thing who lives his days and dies like all the other animals and is forgotten. And yet, he is immortal, too, for both the good and evil that he does live after him."

The southern writer is often obsessed with a sense of guilt and the need for expiation. Robert Penn Warren calls this feeling by its theological name in his poem "Original Sin," and sees it as the inevitable result of our lost innocence; in Allen Tate's "The Wolves" it is a threatening evil to be faced always in the next room; in William Faulkner it may be symbolized by the vicariously shared guilt which Quentin Compson must assume and die to pay for in *The Sound and the Fury*, or the inheritance of the father's which Ike McCaslin vainly tries to repudiate in *The Bear*. This sense of guilt may be the product of the pervasive Calvinism of the region; it may be the product of the poverty and suffering that the region has known; it is certainly in part the result of the guilt associated with slavery in the nineteenth century and the Negro's second-class citizenship in the twentieth—a guilt most thoughtful southerners have felt. In any case it appears to be a hallmark of the serious twentieth-century southern writer. And it is a hallmark that Thomas Wolfe's work certainly bears.

He states his own sense of guilt explicitly in *The Story of a Novel:*

> And through the traffic of those thronging crowds—whose faces, whose whole united and divided life was now instantly and without an effort of the will, my *own*—there rose forever the sad unceasing murmurs of the body of this life, the vast recessive fadings of the shadow of man's death that breathes forever with its dirgelike sigh around the huge shores of the world.
>
> And *beyond, beyond*—forever *above, around, behind* the vast and tranquil consciousness of my spirit that now held the earth and all her elements in the huge clasp of its effortless subjection—there dwelt forever the fatal knowledge of my own inexpiable *guilt*. (pp. 63–64)

In *You Can't Go Home Again* Wolfe explicitly links this sense of guilt with the South, and in turn sees the South as a symbol and in a sense a scapegoat for the national hurt.

Perhaps it came from their old war, and from the ruin of their great defeat and its degraded aftermath. Perhaps it came from causes yet more ancient—from the evil of man's slavery, and the hurt and shame of human conscience in its struggle with the fierce desire to win. It came, too, perhaps, from the lusts of the hot South, tormented and repressed below the harsh and outward patterns of a bigot and intolerant theology. . . . And most of all, perhaps, it came out of the very weather of their lives. . . .

But it was not only in the South that America was hurt. There was another deeper, darker, and more nameless wound throughout the land. . . .

We must look at the heart of guilt that beats in each of us, for there the cause lies. We must look, and with our own eyes see, the central core of defeat and shame and failure. . . . (p. 328)

Thomas Wolfe did not live to complete his representation of his America through the portrait of himself as generic man, and out of the novels, short stories, and letters we piece out the pattern he was trying to follow and we guess at meanings and intentions. One thing seems clear: Wolfe was a southerner, torn by the tensions and issues that thoughtful southerners feel, oppressed as they tend to be with the tragic nature of life, and feeling as they often do a sense of guilt that demands some kind of expiating action. The work he completed had demonstrable southern qualities; the total work, had he lived to complete it, would probably have had these qualities too. The South did, indeed, burn in his blood and on his pages like a "ruined Helen"—beautiful, passionate, and dark with violence and guilt.

The Loneliness at the Core

Thomas Wolfe's *Look Homeward, Angel* fell on critically evil days, and they have taken their toll of its reputation, if not of its steadily increasing number of readers. It was published the month of the 1929 stock market crash, lived the first decade of its existence in the sociological and Marxist-minded thirties, and presented to politically sensitive critics a hero of whom its author approvingly wrote: "He did not care under what form of government he lived—Republican, Democrat, Tory, Socialist, or Bolshevist.... He did not want to reform the world, or to make it a better place to live in." That hero, Eugene Gant, was hardly in tune with the intellectual temper of his times.

It is a frankly autobiographical book, "a story of the buried life," written by a man who, by his own confession, "failed to finish a single book of ... [Henry] James." Yet its whole existence has been during a time when the technical and formal considerations of Henry James have triumphantly established themselves as the proper criteria for fiction. For a book largely devoid of the traditional fictional or dramatic structure, almost naively innocent of "crucial plot," and seemingly dedicated to the lyrical expression of emotion not very tranquilly recollected, the age of Jamesian criticism has proved patronizingly hostile.

As Herbert Muller, by no means an unfriendly critic of Wolfe, has said: "His limitations may be exposed most clearly on his own ground, by setting his novels beside such other autobiographical novels as *Sons and Lovers, Of Human Bondage, A Portrait of the Artist as a Young Man* and *Remembrance of Things Past*. In these the hero is a creation, not a nom de plume, and his life a work of art, not a flood of memories. In this company Wolfe appears a very artless young man."

In such a context of critical opinion it has required effort to maintain a serious attitude toward Wolfe and his first book, *Look Homeward, Angel*, which is almost universally acknowledged to be his best novel— effort that few serious critics have made.

I believe that my experience is fairly typical. I belong to the generation that read *Look Homeward, Angel* when it was new and they were very young. It wove for me an evocative spell as complete as any book ever has. It seemed to me that this was not a book; it was life and life as I knew it. I brought to it, a very young book, the naive and uncritical response of the very young. Such an attitude did not survive, and in a very few years I became aware of the irresponsibility, the rhetorical excess, and the formless confusion of the book.

The Roots of Southern Writing

To go back to *Look Homeward, Angel* and seriously to read it has been an experience in some ways as startling as the initial reading was, and it has made me aware that it is a different book from what I had thought and a much better one.

The standard view of *Look Homeward, Angel* has assumed one of three attitudes: that literal autobiography very thinly disguised constitutes the important portion of the book, that what form it has was given it by the editor Maxwell Perkins rather than its author, and that the book is most interesting in terms of Wolfe's acknowledged and pervasive debt to James Joyce.

The first attitude has resulted in a mass of biographical data, but, as Louis D. Rubin has pointed out, the value of the book must ultimately be determined in terms of its quality as *novel* rather than its accuracy as personal history. The second attitude reached the epitome of critical severity with Bernard DeVoto's "Genius is Not Enough," and Wolfe is today generally credited with the major, if not the sole part in determining the form of his first two books.

The debt to Joyce, although everywhere obvious, seems to me almost nowhere truly significant. The least admirable portions of *Look Homeward, Angel* are those very portions where the ghost of *Ulysses* hovers visibly on the sidelines—portions such as the well-known record of the schoolboys' trip home from school, with its ironic pattern of mixed quotation so reminiscent of Joyce.

I think the first thing that strikes the mature reader who goes back to *Look Homeward, Angel* is the realization that it is a book enriched by a wealth of humor and saved from mawkishness by a pervasive comic spirit. This quality of the book is usually lost on its young readers, because the young very seldom see much amusing in themselves. Yet everywhere in this book one is aware that it is a very young book, not because its attitudes are themselves very young, but because it is a record of the inner and outer life of a very young boy.

The author looks back at youth with longing and love, but also with a steady but tolerant amusement. This is nowhere more apparent than in the hyperbolically presented day-dreams of "Bruce-Eugene" and in the very youthful posturing of the college student so earnestly set upon dramatizing himself. The humor is itself sometimes very poor and very seldom of the highest order. It is satire directed with crude bluntness; it is hyperbole lacking in finesse; it is reductio ad absurdum without philosophical seriousness. Wolfe is not a great comic writer, but his comic sense gives distance and depth to his picture of his youthful self.

For all its rhetorical exclamation about emotion, *Look Homeward, Angel* is a book firmly fixed in a sharply realized and realistically presented social environment. The book comes to us almost entirely through Eugene Gant's perceptions, but what he perceives is very often Altamont and Pulpit Hill (Asheville and Chapel Hill, North Carolina), and he perceives them with a wealth of accurate detail. At this stage of his career Thomas Wolfe had few serious pronouncements to make about man as a social animal (in his later career he was to attempt to make many), but he had a realist's view of his world.

It is a view colored, too, by a broadly agrarian attitude, however much he was contemptuous of the Agrarians as a group. His picture of Altamont is a picture of a place mad with money and size, of a people submerging everything of value in valueless wealth. This view, the sword on which Eliza Gant is first hoist and then eviscerated, extends from the family to the life of the town and finally to the imagery of the whole book. As an example (and it is but one of hundreds), when he hears his idol and brother Ben talking sententious businessman nonsense, "Eugene writhed to hear this fierce condor prattle this stale hash of the canny millionaires, like any obedient parrot in a teller's cage."

Further we perceive as a rediscovery that beneath the extravagant rhetoric, the badly and baldly rhythmic passages—the ones that eager young men reprint as bad free verse—there is a truly lyric quality in Wolfe's writing. With an abnormally keen memory for sensory preceptions, what Wolfe called his "more than ordinary ... power to evoke and bring back the odors, sounds, colors, shapes, and feel of things with concrete vividness," he is able to bring to bear vicariously on our five senses the precise content of a given scene and to make it poignantly and palpably real.

And here he works, not as a rhetorician asking us to imagine an emotion, but as an imagist rubbing "the thing" against our exposed nerve ends and thereby calling forth the feeling. It is, perhaps, in this ability to use authentically the thing to evoke emotion that the finest aspect of Wolfe's very uneven talent appears.

A new look at *Look Homeward, Angel* shows us that it is a book, not only of Eugene's "buried life," but one about tragic loneliness. Few lonelier pictures exist than the ones here that show the insularity within which Eliza and W. O. Gant live. This W. O. Gant, a rich and hungry man in spirit, who was never called by his wife Eliza anything except "Mr. Gant," strove by rhetoric, invective, alcohol, and lust to make somehow an impress on the unresponsive world around him. He is the ultimate tragic center of a book which deals with spiritual isolation almost everywhere.

Certainly the book lacks formal novelistic structure. If its core, as I believe, is W. O. Gant, then it contains a wealth of unresolved irrelevancy. If its central pattern is somehow linked up with brother Ben, as Wolfe seems to feel that it is, then we must regretfully assert that Brother Ben is a failure, the only really dead person in a book noteworthy for the vitality of its characters.

Yet *Look Homeward, Angel* has a consistency and an integrity of its own. In a way different from those indicated above, it presents a world. And as we survey that world and its characteristics, it begins to appear very much like the universe of that surprisingly modern eighteenth-century figure, Laurence Sterne; and the thought impresses itself upon us that Thomas Wolfe has created for Eugene Gant a Shandean world and that his book has something of the inspired illogic of the universe of Walter Shandy and Uncle Toby.

Both *Look Homeward, Angel* and *Tristram Shandy* defy formal analysis. Both are concerned with the education of the very young. Both see that education as essentially the product of the impact of the world outside upon the young mind. Both describe that education through memories in maturity. And both gain a certain quality of detachment through the comic or amused presentation of material, although Sterne's humor is better than Wolfe's and more pervasively a portion of his book.

Both Eugene and Tristram are the products of mismatched parents, both pairs of whom exist in their eternally separate worlds. Both heroes have older brothers who die; both are given to rhetorical excesses; both have a tendency toward unsatisfied concupiscence; and both embarrass us by "snickering," as Thackeray pointed out about Sterne. But these are superficial similarities; more real ones exist in method, language, and theme.

Look Homeward, Angel and *Tristram Shandy* are both ostensibly about their heroes, are records of these heroes' "life and opinions," yet neither Eugene nor Tristram is as real as other characters in their books. Uncle Toby, "My Father," and to a certain extent "My Mother" dominate *Tristram Shandy* and overshadow its narrator-hero. W. O. Gant, Eliza Gant, and Helen Gant dominate *Look Homeward, Angel,* and beside them the viewpoint character, Engene, pales into comparative unreality. Furthermore both books are family novels, peculiarly rich in brilliantly realized, hyperbolically presented familial portraits.

Both Wolfe and Sterne were adept at the precise, fact-laden description in which the thing evokes the feeling. Both were given to the representation of emotional excess in terms of heightened sensibility. Sterne is famous for this characteristic; in Wolfe one needs only to look at the Laura James sequence to see the "novel of sensibility" present with us again. Both men were remarkably proficient at capturing the individual cadences of human speech and reproducing them with sharp accuracy, and both delighted in the rhetorically extravagant; so that their works present, not a unified style, but a medley of styles.

But most significantly of all, both Wolfe and Sterne were oppressed with the tragic sense of human insularity, with the ineffable loneliness at the core of all human life. Walter Shandy sought a word to communicate with wife and brother, and he sought in vain. His wife walked in inarticulate silence beside him. Eugene Gant was striving for "a stone, a leaf, an unfound door." W. O. Gant, with all his exuberance and overbrimming life, remained "Mr. Gant" to a wife who never understood "save in incommunicable gleams."

And the whole problem of life, loneliness, and memory with which in their different ways these two books are concerned is for both writers bound up in the mystery of time and memory. Uncle Toby and Tristram, as well as Sterne, brood amusingly and seriously about kinds of time. For Wolfe and his hero, Time is the great unanswerable mystery and villain of life.

The world of Eugene Gant is a Shandean world. And in that inconsistent, unbalanced, illogical, incongruous, incomplete, and lonely universe, the secret of *Look Homeward, Angel's* sprawling formlessness, its unevenness, and its passages of colossal failure and of splendid success exists.

Unless we demand that all novels be neat and concise, *Look Homeward, Angel* has much to offer us still: a clear, detailed picture of a town; two extravagantly drawn but very living people, Eliza and W. O. Gant; a comic sense that lends aesthetic distance; a poignantly lyrical expression of the physical world of youth; and a picture of the individual's incommunicable loneliness.

Europe as Catalyst for Thomas Wolfe

It is customary to see in an American writer who spent a substantial amount of his artistically formative period in Europe the impact on him of his membership in two national cultures forming either a cosmopolitanism or an expatriated culture. Thus in the nineteenth century many writers seeing Europe in contrast to America found in it an aesthetic and moral challenge and emerged from their experience of the two cultures broadened, deepened, and enriched. This was particularly true of American writers in Italy.[1] In more recent times most American writers seem to have sought in Europe a milieu more congenial to their aspirations and their inner selves than America and have embraced Europe as a truer spiritual—and often physical—home than they could find in the Western Hemisphere. This was true of England in the case of Henry James and T. S. Eliot and of France in the case of the group we commonly call the "Lost Generation."

Neither of these responses describes with any completeness the role that Europe played in the career of Thomas Wolfe, although most of the writers who have attempted to deal in any interpretive way with Wolfe's European experiences have treated him as being basically one of the expatriates. George M. Reeves, Jr., in *Thomas Wolfe et l'Europe*, a detailed examination of Wolfe in Europe, says: "Wolfe appartient au groupe d'écrivains qu'on a appelé La Génération Perdue.... Sa vie suit donc le cycle commun à tout un groupe d'écrivains américains de l'entre-deux guerres: révolte contre les États-Unis, fuite en Europe, et retour en Amérique."[2] And Europe certainly played as great a role in Wolfe's artistic development as it played in the careers of the "Paris Expatriates," whose "recording secretary" and best historian, Malcolm Cowley, included Wolfe as a member of the group and saw his differences as being primarily that he did not serve in World War i as most of the expatriates did and that he preferred Germany to France. Cowley even sees Wolfe's hunger for a lost and unattainable home as typical.[3]

This is a classification with which Wolfe would have been unsympathetic. In a speech at Purdue University in 1938 he said:

> I mention all this ... because of its reference also to a charge that has sometimes been made by some of my friends. One of them, for example, not more than three or four years my senior, is very fixed in his assertion of what he calls "the lost generation"—a generation of which he has been quite vociferously a member, and in which he has tried enthusiastically to include me. "You belong to it, too," he used to say. "You came along

at the same time. You can't get away from it. You're a part of it whether you want to be or not"—to which my vulgar response would be: "Don't you you-hoo me!"

If my friend *wants* to belong to the Lost Generation—and it really is astonishing with what fond eagerness those people hug the ghost of desolation to their breast—that's *his* affair. But he can't have me. If I have been elected, it has been against my will; and I hereby resign. I don't feel that I belong to a lost generation, and I have never felt so.[4]

Yet unmistakably Europe played a significant and perhaps a central role in Wolfe's life and literary career. From his twenty-fourth year, in which he made the first of seven trips to Europe, until his death just before his thirty-eighth birthday, Wolfe spent over one quarter of his time across the Atlantic.[5] In the critical formative period between 1924 and 1931—a period during which he was finding that extended prose fiction was his métier and, after writing *Look Homeward, Angel*, was seeking a theme and a subject matter for the rest of his work—he made five trips to Europe, totaling thirty-four months and representing forty-five percent of his time. A mere listing of the places which he visited or in which he lived for brief periods is impressive. It includes England, France, Switzerland, Italy, Germany, Austria, Czechoslovakia, and Denmark; and it touches almost every famous city which a visitor would normally have seen.[6] The two countries in which he spent the longest periods of time were England and France, although the country to which he felt the warmest spiritual affinity was clearly Germany.

His career as a writer of prose fiction began and flourished during his European travels. His first extended prose narrative, the semi-fictional account of his first voyage abroad, "Passage to England," he began on shipboard in the form of notes which he continued to compile in England. The formal writing of this narrative, which, typically, never appeared in its original form but the subject matter of which was used in portions of several of his books, he began in Tours.[7] He says of Eugene Gant in language remarkably close to that which he used many times about himself that

He had come to Tours, telling himself that now at last, he was going "to settle down and write," that he was going to justify his voyage by the high purpose of creation.... with desperate resolve he sat down grimly now to shape these grand designs into the stern and toilsome masonry of words....

And yet, write he did. Useless, fragmentary, and inchoate as were these first abortive efforts, he began to write now like a madman—as only a madman could write.... And in those words was packed the whole image of his bitter homelessness, his intolerable desire, his mad-

The Roots of Southern Writing

dened longing for return. In those wild and broken phrases was packed the whole bitter burden of his famished, driven, over-laden spirit—all the longing of the wanderer, all the impossible and unutterable homesickness that the American, or any man on earth, can know.

They were all there . . . and in them was the huge chronicle of the billion forms, the million names, the huge, single, and incomparable substance of America.[8]

On his second European trip, while in Paris, he began writing the rough outline of the book which became *Look Homeward, Angel*. In London during that trip the actual final form of the book began to be shaped in the summer of 1926, and much of the first third of the first draft was completed before he returned to New York in December of that year. His third European trip was also given over to intense work on his novel. Thus this first hauntingly evocative record of the autobiographical protagonist Eugene Gant was conceived from the vantage point of England and France and composed out of Wolfe's deep loneliness and hunger for America. It came into being, as he said in *The Story of a Novel*, because he "had felt the bitter ache of homelessness, a desperate longing for America, an overwhelming desire to return."[9]

Shortly after the draft of *Look Homeward, Angel* was completed and submitted to the publishers, Wolfe made his fourth European trip. During this journey he spent a great deal of time in Germany and Austria. He was in Munich during the *Oktoberfest*, a festival celebrating the October beer. During the festival he became embroiled in a fist fight which became a brawl, and he received injuries that placed him for a time in a hospital. While he was hospitalized, he took stock of himself in a foreign land and he came, he says, to a reconciliation with the nature of the world. This reconciliation is the subject matter for the concluding chapters of *The Web and the Rock*, where he and his battered body conclude that "they had discovered the earth together . . . they had discovered it alone, in secrecy, in exile, and in wandering. . . . He knew that we who are men are more than men, and less than spirit."[10] Before he returned home from this fourth trip, he had learned of the interest of Charles Scribner's Sons in publishing *Look Homeward, Angel;* and thus the following year was spent in America putting into publishable form the book which he had written in Europe. It appeared in October 1929.

In May 1930 Wolfe returned to Europe, this time on a Guggenheim fellowship, to begin work on his second novel. He was there for ten months, during which he frantically sought a subject and a theme, an organizing principle for his new book. In *The Story of a Novel* he says of this period:

I think I may say that I discovered America during these years abroad out of my very need of her. The huge gain of this discovery seemed to come directly from my sense of loss. I had been to Europe five times now; each time I had come with delight, with maddening eagerness to return, and each time how, where, and in what way I did not know, I had felt the bitter ache of homelessness, a desperate longing for America, an overwhelming desire to return.

During that summer in Paris, I think I felt this great homesickness more than ever before, and I really believe that from this emotion, this constant and almost intolerable effort of memory and desire, the material and the structure of the books I now began to write were derived. ...It was as if I had discovered a whole new universe of chemical elements and had begun to see certain relations between some of them but had by no means begun to organize the whole series into a harmonious and coherent union.... There was nothing at first which could be called a novel. I wrote about night and darkness in America, and the faces of the sleepers in ten thousand little towns; and of the tides of sleep and how the rivers flowed forever in the darkness. I wrote about the hissing glut of tides upon ten thousand miles of coast; of how the moonlight blazed down on the wilderness and filled the cat's cold eye with blazing yellow. I wrote about death and sleep, and of that enfabled rock of life we call the city. I wrote about October, of great trains that thundered through the night, of ships and stations in the morning: of men in harbors and the traffic of the ships.[11]

Thus he was writing down in notebooks and in great ledgers fragments which later were to find their way into his books and which were records in almost poetic form of his love for and his hunger for his native land. It was here, for example, that he first wrote down what finally became the famous passage on October in *Of Time and the River*. In its notebook form it begins, "And in America the chinquapins are falling. The corn sticks out in hard and yellow rows upon dried ears, fit for a winter's barn and the big yellow teeth of crunching horses; and the leaves are turning, turning, up in Maine,"[12] an obvious foreshadowing of Chapter xxxix in *Of Time and the River*, where these lines are transmuted into this passage, where the sense of contrast, of October remembered in a strange land is present as a hardly distinguishable but still echoing resonance: "Now October has come again which in our land is different from October in the other lands. The ripe, the golden month has come again, and in Virginia the chinkapins are falling. Frost sharps the middle music of the seasons, and all things living on the earth turn home again. The country is so big you cannot say the country has the same October. In Maine, the frost comes sharp and quick as driven nails, just for a week or so the woods, all of the bright and bitter leaves, flare up...."[13]

That year in Switzerland, in Montreux, he found what was to be the theme for much of his work, the theme, as he expressed it, "of wandering forever and the earth again," a very appropriate theme for one possessed as he was by a desperate need for home and an endless urge to wander.[14] He returned in 1931 to America, where he continued to struggle with the desperate energy that he describes with a remarkable frankness in *The Story of a Novel* to merge these experiences into a book. At last over his protests the vast manuscript was sent to the printer in 1934, and the book appeared in 1935 as *Of Time and the River*.

He did not return to Europe until 1935, and then for only two brief periods; but these were periods that seemed to have been profoundly constructive in shaping his final view of the world. In 1935 he was in Paris, London, and Berlin from March until July 4 and discovered that for the Berliners he was an internationally important figure; and in Berlin he had the heady experience of having a great nation literally at his feet—and, of all nations, the one to which, aside from America, he felt the closest kinship. It was natural enough, therefore, that in the following summer he should go again to Berlin to attend the 1936 Olympic games. Then he was gradually forced to see, despite the parties and adulation, the dark death's head beneath the mask of Nazism. Though he had only two years remaining in which to realize the vision which he caught on that occasion and which he expressed most plainly in his short novel "I Have a Thing To Tell You,"[15] this brief journey brought him face to face with a rampant evil that was loose in his world and forced him into a major and soul-searching re-evaluation of his easy acceptance of life and the life principle as unqualified good. As Bella Kussy says, "In Germany under the Nazis he has seen the ultimate political and social effects of that vitalism which has been the supreme impetus and characteristic of his own life and work. Still susceptible to its fascination and power, still conscious of it as basic and essential and all-pervasive in his own life, he sees that he must either accept its social consequences or reject it completely; and he has enough humanity and resolution in him to do the latter." Out of this rejection comes what Miss Kussy calls "Wolfe's new democratic 'social consciousness.' "[16] Unquestionably the greater maturity, social awareness, and objectivity of *You Can't Go Home Again* result in large part from this instruction in the human capacity for evil.

Wolfe's European experiences clearly did serve to broaden him and to enrich him, to instruct him in the nature of his world, and to give him detachment and distance from which to view his subject matter. Europe in this sense was in a major way a catalyst for an intensely American talent. "Catalyst" seems to me the appropriate figure, for a catalyst is an agent, which introduced into a situation where elements are capable of reacting but are not doing so, results in an interaction of these elements without itself participating in the reaction or being changed by it. Between Wolfe and America a reaction occurred that might be called "catalysis," which is defined in *Webster's Third International* as "an action or reaction between two or more persons or forces provoked or precipitated by a separate agent or forces, especially by one that is essentially unaltered by the reaction." Europe served as this separate agent for Wolfe.

His European experiences were by no means unique, nor were his responses to them. They were essentially the response of the self-conscious provincial who elects analysis over adulation and looks upon Europe from the vantage point of an openly American bias. In several respects Wolfe's reaction to Europe was similar to some of Mark Twain's reactions, notably in *The Innocents Abroad*.[17] It is necessary to recognize that, as it did for travelers like Mark Twain, Europe was for Wolfe another frontier of experience but still an essentially American frontier. It was in this respect that he differed most significantly from those members of the "Lost Generation" who turned their backs upon the America of the middle class, the *Saturday Evening Post*, the Saturday night movie, the small town, and the Sunday band concert, and sought in a religion of art practiced in an environment of beauty a substitute for a way of life which they did not admire and in which they could not comfortably live.[18] They clustered around salons and in the offices of little magazines and were a powerful force in the maturing of American literary art. It is difficult to overestimate their value in the development of a sense of form and a formalist critical doctrine in American writing. But Wolfe was never happy or comfortable with them. Wolfe always tended to mock the aesthetes. In his long satiric description of Professor Hatcher's celebrated drama course at Harvard, he had laughed at those who found pretentious art a religious exercise. He was especially contemptuous of their "arty talk," which, he said,

> gave to people without talent and without sincerity of soul or integrity of purpose, with nothing, in fact, except a feeble incapacity for the shock and agony of life, and a desire to escape into a glamorous and unreal world of make believe—a justification for their pitiable and base existence. It gave to people who had no power in themselves to create anything of merit or of beauty—people who were the true Philistines and enemies of art and of the artist's living spirit—the language to talk with

The Roots of Southern Writing

glib knowingness of things they knew nothing of—to prate of "settings," "tempo," "pace," and "rhythm," of "boldly stylized conventions," and the wonderful way some actress "used her hands." And in the end, it led to nothing but falseness and triviality, to the ghosts of passion, and the spectres of sincerity....[19]

In Francis Starwick in *Of Time and the River* he drew a thorough and devastating portrait of a midwesterner who has come East and then to Europe and who embraces all the "shibboleths" of the young art group. One episode that is revelatory of Wolfe's strong preference for America has to do with Starwick's enthusiasm for French names: "But their genius for names is quite astonishing!—I mean, even in the names of their towns you get the whole thing," he says and then mocks the *"horrible"* appropriateness of some of the names in Eugene's region: "Beaverdam and Balsam, and Chimney Rock and Craggy and Pisgah and The Rat.... Old Fort, Hickory, and Bryson City...Clingman's Dome and Little Switzerland...Paint Rock and Saluda Mountain and the Frying Pan Gap."[20] Here the guise of fiction has, for the moment, been dropped; these are quite literal names from the North Carolina mountains.

Wolfe himself was never a part of an artistic group. He was always separate from his fellows, and he lived in a solitary world. He declared in an autobiographical fragment which exists in many versions, one of which Edward Aswell published as "God's Lonely Man": "My life, more than that of anyone I know, has been spent in solitude and wandering.... From my fifteenth year—save for a single interval—I have lived about as solitary a life as a modern man can have. I mean by this that the number of hours, days, months, and years that I have spent alone has been immense and extraordinary."[21] He was a lonely and solitary traveler both at home and in Europe. Furthermore those with whom he came in contact who were even on the edges of the expatriate movements he was offended by, the most startling example being F. Scott Fitzgerald whom he seems to have disliked intensely.[22]

He went to Europe initially with all the romantic expectations of a small town or country boy who loved books. England was for him the enchanted isle, rich in story, rich in all the range of literary associations. He went to England as "Heaven."[23] In London he declared himself to be "now lost in the beauty and mystery and fascination of this ancient and magnificent city."[24] In Paris, on the first journey, he felt himself "entering a new world of art and letters."[25] He made the standard pilgrimages and visited the literary shrines, and was, in general, a wide-eyed and romantic tourist. He was much like George Webber, of whom he wrote: "He was single, twenty-four years old, American. And . . . like certain tens of thousands of [young Americans], he had gone forth to seek the continental Golden Fleece."[26] But he came to see his romantic quest as a little ridiculous and mocked himself in ballad parody: "The night was long, the way was cold: the minstrel young was overbold: he carried in his great valise, two pairs of socks and one chemise; and in his hand, to stay the curse, the Oxford Book of English Verse. Under a sky of leaden grey, he went from Chartres unto Potay, and from that point he journeyed on, until he came to Orléans."[27]

England he continued to like throughout his life. France he cared for hardly at all. The French people he distrusted and disliked, and seemingly only among the peasant class could he find Frenchmen with whom he felt at home. He wrote: "The Frenchman is lacking in true wisdom: he is tragically poisoned in his art, his life, his education...."[28] The Germans, on the other hand, were his father's people; and somehow Germany was for him the Fatherland. It was for him, as he described it as being for George Webber, "the other part of his heart's home, a haunted part of dark desire, a magic domain of fulfillment. It was the dark, lost Helen that had been forever burning in his blood—the dark, lost Helen he had found.... Old German land with all the measure of your truth, your glory, beauty, magic...."[29]

What has been pointed out by many people about Wolfe in relation to New York is also true of his relation to Europe, that he was the perennial provincial, the country boy, fascinated by the city, fascinated by the world; and it was with this open-eyed and provincial astonishment that he looked out upon the Europe which he toured. He once wrote a friend: "What mistakes I failed to make in Paris, I managed to make in various other parts of the continent before I was through. I seem to have been born a Freshman—and in many ways I'm afraid I'll continue to be one."[30]

Not only was he rapidly plunged into the depths of loneliness and masses of mistakes on these solitary pilgrimages, he also was angered by attacks upon America of the sort that was common among the expatriate groups; and he rose vigorously to the defense of his native land in terms that would have been appropriate in the Rotary Club of his native Asheville. He said, for example, in one letter to his mother:

American vulgarity and American Philistinism is a source of much satire and jest; also the American tourist who spends his money here[.] I suppose, like all nations, we have our vulgarities; but I have seen no group of people more vulgar in its manners, its speech, and the tone of its voice than the French middle class[.] And no matter how materially-minded our own people have been, or are now, there is a certain satisfaction in knowing that, at least, they wash themselves with some regularity.

I shall never go about waving my country's flag—I believe I recognize

The Roots of Southern Writing

a great many of our faults, but the faults I recognize are not the faults Europeans accuse us of. That is what sometimes annoys me. They may curse us all they please if they only curse us for sins we have committed; but they are forever cursing us for things we are not guilty of.[31]

These European experiences would hardly have been the raw materials for a writer aiming at a well-made novel of the school of Flaubert or Henry James; and to appreciate fully what Europe contributed to Wolfe, it is necessary to recognize that his true subject and his consistent one, binding together into a unity the diffuse parts of his sprawling books, is his own deep immersion in experience and, in particular, the experience of being an American. He is not a novelist in the true sense of the word; he is a maker of epics; and, like Whitman, he recognized that the American epic was ultimately the song of the democratic man sung by himself. In his common experiences of the length and breadth, the light and darkness, the beauty and the ugliness of his land and his people, Wolfe found the subject for his work. In attempting to realize it, he created self-contained, dramatic, lyric, and rhapsodic passages which become, like the segments of *Leaves of Grass,* short but total records of parts of his experience. What Europe gave him more than anything else was not its storied history or the beauty of its landscape or the grace of its culture or the ability to associate with great men but simply a sense of difference, an awareness that somehow these differences defined what it is to be American. He went to Europe not to escape but to seek the dream of a paradise. He found not paradise but loneliness. Out of that loneliness came his subject. Out of that subject came a desperate awareness that the American artist must seek and find new traditions and new methods.

What emerges finally from his experience with Europe is not his expatriation or necessarily any internationalism in his cultural view but rather awareness of an artistic task that the American writer must undertake in difficulty and with fear but in which he must succeed if, as Wolfe sees it, he is to be both artist and American. Without Europe his relationship to his own land and his own past might never have been clear to him. Hence Europe was a catalyst, not an agent in the reaction; and out of that catalysis came the declaration with which he closed *The Story of a Novel,* perhaps as profound a judgment about the complex fate of being an American as he was ever to make:

It is not merely that in the cultures of Europe and of the Orient the American artist can find no antecedent scheme, no structural plan, no body of tradition that can give his own work the validity and truth that it must have. It is not merely that he must make somehow a new tradition for himself, derived from his own life and from the enormous space and energy of American life, the structure of his own design; it is not merely that he is confronted by these problems; it is even more than this, that the labor of a complete and whole articulation, the discovery of an entire universe and of a complete language, is the task that lies before him.

... Out of the billion forms of America, out of the savage violence and the dense complexity of all its swarming life; from the unique and single substance of this land and life of ours, must we draw the power and energy of our own life, the articulation of our speech, the substance of our art.

For here it seems to me in hard and honest ways like these we may find the tongue, the language, and the conscience that as men and artists we have got to have. Here, too, perhaps, must we who have no more than what we have, who know no more than what we know, who are no more than what we are, find our America.[32]

Thus did the catalytic Europe bring the artist Wolfe to an awareness of his subject America. As Kathleen Hoagland said of Wolfe, "I know why he writes like he does. He's in love with America."[33] Europe made him achingly aware of that love.

The Unity of Faulkner's
Light in August

The nature of the unity in William Faulkner's *Light in August,* in fact, even the existence of such unity, has been seriously disputed by his critics. The debate has ranged from Malcolm Cowley's insistence that the work combines "two or more themes having little relation to each other" to Richard Chase's elaborate theory of "images of the curve" opposed to "images of linear discreteness."[1] Those critics who see a unity in the novel find its organizing principle in theme or philosophical statement—"a successful metaphysical conceit," a concern with southern religion, the tragedy of human isolation, man's lonely search for community—but they fail to find a common ground for the unity they perceive because they neglect to evaluate properly the objective device which Faulkner employs in the novel as an expression of theme.[2] That device is the pervasive paralleling of character traits, actions, and larger structural shapes to the story of Christ. Viewed in terms of this device the novel becomes the story of the life and death of a man peculiarly like Christ in many particulars, an account of what Ilse D. Lind has called "the path to Gethsemane which is reserved for the Joe Christmases of this world."[3] However, that account is in itself perverse, "a monstrous and grotesque irony,"[4] unless the other strands of action in the book—the Hightower story and the Lena Grove story—are seen as being contrasting portions of a thematic statement also made suggestively by analogies to the Christ story. This essay is an attempt to demonstrate that such, indeed, is the basic nature of the novel and that it has a unity which is a function of its uses of the Christ story.

The parallels between Christ and Joe Christmas, the leading character in the novel, have not gone unnoticed. However, although many critics have commented in passing on their presence, they have usually been dismissed as casual or irresponsible.[5] But the publication of *A Fable,* with its very obvious and self-conscious use of Christian parallels in highly complex patterns, forces us to accept Faulkner's concern with the Christ story as profoundly serious, and recent criticism has also shown us that such a concern is not a late occurrence in his work.[6] Furthermore, in an interview, Faulkner talked very directly about the use of Christian materials in *A Fable* and the function that such material has in a novel. He said:

In *A Fable* the Christian allegory was the right allegory to use. Whatever its [Christianity's] symbol—cross or crescent or whatever—that symbol is man's reminder of his duty inside the human race. Its various allegories are the charts against which he measures himself and learns to know what he is.... It shows him how to discover himself, evolve for himself a moral code and standard within his capacities and aspirations. ... Writers have always drawn, and always will, of the allegories of moral consciousness, for the reason that the allegories are matchless.[7]

Apparently Faulkner intends to use parallels to Christ as devices to invest modern stories with timeless meanings; and Christian allegory, when it appears in his work, may justifiably be viewed as a means of stating theme. Dayton Kohler correctly says, "Faulkner's treatment of Hebraic-Christian myth is like Joyce's use of the Homeric story in *Ulysses* and Mann's adaptation of Faustian legend in *Doctor Faustus*."[8] It is a pervasive and enriching aspect of the total book, and we expect to see it bodied forth, not only in fragments and parts, but in the complete design.

Light in August consists of three major and largely separate story strands, what Irving Howe has called "a triad of actions." These strands are the story of Joe Christmas, his murder of Joanna Burden, and his death, together with long retrospective sections that trace his life in considerable detail from his birth to the night of Joanna's death; the story of Gail Hightower, his reintroduction into life through Lena Grove and Joe Christmas, and his return to life-in-death, together with retrospective and narrative sections on his marriage and his ministry; and the story of Byron Bunch and Lena Grove, of her search for the father of her illegitimate child, and of its birth. These strands are tied loosely together by the accident of time, some interchange of dramatis personae, and by the almost mechanical device of having characters in one strand narrate events in another. Lucas Burch, the father of Lena Grove's bastard child, is Joe Christmas's helper and would-be betrayer. Byron Bunch, Lena's loving slave, is a friend of Hightower, narrates much of the Joe Christmas story to Hightower and is himself the retrospective narrator for a good deal of Hightower's eary story. Joe Christmas's grandmother attempts, with Bunch's assistance, to persuade Hightower to save her grandson, and Joe turns to Hightower in the last moments of his life. Hightower assists at the birth of Lena's child, and Joe's grandmother confuses Lena with her daughter Milly and Lena's child with Joe as a baby. However, these links are not sufficient to tie the triad of actions into "a single action that is complete and whole."

A certain mechanical unity is imposed upon the novel through Faulkner's establishing the action of the story in the ten days between Joe

The Roots of Southern Writing

Christmas's killing Joanna Burden and his being killed by Percy Grimm. However, the significance of these present actions is to be found in the past, and the bulk of the novel actually consists of retrospective accounts of that antecedent action. Faulkner attempts to preserve a sense of present action as opposed to antecedent action by the device of telling in the present tense all events that are imagined to be occurring in a forward motion during these ten days, and in the past tense all retrospective and antecedent events.

There are also three distinct bodies of material in the book: formal Protestant religion, sex, and the Negro in southern society. Each of the story strands deals predominantly with one of these matters but contains the other two in some degree. The story of Joe Christmas is centered on the problem of the Negro in southern society; the Gail Hightower story is centered in the Protestant church; and the sexual element is the controlling factor in the story of Lena Grove, her search for the father of her child, and Byron Bunch's love for her. The interplays of these materials among these separate story strands help to knit the parts of the novel into a whole, but these bodies of material and the stories constructed from them find their most significant thematic expression as contrasting analogues of the Christ story.

The most obvious of the Christ analogues is in the story of Joe Christmas. Faulkner establishes numerous parallels between Joe Christmas and Christ, some of which are direct and emphatic and some of which are nebulous, fleeting, almost wayward. Strange dislocations in time occur; events in Christ's life have multiple analogies and are sometimes distributed over long periods of time. The parallels often seem perverse and almost mocking, yet they all seem to invite us to look at Joe Christmas as a person *somehow like Christ in certain aspects*. Around his birth and his death events are closely parallel to those in Christ's life; in the middle period of his life the analogies grow shadowy and uncertain.

Joe is the son of an unmarried mother, and the identity of his father is hidden from him and from the world. He is found on Christmas day on the steps of an orphans' home, and he is named Joseph Christmas, giving him the initials J.C. His grandfather says that God "chose His own Son's sacred anniversary to set [His will] a-working on" (p. 363).[9] When he is five, his grandfather spirits him away by night to Little Rock to save him from the orphanage authorities who has discovered that he has Negro blood. After he is returned, he is adopted by the Simon Mc-Eacherns, and upon his first entering their home Mrs. McEachern ceremoniously washes his feet. The stern Calvinism of Simon McEachern represents the accepted religious order of Joe's world, an equivalent of the Pharisaic order of Christ's, and Joe achieves what he later senses to be manhood and maturity when at the age of eight he sets himself against the formal codification of that order by refusing to learn the Presbyterian catechism. He rejects three temptations: Mrs. McEachern's food and the feminine pity which it represents, the Negro girl whom he refuses when he is fourteen, and McEachern's attempt by means of a heifer to purchase Joe's allegiance to his orthodox conventions. He also rejects food three times, as Robert D. Jacobs has pointed out.[10] Once, when he is taken into Mottstown at the age of eighteen by his foster father, Joe goes to a restaurant where he meets Bobbie Allen and begins to learn about the larger world of which he is a part, the restaurant being a kind of carnal temple and Bobbie and its owners being priests of that world.

His middle years are cloaked in obscurity, but at the age of thirty he comes to Jefferson, and there he is first introduced to us as a man with a name that is "somehow an augur of what he will do" (p. 29). He is rootless, homeless, "no street, no walls, no square of earth his home" (p. 27). For three years he works in Jefferson. At first he works in the sawmill with Brown who is later to betray him, and Faulkner refers to them as "master" and "disciple" (pp. 40–41). He becomes the lover of a nymphomaniac, Joanna Burden, who, after reveling for a while in depravity, tries to convert him to the Pharisaic religious order, when sex is no longer interesting to her.

Then one Friday night he kills her, striking in self-defense against her use of a pistol to force him to subscribe through prayer to her religion. He flees, and he is betrayed, although ineffectually, by his "disciple" Brown for $1000. On the Tuesday of his week of flight, the day of Holy Week on which Christ cleansed the temple, he enters a Negro church and, using a table leg, drives out the worshippers. On Thursday night, the night of the Last Supper, he finds himself in the cabin of what he calls a "brother" and a meal mysteriously appears before him. Jacobs observes that "this Christ has no disciple except himself and always must eat alone."[11] Faulkner says, "It was as though now and at last he had an actual and urgent need to strike off the accomplished days toward some purpose, some definite day or act" (p. 317). The next morning he frantically questions to learn the day of the week, and, finding it to be Friday, sets his face steadfastly toward Mottstown. Although up to this time he has been walking, he now enters the village riding with a Negro in a wagon drawn by mules. First he gets a shave and a haircut; then a man named Halliday recognizes him and asks, "Aint your name Christmas?" Faulkner reports, "He never denied it. He never did anything" (p. 331). Halliday hits him twice in the face, so that his forehead bleeds. His grandfather, who, being a stern Calvinist, speaks for the Pharisees,

The Roots of Southern Writing

tries to incite the crowd to violence, shouting, "Kill him. Kill him" (p. 327). The mob, however, leaves him into the "law." He is moved from Mottstown to Jefferson, another legal jurisdiction, and the Mottstown sheriff yields his responsibility happily. In Jefferson he is guarded by volunteer National Guardsmen, who spend their time gambling. He escapes from the sheriff in the town square, runs to a Negro cabin where he steals a pistol, and then runs to the home of the ex-minister Hightower, where he is shot by the leader of the guardsmen, a self-important soldier. As Joe is dying, the guardsman takes a knife and mutilates him, so that "from out the slashed garments about his hips and loins the pent black blood seemed to rush like a released breath" (p. 440). And Joe Christmas, at thirty-three, as Gail Hightower had earlier prophesied that he would, becomes "the doomed man . . . in whose crucifixion [the churches] will raise a cross" (p. 348).

These parallels have been dismissed as insignificant, I believe, because critics have looked for a theological saviour, whose death becomes an effective expiation for man's guilt, and viewed in these terms Joe Christmas is a cruel and irreverent travesty on Christ. However, Faulkner has defined the function of allegory to be a chart against which man can measure himself and learn "to know what he is." And Christian allegory uses Christ as "a matchless example of suffering and sacrifice and the promise of hope" (*Paris Review*, p. 42). The Christ to whom Faulkner parallels Joe Christmas is not the Messiah of St. Paul's epistles but the suffering servant of Isaiah, who is described thus:

> he hath no form nor comeliness; and when we shall see him, there is no beauty that we should desire him.
>
> He is despised and rejected of men; a man of sorrows, and acquainted with grief: and we hid as it were our faces from him; he was despised, and we esteemed him not. . . .
>
> He was oppressed, and he was afflicted, yet he opened not his mouth: he is brought as a lamb to the slaughter, and as a sheep before her shearers is dumb, so he openeth not his mouth.
>
> He was taken from prison and from judgment: and who shall declare his generation: for he was cut off out of the land of the living: for the transgression of my people was he stricken. (Isaiah 53: 2–3, 7–8)

The central fact in this story of the suffering servant Joe Christmas is his belief that he bears an imperceptibly faint strain of Negro blood, an ineradicable touch of evil in the eyes of the society of which he is a part and in his own eyes as well. This Negro blood exists for him as a condition of innate and predetermined darkness, a touch of inexorable original sin, a burden he bears neither through his own volition nor because of his own acts. In the lost central years of his life his sense of this innate damnation leads him to shock his many women with confessions of his Negro blood (p. 211). At last he finds a woman who is not shocked.

> She said, "What about it? ... Say, what do you think this dump is, anyhow? The Ritz hotel?" Then she quit talking. She was watching his face and she began to move backward slowly before him, staring at him, her face draining, her mouth open to scream. Then she did scream. It took two policemen to subdue him. At first they thought that the woman was dead.
>
> He was sick after that. He did not know until then that there were white women who would take a man with a black skin. He stayed sick for two years. (p. 212)

It is from this aspect of himself that Joe runs in such fatal and precipitant flight down "the street which was to run for fifteen years" (pp. 210, 213).

Hightower equates this Negro blood in Joe to "poor mankind" (p. 93); and Joe, running from the Negro quarter of the town, sees it as the "black pit," and thinks, "It just lay there, black, impenetrable.... It might have been the original quarry, abyss itself" (p. 108). It is this black blood that stands between Joe and a natural life. It is his belief in it that stands between him and his becoming "one with loneliness and quiet that has never known fury or despair" (p. 313). And it is this black blood which, in Joanna Burden's impassioned view of the "doom and curse" of the Negro, casts a "black shadow in the shape of a cross" (p. 239).

Gavin Stevens believes that Joe Christmas's actions, after he escapes in the town square, were the results of a series of conflicts between his black blood, which is a form of evil, and his white blood, which represents his humane and good impulses. This conflict reaches its climax when the black blood leads him to strike the minister to whom he had run for help, but, Stevens says: " 'And then the black blood failed him again, as it must have in crises all his life. He did not kill the minister. He merely struck him with the pistol and ran on and crouched behind that table and defied the black blood for the last time, as he had been defying it for thirty years. He crouched behind that overturned table and let them shoot him to death, with that loaded and unfired pistol in his hand' " (p. 425).[12] After Percy Grimm shoots Joe down, he mutilates him, and then, with the crowd watching, "the pent black blood" rushes from him. Faulkner says:

> It seemed to rush out of his pale body like the rush of sparks from a rising rocket; upon that black blast the man seemed to rise soaring into

The Roots of Southern Writing

their memories forever and ever. They are not to lose it, in whatever peaceful valleys, beside whatever placid and reassuring streams of old age, in the mirroring faces of whatever children they will contemplate old disasters and newer hopes. It will be there, musing, quiet, steadfast, not fading and not particularly threatful, but of itself alone serene, of itself alone triumphant. (p. 440)

This is Joe Christmas' crucifixion and his ascension, and this outrushing and ascending stream of black blood becomes his only successful act of communion with his fellowmen. Through it, a symbol of his Negro qualities shed for sexual reasons in the house of a man of religion, Joe Christmas becomes one of the "charts against which [man] measures himself and learns to know what he is ... a matchless example of suffering and sacrifice ..." (*Paris Review*, p. 42).

Joe's life is also shaped by sexual distortions, perversions, and irregularities. His mother was unmarried; his grandfather's righteous anger at her impurity and at what he believes to be the Negro blood in Joe's father makes him kill Joe's father and refuse his mother the medical assistance which would have prevented her death at his birth. This anger sends Joe into the world an orphan. His accidental witnessing of the illicit relations between an orphanage dietician and an intern results in the dietician's learning of his Negro blood and in his being adopted by the McEacherns. At fourteen, when Joe's turn comes in a group assignation with a Negro girl, he is repelled by the "womanshenegro" and it is against "She" that he struggles and fights, until "there was no She at all" (pp. 146–147). Significantly this early sexual experience is allied in Joe's mind with the Negro.

The menstrual period becomes for him a symbol of darkness and evil. Learning about it from boys' conversation, "he shot a sheep. ... Then he knelt, his hands in the yet warm blood of the dying beast, trembling. ... He did not forget what the boy had told him. He just accepted it. He found that he could live with it, side by side with it" (p. 174). This blood sacrifice he is to duplicate himself in his death. But three years after killing the sheep, when he confronts the idea again in connection with Bobbie Allen, it fills him with horror. "In the notseeing and the hard-knowing as though in a cave he seemed to see a diminishing row of suavely shaped urns in moonlight, blanched. And not one was perfect. Each one was cracked and from each crack there issued something liquid, deathcolored, and foul" (pp. 177–178). This image of the urn is to appear crucially in each of the major story strands.

Woman thus becomes for Joe a symbol and source of darkness and sin, the dark temptress who is viewed with revulsion alternating with attraction. Joseph Campbell expresses such a duality in attitudes toward women in terms that might have been designed to define Joe's feeling when in his study of religion and mythology he says:

> Generally we refuse to admit within ourselves or within our friends, the fullness of that pushing, self-protective, malodorous, carnivorous, lecherous fever which is the very nature of the organic cell....
>
> But when it suddenly dawns upon us, or is forced to our attention, that everything we think or do is necessarily tainted with the odor of the flesh, then, not uncommonly, there is experienced a moment of revulsion: life, the acts of life, the organs of life, woman in particular as the great symbol of life, become intolerable.[13]

Simon McEachern's harsh and grimly puritanical ideal of chastity drives Joe to the prostitute Bobbie Allen, appropriately named for the hard-hearted heroine of the southern folk version of the Scottish ballad "Barbara Allen."[14] And this cheap and cruel woman is Joe's closest approach to love and acceptance, and she at last turns upon him, screaming against his Negro blood.

This pattern of unhappy if not unnatural sex reaches its climax for Joe Christmas with the puritanical nymphomaniac Joanna Burden. In a sense, the ministry that Joe performs during his three years in Jefferson is to call to life in this cold, barren woman the primitive sex urge; as he expresses it, "At least I have made a woman of her at last" (p. 223). But what he awakens in her is not a natural urge, but an unnatural and perverted one, for she was too old to bear children, too old to serve the purposes of nature. Faulkner says, "Christmas watched her pass through every avatar of a woman in love.... He was aware of ... the imperious and fierce urgency that concealed an actual despair at frustrate and irrevocable years.... It was as though he had fallen into a sewer" (pp. 244, 242). Having perverted his "ministry," she finally denies it and attempts to force him into her sterile religious patterns. It is then that he kills her in an act of self-defense, for she had tried to shoot him; and in an act of spiritual self-preservation, for he could live only by refusing to pray with her; but in an act of suicide, for he could not himself long survive her killing.

It is in the Joanna Burden episode that the sexual material of the Joe Christmas story reaches its fullest statement. It is in her episode, too, that the union of this material with the idea of Joe's Negro blood is most clearly stated, for Joanna is the daughter of a northern father in a southern town. From her childhood she had been taught that the Negroes were "a race doomed and cursed to be forever and ever a part of the white race's doom and curse for its sins" (p. 239) and that "in order to rise, you must raise the shadow with you . . . the curse of the white race is the black man who will be forever God's chosen own because He once cursed Him!" (p. 240). She first befriends Joe because he is a Negro. And when the flames of her sexual desires die out she wishes to send him to law school and to have him administer her numerous charities for Negro people, but this involves an acceptance of his Negro status, and such acceptance is intolerable to Joe.

Joanna serves adequately to link these two matters, sex and the Negro, to religion, for she is a conventionally devout person; and when she attempts to shoot Joe, thus forcing him to kill her, it is because he refuses to join her in her return to religion through prayer.

The formal Protestant religion, an aspect of which Joanna represents, has been haunting Joe from before his birth. His grandfather Eupheus Hines is a half-mad religious zealot with a special and spiteful hatred of women, of what he calls "abomination and bitchery." He believes that God speaks directly to him telling him how to execute His vengeance on earth. In the narrow, vindictive, cruel God to whom Eupheus listens may be seen the primitive Protestant Old Testament Jehovah of anger and jealousy. The Negro has been singled out for the special wrath of this God, and Hines goes about as a quasi minister to Negro congregations preaching to them of God's disfavor. He becomes a kind of perverted and evil divine father for Joe, and he pursues passionately his desire to destroy his grandson. Although his religion is unorganized and brutally primitive, he seems to speak on the lowest level of the religious order and attitudes of Joe's world.

Simon McEachern, Christmas's foster father, into whose hands he is committed when he passes from the orphanage and Hines's control, is a Presbyterian elder. He attempts to instill through grim authority the cheerless pattern of Calvinistic conduct and belief. His only weapon is the flail, and to him love is a deplorable weakness. The crucial occurrence in Joe's relationship with him comes when McEachern attempts unsuccessfully to force Joe to learn the Presbyterian catechism. Finally Joe strikes McEachern down in murderous rage when his foster father comes between him and the closest thing he has known to love, Bobbie Allen.

When Joe is running away after killing Joanna, he reenacts Christ's cleansing of the temple by interrupting a Negro church service and driving out the worshippers with a table leg. His grandmother, anxious to give him a respite from the punishment he is to suffer, turns to the disgraced Presbyterian minister Hightower and asks him to give Christmas an alibi for the time of Joanna's murder. She tells Joe to go to the minister. When he escapes in the town square, he turns first to a Negro cabin and then to Hightower, but he strikes the minister down, as he has struck down the others who have symbolized church to him.

Significantly organized religion is represented by the Presbyterian Church rather than the Baptist or the Methodist, both of which are numerically superior to the Presbyterian in Faulkner's country.[15] Yet Faulkner is remarkably ignorant of the government and instruction of that church. He gives it an episcopal government quite contrary to the government by elders from which it gains its name (pp. 456–457).[16] He seems naively ignorant of how the catechism is learned, for he has Joe Christmas standing silent with the book in his hands, as though the catechism were a litany to be recited rather than a group of answers to be repeated to questions (pp. 137–146). However, the Presbyterian Church is the doctrinal church of the Protestant sects, the church of unrelenting Calvinism.[17] As such it represents the Pharisaic order and is an example of what man does in codifying into cold ritual and inhumane form the warm and living heart of religion.

It is against the dead order of his world as it is defined by this formal religion that much of Joe's rebellion is directed. He defines himself by rebellion against McEachern's catechism and grim and inhumane morality, against Joanna Burden's attempt to force him into her religious patterns, against a symbol of the organized church when he strikes out in flailing anger against the Negro congregation, and against the exminister Hightower when he strikes him down. He is pursued and harried by the organized church of his day in a way suggestive of that in which Christ was pursued and harried by the Pharisees.

Joe Christmas is like Christ, so many of whose characteristics his creator has given him, in that he bears our common guilt, symbolized by his Negro blood, that he is denied by the world; and that he is ultimately offered as a blood sacrifice because of the "original sin" he bears. But he is not Christ; he is a rebelling and suffering creature, embittered, angry, and almost totally lacking in love. In his ineffectual death is no salvation. His is a futile and meaningless expiation of his "guilt."

The religious subject matter is pervasive in *Light in August*. The sounds of church bells and of choirs echo throughout the novel, and it is shaped in part by the Protestantism of the South; but the Gail Hightower story strand is the one most completely, although by no means exclusively, drawn from this subject matter.

Hightower is the grandson of a Confederate soldier killed in a raid in Jefferson during the Civil War. He is the son of a pacifist, an abolitionist, a "phantom ... who had been a minister without a church and a soldier without an enemy, and who in defeat had combined the two and be-

The Roots of Southern Writing

come a doctor, a surgeon" (p. 449). Hightower goes to the seminary seeking an asylum from the world and a means of rejoining his grandfather's ghost at Jefferson. "He believed with a calm joy that if ever there was shelter, it would be the Church; that if ever truth could walk naked and without shame and fear, it would be in the seminary. When he believed that he had heard the call it seemed to him that he could see his future, his life, intact and on all sides complete and inviolable, like a classic and serene vase, where the spirit could be born anew sheltered from the harsh gale of living and die so, peacefully, with only the far sound of the circumvented wind..." (p. 453). This "classic and serene vase...intact and inviolable" is in contrast to the urn with cracked sides and deathcolored fluid which Joe Christmas imagined he saw when the revolting animal facts of reproduction were forced upon him.

While in seminary Hightower marries a girl who is desperately seeking escape from her life as the daughter of one of the seminary teachers. He marries her because he quite correctly believes that she has sufficient influence with the authorities in the church to get for him a call to Jefferson. But once he reaches Jefferson he proves ineffectual in every sense. His sermons are half-mad rhapsodies on the last cavalry charge of his grandfather. The members of his church protest that he is using "religion as though it were a dream" (p. 56). His church and his wife, along with everything in the present, seem to him to be meaningless, held in suspension, while reality is "the wild bugles and the clashing sabres and the dying thunder of hooves" (p. 467). So that, like that other solipsist in Allen Tate's poem,

You hear the shout [of brave men at war]—the crazy hemlocks point
With troubled fingers to the silence which
Smothers you, a mummy, in time.[18]

His frustrated wife is driven into a pattern of promiscuity which culminates in her suicide and in his being shut out in disgrace from his church. But he lives in Jefferson—a flaccid, fat, breathing corpse. Although the possibilities of an effective ministry for him have long since passed, he remains a symbol of the church and its truth to the simple religious man, Byron Bunch.

He is called back to an actual ministry to man by Bunch when that man sends him to help Lena in childbirth and he has to deliver the baby. He is asked by Bunch and by Joe's grandmother to reassume his ministry by championing Joe's cause and giving him an alibi. As Byron introduces the request, he apologizes and yet insists, " 'But you are a man of God. You cant dodge that.' " Hightower protests, " 'I am not a man of God,' " and he argues that the town and the church had chosen that he should not be; but Byron answers, " 'You were given your choice before I was born, and you took it. . . . That was your choice. And I reckon them that are good must suffer for it the same as them that are bad' " (pp. 344–345). At the last moment, Hightower attempts to do what Byron and Mrs. Hines have asked and to save Joe by telling the lie, but the attempt is vain, for when Joe, escaping, turns to him, it is with raised pistol to strike him down. Yet Hightower has been given by these actions a sufficiently clear vision of the way in which he has betrayed his ministry for him to understand himself. Christmas is for him, indeed, the chart "against which he measures himself and learns to know what he is."

In the senses that Hightower accepts a "call" to the ministry not as a field of service but as a sanctuary from the "harsh gale of living"; that he is absorbed in the past rather than the present—a past appropriately, for a southern minister, built on a false view of Confederate heroism (the cavalry charge is a hen-house raid)—that his aloofness prevents his ministering to suffering mankind; that he has a sharp sense of the ethical values in the human situation (he can properly instruct Byron, for example) but lacks the human sympathy that would make him act on his knowledge—in these senses, he exemplified qualities which Faulkner sees in religion. In Hightower's dying vision of truth:

> He sees himself a shadowy figure among shadows . . . believing that he would find in that part of the Church which most blunders, dream-recovering, among the blind passions and the lifted hands and voices of men, that which he had failed to find in the Church's cloistered apotheosis upon earth. . . . [He sees] that that which is destroying the Church is not the outward groping of those within it nor the inward groping of those without, but the professionals who control it and who have removed the bells from its steeples. . . . He seems to see the churches of the world like a rampart, like one of these barricades of the middleages planted with dead and sharpened stakes, against truth and against that peace in which to sin and be forgiven which is the life of man. (p. 461)

Hightower is here seeing himself and his failure as microcosmic patterns of the failure of the religious spirit in his world. His is not the harsh failure of understanding or vision which the institutional church can sometimes represent and which is shown in this novel in McEachern and Eupheus Hines; for Hightower had known the meaning of the church and of its call to service: "He had believed in the church, too, in all that it ramified and evoked" (p. 453). But this vision has been smothered by his retreat from a positive engagement in life. One evening, listening to the organ music from the Sunday evening prayer meeting, he broods:

The organ strains come rich and resonant through the summer night, blended, sonorous, with that quality of abjectness and sublimation, as if the freed voices themselves were assuming the shapes and attitudes of crucifixions, ecstatic, solemn, and profound in gathering volume. Yet even then the music has still a quality stern and implacable, deliberate and without passion so much as immolation, pleading, asking, for not love, not life, forbidding it to others, demanding in sonorous tones as though death were the boon, like all Protestant music. . . . Listening, he seems to hear within it the apotheosis of his own history, his own land, his own environed blood. . . . (p. 347)

Malcolm Cowley has noted Faulkner's tendency to turn Freudian method backward, producing "sexual nightmares" that are in reality symbols on another level,[19] and in the story of Gail Hightower that method is well illustrated. As in a sense the "ministry" of Joe Christmas in Jefferson may be viewed as sexual, so in a more pronounced sense the ministry of Hightower is pictured through sexual parallels: the story of his marriage is in miniature the story of his religious failure.

Hightower is impotent. Faulkner says of him, "[It was] as though the seed which the grandfather has transmitted to him had been on the horse too that night and had been killed too" (p. 59), and he instinctively is drawn to Tennyson's poetry, which, Faulkner says, is "like listening in a cathedral to a eunuch chanting in a language which he does not even need to not understand" (p. 301). He marries, not for the love of his wife, but to use her to secure the pastorate at past-haunted Jefferson, and she is driven to destruction by his impotence and neglect. He fails equally the church which he neglects her to serve, and he finally realizes that these two failures are in truth the same one. He says:

I served it [the church] by using it to forward my own desire. I came here where faces full of bafflement and hunger and eagerness waited for me, waiting to believe; I did not see them. Where hands were raised for what they believed that I would bring them; I did not see them. I brought with me one trust, perhaps the first trust of man, which I had accepted of my own will before God [i.e., his duty to his wife]; I considered that promise and trust of so little worth that I did not know that I had even accepted it. And if that was all I did for her, what could I have expected? what could I have expected save disgrace and despair and the face of God turned away in very shame? Perhaps in the moment when I revealed to her not only the depth of my hunger but the fact that never and never would she have any part in the assuaging of it; perhaps at that moment I became her seducer and her murderer, author and instrument of her shame and death. (pp. 451–452)

The Unity of Light in August

One of man's basic duties is to the natural order of things, a duty to the race and its propagation. On the one occasion when Hightower works in harmony with that natural order and not against it—on the occasion of his assisting at the birth of Lena's son—he experiences a sudden rejuvenation, a sense of strength and rightness, and he puts away his Tennyson for the redder meat of Shakespeare's *Henry IV* (pp. 382–383). And in his vision of truth he sees man's duty to propagate the race as his "first trust," a duty so elemental that a failure here is a total failure (p. 462).

The stories of Christmas and Hightower are counterparts of the same story, but with reversed roles for the characters. The parallels of Gail Hightower to Joanna Burden are marked. Both are the entangled victims of the heroic past, even to the point of both being the descendants of abolitionists. Both are practically sterile; both destroy those in intimate physical relation to them; both follow religions inadequate to meet their actual problems; both represent distortions and perversions of the natural order as it is represented by normal sexual life and reproduction.

Joe Christmas in his self-destructive relation to Joanna Burden has a parallel role to that of Hightower's doomed wife. Both represent comparatively normal basic urges; both are in quite emphatic ways the victims of the impotence of those to whom they are attached; both are offered religious solace—Mrs. Hightower by the women of the church and Joe by Joanna's attempt to convert him; both reject such solace and elect death.

Thus the stories of Joe Christmas and Joanna Burden and of Gail Hightower and his wife become contrasting personal and institutional aspects of the religious aspirations and frustrations of man, as symbolized by deviations from the sexual norm. Ward Miner is only partly correct when he says, "In *Light in August* the force which destroys Christmas, Hightower, and Miss Burden is institutional Christianity."[20] For Joanna Burden is a destroyer rather than a victim, and she destroys through the same atrophy of natural feeling that has ruined the church as institution. Furthermore Hightower is a symbol of the atrophy of the religious spirit, a figure indicating how and why the churches fail, rather than a victim of such failure. He is withdrawn from life, remote, indifferent; Faulkner speaks of "his dead life in the actual world" (p. 346).

These stories are finally merged, in a plot sense, near their conclusions by Joe's turning to Hightower, and they then stand as contrasting and complementary portions of the novel—contrasting in that the roles of the actors are reversed and complementary in that both are stories of "suffering and sacrifice" and of the failure of man to find and execute

The Roots of Southern Writing

what Faulkner calls "his duty inside the human race" (*Paris Review*, p. 42).

The stories of Lena Grove and Byron Bunch form more than a pastoral idyll within which the violence of the other stories plays itself out. They establish a norm for the other actions, a definition of the natural order against which the perversions and distortions of the other stories are to be set. Here it is sex which is the principal subject matter.

Lena Grove in her calm and tranquil way is seeking Lucas Burch, the father of her child whose birth is imminent. Traveling alone in the confident belief that he is waiting for her, she arrives in Jefferson on Saturday morning, the first day of Joe Christmas' flight. At the sawmill to which she has been directed she meets a good, devout, earnest man, Byron Bunch, whose name is a southern colloquialism for "crowd" or "masses." He immediately recognizes that Burch is "Brown," Joe Christmas's partner and now would-be betrayer, and he decides to shield her from a knowledge of the murder and of who Burch is. Bunch seems to possess on a primitive and unthinking level that aptitude for religious sentiment which Hightower betrays. He and Hightower can talk together, and Hightower has been his religious mentor. He shares with Hightower, too, a desire to retreat from the evils of the world. He is working on Saturday in order to escape temptation; when Lena comes, he says, "Out there where I thought the chance to harm ere a man or woman or child could not have found me. And she hadn't hardly got there before I had to go and blab the whole thing [that Burch was in Jefferson]" (p. 284). But Bunch falls hopelessly and completely in love with Lena, and thus he involves himself increasingly in the problems from which he had been fleeing and attempts to involve Hightower too. He sees that Hightower is present to assist at the birth of a baby, sees that the sheriff sends Burch to the cabin to be confronted by Lena and their son, and learns, since he loves Lena, that the fact of that son certifies the other and antecedent fact of Lucas Burch: "Then he heard the child cry. Then he knew . . . that there had been something all the while which had protected him against believing, with the believing protected him. . . . he thought . . . *she is not a virgin. . . . It aint until now that I ever believed that . . . there ever was a Lucas Burch*" (p. 380). But Byron, learning to face the evil he has been fleeing, faces it completely because he loves Lena. When Burch flees from Lena's cabin, Byron confronts him at the railroad tracks and fights him although the conflict is hopeless. Thus he earns the right to go with Lena, like another Joseph going with Mary, as she continues her journey on into Tennessee, but without real hope of other pleasures than those of serving her.

The Unity of Light in August

Lena Grove herself is almost an earth-mother symbol. She moves with tranquil ease and unflagging faith through the world. "She advanced in identical and anonymous and deliberate wagons as though through a succession of creakwheeled and limpeared avatars, like something moving forever and without progress across an urn" (p. 5), Faulkner tells us, and she thus becomes a third aspect of the urn or vase image, one neither removed and inhuman like Hightower's or horribly imperfect and repulsive like Joe's, but simply right and natural and combining both.[21] When she senses the child within her, "she sits quite still, hearing and feeling the implacable and immemorial earth, but without fear or alarm" (p. 26). At the birth of her child, Hightower observes, "More of them. Many more. That will be her life, her destiny. The good stock peopling in tranquil obedience to it the good earth; from these hearty loins without hurry or haste descending mother and daughter" (p. 384). Faulkner said of her, "It was her destiny to have a husband and children, and she knew it and so she went out and attended to it without asking help from anyone. . . . She was never for one moment confused, frightened, alarmed. She did not even know that she didn't need pity" (*Paris Review*, p. 50). In one sense she symbolizes the basic natural order in a way very like Whitman's "placid and self-contain'd" animals in "Song of Myself."[22] But in another sense she is the "Queen Goddess of the World," whose rightness in the order of things stands in religious contrast to the Dark Temptress, the symbol and source of sin. In some form or other both always exist in religions.[23] In traditional Christian symbolism they are the Virgin and the Whore of Babylon.

To the degree that Lena Grove symbolizes this earth-mother, Byron Bunch, the simple, good, and unthinkingly religious man, symbolizes the loving service of this natural order which the mass of mankind renders. Together they form a religious symbol of a stable order.

This elemental and eternal aspect of Lena is further enhanced by Faulkner's presenting her story and that of Byron Bunch largely in the present tense. The bulk of the stories of Joe Christmas and of Gail Hightower come to us through elaborate patterns of retrospect and character narration, so that they are in the past tense, and Faulkner is, as we have already noted, anxious to maintain a distinction between present action and antecedent action. Yet the use of the present tense for most of the Lena Grove story and for comparatively little of the other stories gives her narrative a special quality, for the present tense is the tense of eternal truths, of continuing and forever reduplicating actions; the past tense stamps the action with tragic finality. Faulkner said, "Time is a fluid condition which has no existence except in the momentary avatars of individual people. There is no such thing as *was*—only *is*" (*Paris Review*, p. 52). Lena belongs in the world of eternal truths, in the world of *is*.

This serene and calm and eternally hopeful mother who comes a journey to give birth to her fatherless child in a strange place has similarities, too, to Joe's mother Milly Hines. Both are unwed; both suffer from family disapproval, although in differing degrees; both have lovers who are disreputable betrayers. But their similarity is most apparent in the children they bear. Lena's son is presented as a new Joe. When he is born, old Mrs. Hines confuses him with Joe Christmas as a baby, saying, " 'It's Joey. . . . It's my Milly's little boy' " (p. 376), and she settles down grimly to protect him against Eupheus, lest he be stolen away again. The child sets into motion once more what Gavin Stevens calls her "hoping machine" (p. 421). He says, " 'I dont think that it ever did start until that baby was born out there this morning, born right in her face, you might say; a boy too. And she had never seen the mother before, and the father at all, and that grandson whom she had never seen as a man; so to her those thirty years [since she had seen Joe] just were not' " (pp. 421–422). Lena herself gets confused as to the parentage and identity of the child. She says, " 'She [Mrs. Hines] keeps on calling him Joey. When his name aint Joey. And she keeps on . . . talking about—She is mixed up someway. And sometimes I get mixed up too, listening, having to . . .' " (p. 387). For Hightower the birth is a rejuvenating act. He goes home thinking, "Life comes to the old man yet. . . ." Usually he sleeps a great deal. "He goes to the door [of his bedroom] and looks in, with that glow of purpose and pride, thinking, 'If I were a woman, now. That's what a woman would do: go back to bed to rest.' He goes to the study. He moves like a man with a purpose now, who for twentyfive years has been doing nothing at all between the time to wake and the time to sleep again" (p. 383). Lena's child is indeed a "newer hope."

Faulkner commented on the "trinity" represented in *A Fable* "by the young Jewish pilot officer who said 'This is terrible. I refuse to accept it, even if I must refuse life to do so,' the old French Quartermaster General who said, 'This is terrible, but we can weep and bear it,' and the English battalion runner who said, 'This is terrible, I'm going to do something about it' " (*Paris Review*, pp. 42–43). In one sense Hightower is like the Jewish pilot who refused life; Joe Christmas is like the quartermaster general who could weep and bear it; and Lena's son bears the eternal hope that this one is the one who will do something about it. Thus Faulkner's threefold Christ is complete: the Christ who is "a matchless example of suffering and sacrifice and the promise of hope" (ibid., p. 42).

The Unity of Light in August

Hightower is a symbol of suffering, however impotent and inward; Joe Christmas is a symbol of sacrifice, however private and ineffectual; and Lena's child is a symbol of hope.

This son of Lena has almost no plot relation to Joe: their links are temporal and accidental; their life lines never cross. More binds them, however, than the accident of Mrs. Hines's confusion or the similarities between their mothers. Both are the volitionless inheritors of a social stigma transmitted through their parents: in Joe's case the suspected taint of Negro blood, in the baby's case the fact of his being born out of wedlock. These facts are stigmata that isolate their bearers from their fellowmen, distinguishing them as in some sense "guilty," because of the attitudes of society; and in the puritanical and race-conscious Yoknapatawpha County in which the novel is laid they are blots that have the implication of immitigable evil. It is in order that Lena's son may not achieve the social acceptance of having a legal father that Byron Bunch must go with the mother and the young child as an unwed rather than a wed Joseph as they leave Jefferson and Mississippi. Both Joe and the child bear the social stigmata that are the outward signs of inward states. And Faulkner has so juxtaposed them that they suggest that everyman, like Joe, like Lena's son, has laid upon him the intolerable burden of human institutional coldness and inadequacy (here represented by the church and the atrophy of the religious spirit), the obligations and the abuses of the natural order (here represented by sex), and the accumulated human guilt or original sin (here represented by the bastardy and the tainted blood). And they suggest, too, that everyman is charged with rebelling against these oppressions, and that it is this rebellion, this refusal to accept which is the divine in man, the secret of his hope, the key to "a spirit capable of compassion and sacrifice and endurance," the qualities that assure that "he will prevail."[24]

The three concluding chapters, drawing together the three main strands of the story, suggest by their content and method this same threefold view. Chapter xix tells, belatedly from a narrative sense, of the death of Joe Christmas, ending as his yielding-up of the black blood in death imprisons him in the spectators' "memories forever and ever" (p. 440); thus we see Joe last in his sacrificial dying. Chapter xx shows us Hightower, whose understanding of the situations has been sharp but whose sympathy has been too frail to support action, as finally he views the world, himself, and his ministry honestly; thus we see him last in his awareness that he has failed the church (and implicitly that the church has thus failed) because he failed in the primary human relations, that the religious spirit must express itself in service to those like Joe and Lena. In Chapter xxi Lena, Byron, and the child move toward Tennes-

The Roots of Southern Writing

see, and the narrative comes to us through the detached, comic report of a furniture dealer; thus the child of hope and the earth-mother are seen at last, as Lena had been at first, moving serenely and dispassionately through the world of men and seasons, remote and somehow eternal, preserved in the amber of the comic spirit.

None of these characters are in themselves alone adequate representations of the Christ story or of those elements in it which have special meaning for Faulkner; but each of them is a representation of certain limited aspects of Christ, so that we may look upon them all and the complex pattern of actions through which they move and see, as it were, the dim but discernible outline of Christ as the organizing principle behind them. Viewed in such terms as these the separate story strands are fused into a thematic whole, and it is a whole unified by Faulkner's extensive use of the Christ story and his application of a non-theological interpretation in which Christ is the suffering servant of Isaiah, the archetype of man struggling against the order and condition of himself and his world. In a sense he would have us look upon the impotent, suffering despair of Hightower, the "old disaster" of the sacrificially dead Joe Christmas, and the "newer hope" of Lena's son and to say of them all, with Walt Whitman:

> . . . I think this face is the face of the Christ himself,
> Dead and divine and brother of all, and here again he lies.[25]

Absalom, Absalom!
The Historian as Detective

Absalom, Absalom! is a study in history and myth, and it is also a study in refractions, in inflections, and in innuendoes. On one level, at least, it is the account of Thomas Sutpen and his self-destructive effort to achieve his "design," a Greek tragedy laid in nineteenth-century Mississippi. *Absalom, Absalom!* is also a study in kinds of knowledge, in ways of knowing. It is, in this sense, a very modern book, for it shares the contemporary concern with how a tale is told as being fully as significant as what it tells; and in Faulkner's convoluted and incantatory narrations the drama of the tellers and their struggle with the nature and quality of truth are fundamental to the work.

Cleanth Brooks has argued that Thomas Sutpen espouses a "design" that he does not understand and pursues it with Yankee abstraction and calculation, that he is, indeed, foreign to the culture in which he is located. Others, notably Olga Vickery and Ilse Lind, have seen Sutpen as a personal representation of the Old South and its sin. Faulkner himself denied that Sutpen was typical, asserting that what the Civil War did to him it did not do to the other plantation owners of his region and that the key to Sutpen's story is in his *hybris*, in his intemperate and impersonal seeking for sons and in the irony (like that of a Greek tragedy) by which he gained too many and was destroyed by them. If, however, Sutpen's destiny is shaped by his destructive and overreaching ambition, it is certainly the quality of life in the South and particularly the issue of slavery and the inhumanity of racial discrimination that are the mechanics by which his *hybris* is brought low. Thus the fable in which Sutpen is imprisoned speaks powerfully of the guilt of slavery, whether Sutpen is a representative southerner or not.

The complicated plot of the novel—enough for a 1,500-page book if it were told in orthodox dramatic scenes—comes to us through the rhetoric and the brooding speculation of four people, none of whom fully understands what happened—particularly in the puzzling murder of Charles Bon by Henry Sutpen. Rosa Coldfield tells a part of the story to Quentin Compson on the night before she takes him on his first visit to Sutpen's Hundred. On this same night Quentin's father tells him what his grandfather knew, and later writes Quentin at Harvard telling him of Miss Rosa's death. And Quentin and his Harvard roommate, Shreve McCannon, take these narratives and Quentin's own very limited experience and attempt to piece from them what happened and what it meant.

When Faulkner was at the University of Virginia, a student asked him, "In *Absalom, Absalom!* does any one of the people who talks about Sutpen have the right view, or is it more or less a case of thirteen ways of looking at a blackbird with none of them right?'" To which he replied, "'That's it exactly.'" I don't know whether either Faulkner or the student knew how perfectly Wallace Stevens's poem, "Thirteen Ways of Looking at a Blackbird," with its sense of the unknowable aspects of even the simplest reality, with its "indecipherable cause" traced in "the shadow," defines the nature of the problem which the novel explores; but if neither did, it was a most fortunate accident that led to their use of the figure from Stevens. For the novel does, indeed, come to us through intensified rhetoric and suggestion—what Stevens calls "the beauty of inflections / Or the beauty of innuendoes." And, although Rosa Coldfield, Mr. Compson, and Quentin and Shreve all talk like Faulkner and no one else on earth when the frenzy of passion or rhetoric is upon them, they view the action of the novel from startlingly different angles, see markedly different things, and reach contradictory conclusions. Even in the similarity of their incantatory rhetoric, they do shade by mood and rhythm and figure what we know through their accounts—Miss Rosa by hysterical "demonizing" and Mr. Compson by elaborate literary allusion and weary irony, for example. Each working with a meager handful of facts and a rich flood of imagination traces in his divergent ways "in the shadow / An indecipherable cause."

Absalom, Absalom!, despite its concern with historical issues, cannot be considered a historical novel in the classic sense of Scott's works, which are, as Georg Lukács has expressed it, echoing Balzac, "the broad delineation of manners and circumstances attendant upon events, the dramatic character of action." For Faulkner's models we must turn to two other and, although seemingly different, quite related sources: the Greek drama and the detective story. Many, including Faulkner himself, have pointed out the parallels of the House of Sutpen to the House of Atreus, of *Absalom, Absalom!* to Aeschylus' *Oresteia*. In literal construction, however, the novel is closer to the standard detective story, a fact that should not come as a surprise to any Faulkner student. He wrote detective stories and published some of them in *Ellery Queen's Mystery Magazine. Knight's Gambit* is a collection of detective stories, and *Intruder in the Dust* is virtually a detective novel. In that interesting accumulation of books which he left in his several libraries are the works of thirty-one detective story writers, including such masters of the craft as John Dickson Carr, Ellery Queen, Rex Stout, Agatha Christie, and Dorothy Sayers. That a novel based on concepts from Greek tragedy should be cast in the structural form of a detective story also should not be surprising; as W. H. Auden pointed out many years ago, the detective story is the Greek recognition scene played as an end in itself.

In structure the detective story is really a double tale: the actual crime, with its motive and its action, is the core of the book, but it has taken place before the detective story proper begins. That story is the record of the attempts to utilize the clues and discovered facts in uncovering the truth about that past crime. Thus the dramatic action of the detective story is in the present and is made up of attempts to discover the past. It has two protagonists: the detective, working in the present, and the murderer, who worked in the past. One of its most common patterns is dialectical, with two characters in the present action debating the proper interpretation of data discovered from the past. It tells its two stories in a complexly involved way: one is told in straightforward fashion and the other is given in fragments in a seemingly accidental order that is determined by discoveries in the present not by normal sequence in the past. In fact two distinct patterns of conflict occur in the detective story: in the first the murderer is in opposition to his victim and finally kills him; in the second the detective is in opposition to the murderer and finally unmasks him.

In essence the detective story is a form which puts a high premium on the interpretation of the past. Auden's argument that it is like the Greek recognition scene is based on content rather than form; the recognition scene is important in bringing the present to an awareness of the past and thus producing a reversal of fortune in the present. The detective story is much more concerned with understanding the past through interpretation; it is almost epistemological in its concern. *Absalom, Absalom!* is like the detective story form in its persistent attempt to understand the past from a group of partially perceived fragments. It follows the formula of the detective story only occasionally and unevenly, and its present seekers after an understanding of the past come finally to play the roles of historians and artists rather than amateur detectives or prosecuting attorneys.

The questions that actuate *Absalom, Absalom!* are largely questions of motive and of causation, of not who but why. They center in large part on the role of Charles Bon and his motives and on Henry Sutpen's reason for killing him, an event that has puzzled everyone for forty-five years at the time of the forward action of the novel. The search for motive and causation ranges far in the book and involves almost all the characters who participate in the past action. Significantly it is carried on most extensively by two people in a Harvard dormitory room who try to reason out what must have happened in Mississippi a half century

The Roots of Southern Writing

before. These two are Quentin Compson, who had accompanied Miss Rosa on both the trips she made to Sutpen's Hundred after Henry's return and who had there received the "key" fact—that of Charles Bon's Negro blood, a fact which is the central and organizing "clue" that had not been known before; and Shreve McCannon, a Canadian who knew nothing about Yoknapatawpha County, its people, or its way of life. Their reconstruction rests on the narratives of Miss Rosa and Mr. Compson, on Quentin's new information (although Faulkner never tells us just how he gets it), and upon Mr. Compson's letter. The special information which Quentin has is withheld from the reader until the very end of the novel, for it is the data that order and give meaning to the whole narrative, at least in a plot sense, as it is a central clue to southern history. Thus Miss Rosa, General Compson (as reported), Mr. Compson, and the town of Jefferson are all ignorant of the fundamental facts that precipitated the fatal action at the gates to Sutpen's Hundred when Henry Sutpen killed Charles Bon in 1865.

In speculating upon this data and giving it the clothing of imaginary conversations and actions, Shreve and Quentin take the dry bones of historical data and create from them the substance of history and of legend. In so doing their approaches are interestingly different, as are the approaches of all the others who comment on the events: Miss Rosa, seeing Sutpen as a demon, a devil incarnate, and talking always out of her sense of outrage and indignity; Mr. Compson, struck with the parallels to the Greek tragedies, seeing Sutpen as an example of *hybris*, and talking with a wondering, cynical irony; Shreve, seeing in Charles Bon with his Negro blood the true key and meditating on the meaning of the events for him and the quality of his motives and the social implications of his actions; Quentin, identifying himself with Henry, obsessed with the struggle of the inheritor of the ancestral guilt, with the issue of incest, with the almost existential problem which is not only Henry's but his own and was, before the school year had ended, to bring him to the suicide already described in *The Sound and The Fury*.

In a fragmentary story, told in outline with elaborate speculation and chronological dislocation, any or all of these views are possible. Commenting on the meaning of the book and on its structure, Faulkner said:

> No one individual can look at truth. It blinds you. Someone else looks at it and sees a slightly awry phase of it. But taken all together, the truth is in what they saw though nobody saw the truth intact. So these are true as far as Miss Rosa and Quentin saw it. Quentin's father saw what he believed was truth, that was all he saw. . . . It was, as you say, thirteen ways of looking at a blackbird. But the truth, I would like to think, comes out, that when the reader has read all these thirteen different

ways of looking at the blackbird, the reader has his own fourteenth image of that blackbird which I would like to think is the truth.

Well, each critic has constructed his own fourteenth way of looking at this particular blackbird, and none of them seems to be the truth, although some of the truth is in all of them.

If, using the analogy to detective fiction, the deed in the past is imperfectly imprisoned in a few partially known facts and can be understood in the present only through meditation and imagination, then we can say that history is both a mass of inert and most partial factual data and that it is also the product of the process of brooding over these data with logic and imagination. Thus *Absalom, Absalom!* is both history and the drama of the historical inquiry viewed together.

Actually Quentin and Shreve represent two radically different ways of looking at the data of history and, in a sense, these ways define the difference between the historian and the artist. Each identifies himself with a different character—Quentin with Henry Sutpen, Shreve with Charles Bon. Each finds through this identification an answer to the riddle which he is asking; for the significance of the answer is always framed by the nature of the question. Quentin's is personal, intense, larger than life. Shreve's is a logical construct centering in a social meaning. The task that they both face in knowing that past Mr. Compson describes well in the novel:

"We have a few old mouth-to-mouth tales; we exhume from old trunks and boxes and drawers letters without salutation or signature, in which men and women who once lived and breathed are now merely initials or nicknames out of some now incomprehensible affection which sound to us like Sanskrit or Chocktaw; we see dimly people, the people in whose living blood and seed we ourselves lay dormant and waiting, in this shadowy attenuation of time possessing now heroic proportions, performing their acts of simple passion and simple violence, impervious to time and inexplicable."

That is Quentin's world and the intensely personal nature of his problem; for he is seed of their seed, bone of their bone; and they loom for him, as they did for his father, as vast phantasmagorial figures, out of primordial time, defining self and society and sin. The black shadow of slavery and of racial injustice is his, and the people of his region have deep moral meaning to him, meaning that transcends their social history.

To him it little matters that Mississippi was still virtually a frontier at the time of Sutpen's climactic tragedy in 1865 or that it had emphatically been a frontier in 1833 when Sutpen arrived to impose his dream of grandeur on this "postage stamp of earth." It does not matter that the shadows that Sutpen and the others cast in life hardly stretched beyond the bounds of Yoknapatawpha County, that they were farmers, small businessmen, middle-class entrepreneurs, men whose lives shook or shaped no national structures, however much they might dream of themselves in a world of baronial splendor. For Quentin they smacked of elemental truths; they loomed larger than life; they flung gigantic challenges across lurid skies against the very gods. His treatment of them was legendary, mythological, imaginary, and creative. Mr. Compson said of the one letter from Charles Bon that Judith kept that it was an "undying mark on the blank face of the oblivion to which we are all doomed." It is to him and to his son not a datum for a footnote, not a straw in the rising wind of social history, but an act—"an undying mark" —of permanence and value.

Not so Shreve McCannon, native of Alberta, Canada, student in Cambridge, Massachusetts, and ignorant of the South and having to have its climate and its seasons and its plants explained to him. This Shreve, studying to become the physician which Faulkner tells us in an appendix that he became, sees in the compulsive narrative of Quentin about the House of Sutpen, not another telling of the *Oresteia* but a symbol of the South's social history, a way of understanding the nature of the southern experience. He approaches with logic and reason, with the careful piecing together of data, the whole problem of what happened and why, as the scientific historian would. Listen to him for a moment as he tries to deal with the issue of whether it was Henry or Bon who was wounded at Shiloh:

> "Your old man was wrong . . . ! He said it was Bon who was wounded, but it wasn't. Because who told him? Who told Sutpen, or your grandfather either, which of them it was who was hit? Sutpen didn't know because he wasn't there, and your grandfather wasn't there either because that was where he was hit, too, where he lost his arm. So who told them? Not Henry, because his father never saw Henry but that one time and maybe they never had time to talk about wounds and besides to talk about wounds in the Confederate Army in 1865 would be like coal miners talking about soot; and not Bon, because Sutpen never saw him at all because he was dead—it was not Bon, it was Henry; Bon that found Henry at last and stooped to pick him up and Henry fought back, struggled, saying, 'Let be!' "

Was ever logic more triumphantly—and casuistically—applied to reach a conclusion supported purely on negative reasoning? One is reminded of the police officer reaching a fallacious conclusion through spurious reasoning, only to be set right by the amateur, of Sergeant Heath and Philo Vance, of Inspector Cramer and Nero Wolfe, of Inspector Hadley and Dr. Fell.

It is little wonder that Faulkner, speaking in his own person as author for one of the few times in the novel, referred to the place where Shreve and Quentin debated in a dark New England night as "the cold room ...dedicated to the best of ratiocination ...this room not only dedicated to it but set aside for it and suitably so since it would be here above any other place that it ...could do the least amount of harm." And he added that Shreve was "saying No to Quentin's Mississippi shade who in life had acted and reacted to the minimum of logic and morality, who dying had escaped it completely, who dead remained not only indifferent but impervious to it, somehow a thousand times more potent and alive."

Donald M. Kartiganer has maintained that the ultimate value of these experiences is discovered in the novel by the imaginative exploration of meaning. "The most vital truth of *Absalom, Absalom!*," he says, "is that the possibility of value depends entirely on the ability of the human imagination to create it." But that creation is Quentin's role, not Shreve's, is that of the artist not the historian, and it is vested in personal and humane values not social or historical ones. Shreve, when his rhetoric gets rolling sounds like Faulkner and hence like all the others—but this is not peculiar to *Absalom, Absalom!*, for the lowliest and most illiterate Snopes talks like Faulkner when the rhetorical urge is upon him. We must judge Shreve's position, not by the tone of these incantatory speculations but by the conversations and conclusion which he expresses in his own voice. Then his is the cold logic of the outsider, the reason of the "iron New England dark," the method of the historian who pieces together patterns of cause and effect in a social world whose history he is constructing by reason from data. For Shreve finally there are no phantasmagorial figures, drawn larger than life and bestriding the Mississippi earth in vast outline beneath portentous skies. These people are just what they are in mundane actuality. Sutpen is a small plantation owner like, Shreve falsely believes, thousands of others and thus typical of the South. His children, both white and of mixed blood, are doomed by their strange environment to extinction. In Shreve's hands is the play of social forces—he even interrupts Quentin to say, " 'Wait, wait, let me play' "—and the fundamental questions he asks are social questions. When he finally sums up what he has learned through this intense exploration of the South, it is very simple:

"So it took Charles Bon and his mother to get rid of old Tom, and Charles Bon and the octoroon to get rid of Judith, and Charles Bon and

The Roots of Southern Writing

Clytie to get rid of Henry; and Charles Bon's mother and Charles Bon's grandmother got rid of Charles Bon. So it takes two niggers to get rid of one Sutpen, dont it. . . . Which is all right, it's fine; it clears the whole ledger, you can tear all the pages out and burn them, except for one thing. . . . You've got one nigger left. One nigger Sutpen left. Of course you can't catch him and don't even always see him and you never will be able to use him. But you've got him there still. You still hear him at night sometimes. . . .

"I think that in time the Jim Bonds are going to conquer the western hemisphere. Of course it won't quite be in our time and of course as they spread toward the poles they will bleach out again like the rabbits and the birds do, so they won't show up so sharp against the snow. But it will still be Jim Bond; and so in a few thousand years, I who regard you will also have sprung from the loins of African kings."

And, of course, he is right—in his way, which is that of the social historian. It's certainly one way of looking at a blackbird, and it would be foolishness to deny that Faulkner posited this as a possible way for us. But it is not this view of history, however accurate, that gives *Absalom, Absalom!* its power or that makes it one of Faulkner's greatest imaginative creations and one that speaks with thundering power of the traditional tragic view of man. That power comes, instead, from a sense of these beings as more than pawns on a chessboard of social history, as more than data to be tabulated and categorized; it comes from knowledge not rational or rationalized but knowledge, in Allen Tate's term, "carried to the heart." Above and behind Faulkner's view is a sense of cosmic order and justice, a world of human values against which man may try himself, a preordained justice that strikes a final balance regardless of the immediate outcome. Hence history for Faulkner, whether the social history of the South or the efforts of the historian to construct that history, such as Shreve makes, is always a means toward an end, always a fable rather than a fact, always meaningful in what it says of man rather than in what man says of it. Shreve and Quentin collaborate in the reconstruction of the history of the House of Sutpen, and each of them is essential to the other. Without Quentin's data Shreve's historical and sociological construct would not have been possible. Yet Shreve's construct teaches—forces, one is almost moved to say—Quentin to see and to accept the reality of both his past and his present. In a sense Shreve forces Quentin's knowledge of his past out of demonizing and romanticizing and into recognizing the role that Negro slavery has played in the drama of his region. Significantly it is Quentin, of the youngest generation, that finds the crucial key to the mystery and is given the power to interpret the actions of old and hidden crimes.

That Faulkner could have been as thoroughly modern as he was in *Absalom, Absalom!*, could have engaged with great success in the contemporary artistic gambit of how we know rather than what we know, and still have used these startlingly new techniques to assert things about man that Aeschylus and Sophocles had stated, and even have borrowed names—such as Clytemnestra—and scenes—such as the burning of Sutpen's Hundred, which has a direct debt to the dénouement of Euripides' *Orestes*—is a signal achievement both for his art and for his conscience. In accepting the Nobel Prize for Literature, Faulkner declared that it is "the problems of the human heart in conflict with itself which alone can make good writing because only that is worth writing about," and he urged the writer to leave "no room in his workship for anything but the old verities and truths of the heart, the old universal truths lacking which any story is ephemeral and doomed—love and honor and pity and pride and compassion and sacrifice."

History is one of the materials of that workshop and Faulkner would never have considered excluding it; but the recording of history is not an objective of the artist. To the limited view of the scientific historian, whom Shreve in his detachment to some extent represents, Faulkner, with all his reverence for the past and its meaning, does not give a place of highest honor. That high place is reserved for the imagination of the artist, which can transmute the data of history into the enlarged reality of art, which can translate sociological data into the eternal problems of human culpability and compassionate feeling. Faulkner's "postage stamp of earth" has stretched out to the four corners of the world, and the middle-class planters and farmers and storekeepers of Yoknapatawpha County can body forth man's enduring tragedy.

Her Rue with a Difference

Nathaniel Hawthorne once stated his intention "to achieve a novel that should evolve some deep lesson and should possess physical substance enough to stand alone."[1] He was describing the ambition of many writers of fiction, but his remark is peculiarly appropriate to the work of Flannery O'Connor, a brilliantly gifted writer whose death at the age of thirty-nine silenced one of the finest voices of American fiction. Hawthorne's statement is particularly useful in looking at Miss O'Connor's work because of his separation—or at least his distinction—between meaning and matter, a distinction often overlooked by the numerous reviewers who have seen Flannery O'Connor as simply another writer of southern Gothic and have easily grouped her with other southern writers of the grotesque such as Erskine Caldwell, Carson McCullers, Truman Capote, and Tennessee Williams. Indeed Caroline Gordon once derisively quoted the assertion of a critic that "if the name of the author were deleted it would be hard to tell a story by Miss O'Connor from a story by Truman Capote, Carson McCullers or Tennessee Williams."[2]

However wrong that critic was, there certainly can be little question that Miss O'Connor was a southern writer. The South, particularly that of piedmont Georgia and eastern Tennessee, is what she called her "country." "The country that the writer is concerned with in the most objective way is," she said, "... the region that most immediately surrounds him, or simply the country, with its body of manners, that he knows well enough to employ."[3] Out of this South and its people she quarried the "physical substance" which gave her work the living elements of successful fiction.

But, as has been obvious to all but the most unperceptive of her critics, this "physical substance" for her was not an end in itself; she hungered passionately for meaning and worked hard to "evolve" from her country "some deep lesson." Here, too, she was a part of a "southern literary tradition." For if she seemed in immediate subject matter to belong to the "school of the Southern Gothic," she seemed also to find in the southern experience a lesson for the present, as did the Agrarians, or a cosmic truth, as did the apocalyptic mythologizers like Faulkner. Such association with any southern "school," whether it be Agrarian or that preoccupied, as she said, "with every thing deformed and grotesque,"[4] irritated her. She declared, "The woods are full of regional writers, and it is the great horror of every serious Southern writer that he will become one of them."[5] I not only sympathize with her attitude; I also find her relation to the southern literary tradition to be unusual and illuminating both about her and about the tradition itself. Indeed, in looking at her native Georgia, like many modern southerners, Miss O'Connor's vision was touched with rue, but she wore her "rue with a difference"—a difference that helps to define her essential quality and to give us a deeper insight into her "country," both of soil and spirit.

Geographically hers was a special South, remote from the moss-draped melancholy great oaks and the stable social order of the Atlantic seaboard and equally distant from the tropical lushness and fecundity of the gulf-coast Deep South. She knew and wrote of piedmont Georgia and eastern Tennessee—a rolling, sparsely wooded land where both the spring freshlets and the ravishing plow pierce its surface to leave gaping wounds of dark red clay. It is cotton country, made up of small farms, small towns, and widely-spaced small cities—a country at the mercy of capricious weather and the vicissitudes of the cotton market, which has been in a fluctuating state but one that has always remained depressed since the 1920s. It is a land wracked by diseases peculiar to poverty, by a vicious sharecropper system, by little education, and by a superstitious, intense, pietistic but nontheological religious passion. Hers is not the South of the Virginia Tidewater or the Carolina Low Country, regions that are nominally Episcopal in religion, aristocratic in dream if not in fact, and tied to a past culture that revered learning, practiced law, and dreamed of a republican government of merit founded upon the doctrines of the eighteenth-century enlightenment.

Miss O'Connor's segment of the South was settled, in large measure, by the Scotch-Irish who came down the inland cattle trails from Pennsylvania. By 1790 the Scotch-Irish represented over a quarter of a million Americans. They had entered principally through the ports of Philadelphia, Chester, or New Castle, and had followed the Great Valley westward for about a hundred miles, until tall mountains blocked their trail. Then they had turned south into Virginia, the Carolinas, Tennessee, and Georgia. They were a poverty-stricken, harsh, impetuous people, with a deep sense of integrity, a tendency to make their own laws, and to worship God with individual and singular fervor. Once in the southern piedmont, they fanned out to encompass the region, and to help define its qualities, among whose most noticeable characteristics was a widespread social crudity marked, as even the sympathetic historians of the Scotch-Irish point out, by brutal fights, animal cruelty, and folk hilarity.[6] The journal of the Anglican Reverend Charles Woodmason is a graphic account of the shocking effect which this primitive

The Roots of Southern Writing

life made upon a Tidewater minister who visited it and saw its chief characteristics as lawlessness, vile manners, ignorance, slovenliness, and primitive emotionalism in religion.[7] These people's pragmatic frugality, their oversimplified—almost folk-version—Calvinistic religion, and their intense individualism formed a distinct but not always attractive culture. Here, in the foothills near the early rises of the mountains, the Scotch-Irish were joined by the refugees and malcontents of the established seaboard society to form a harsh and unmannered world.

There has not been a time since the eighteenth century when this piedmont South has lacked chroniclers, and there has been a remarkable unanimity of opinion and attitude toward its inhabitants by its recorders. William Byrd in his *History of the Dividing Line* (1728) and *A Journey to the Land of Eden* (1733) portrayed back-country North Carolinians with a detached amusement and a sense of their comic grotesqueness. Augustus Baldwin Longstreet described these people in the sketches which he wrote for newspapers in the 1820s and 1830s and collected as *Georgia Scenes* in 1835. Here the detached view of a cultivated lawyer and judge established a vantage point which gave aesthetic distance to his portraits of the cruel, unlearned, but shrewd denizens of the piedmont, weighing these people against the implicit concept of the ordered seaboard society which Judge Longstreet revered. As a result the figures in *Georgia Scenes* are comic grotesques. The early novels of the southern frontier describe these same kinds of people and similarly judge them against an aristocratic social order, a method common to William Gilmore Simms's "Border Romances"—notably *Guy Rivers* (1834), which is laid in Miss O'Connor's native Georgia.

In the local color movement of the latter part of the nineteenth century, three Souths existed—the plantation South of Thomas Nelson Page, the Deep South of George Washington Cable and Kate Chopin, and the Tennessee-Georgia South of writers like "Charles Egbert Craddock" (Mary Noailles Murphree). And three differing attitudes were presented: Page's was an apologia through the portrayal of a glorious past, Cable's a social concern through an impassioned attack on the social and racial evils of his world, and Miss Murphree's a whimsical interest through a summer visitor's condescension to the illiterate Tennessee mountaineer.

Faulkner's *Absalom, Absalom!* has a theme pertinent to these issues, and is in one sense at least almost an historical allegory of these three Souths. In it Thomas Sutpen, from the Virginia piedmont, encounters Tidewater aristocracy which he admires but to which he is refused entrance, and he goes to Mississippi, by way of the Caribbean, to attempt to create on Sutpen's Hundred by violence, greed, and lust, the outward signs of an inner grace which he can envy but cannot understand or truly possess.

It is with these piedmont people whose literary representation has always been as grotesques that Miss O'Connor deals; they constitute the "physical substance" out of which she fashioned her vision of reality. In our time these same groups of southerners have been the subject matter of Erskine Caldwell, Carson McCullers, and the southern Gothic school in general.

The representation of the grotesque is a characteristic of much twentieth-century writing, southern and otherwise. In a fruitful and provocative essay, "The Grotesque: An American Genre," William Van O'Connor, who includes Miss O'Connor among the writers he discusses, states that the representation of an inverted world in which "what most of us would take to be normal is presented as monstrous" results from the fact that "the old agricultural system depleted the land and poverty breeds abnormality; in many cases people were living with a code that was no longer applicable, and this meant a detachment from reality and loss of vitality."[8] Although he sees "clear antecedents" in Edgar Allan Poe and finds the genre practiced by Caldwell, Faulkner, Robert Penn Warren, Eudora Welty, Carson McCullers, and Tennessee Williams, all of whom certainly use southern grotesques, his emphasis on a decayed order and lost wealth, an emphasis pertinent to many southern writers, does not seem to apply very well to Miss O'Connor's works.

He comes much closer to her position when he quotes Thomas Mann on the grotesque as resulting from the fact that modern art "has ceased to recognize the categories of tragic and comic.... It sees life as tragicomedy, with the result that the grotesque is its most genuine style ... the only guise in which the sublime may appear."[9] Miss O'Connor seemed to have the same view of the grotesque. In a preface written in 1962 for a reprinting of *Wise Blood* she said, "It is a comic novel about a Christian *malgré lui*, and as such, very serious, for all comic novels that are any good must be about matters of life and death" (p. 8). For, while there is no question that Flannery O'Connor deals with southern characters who are grotesques, the grotesque element in her work has other sources than the heat of social anger which warms Erskine Caldwell's or the sense of the absurdity of human existence which shapes the grotesqueries of our young existentialists.

She is more nearly central to the southern literary tradition in her persistent passion for order. Confronted with a modern, mechanized, scientifically-oriented world, the leading literary spokesmen for the South have usually shared the discomfort that most producers of humane art experience in the presence of the mechanical, and, like the twelve at Vanderbilt in 1930, they "tend to support a Southern way of life against what may be called the American or prevailing way."[10] Almost all artists feel a hunger for meaning, a need for structure, and rage for order in existence, and believe that the human spirit should never calmly surrender its endless search for order. Twentieth-century writers confronted by the spectacle of the mechanized culture of America have taken many different roads to many different regions of the spirit. Some have sought in art itself a kind of solipsistic answer to the need of order and thus have made a religion of art. Some have sought in activist movements bent on social change a way to establish meaning in the world. The southerner, predisposed to look backward as a result of his concern with the past,[11] has tended to impose a desire for a social structure that reflects moral principles and he has tried to see in the past of his region at least the shadowy outlines of a viable and admirable moral-social world. Allen Tate said, in 1952, in a retrospective glance at the Agrarian movement:

> I never thought of Agrarianism as a *restoration* of anything in the Old South; I saw it as something to be created, as I think it will in the long run be created as the result of a profound change, not only in the South, but elsewhere, in the moral and religious outlook of western man.... What I had in mind twenty years ago ... presupposes, with us, a prior order, the order of a unified Christendom.... If there is a useful program that we might undertake in the South, would it not be towards the greater unity of the varieties of Southern Protestantism, with the ultimate aim the full unity of all Christians? We are told by our Northern friends that the greatest menace to the South is ignorance; but there is even greater ignorance of the delusion of progressive enlightenment.[12]

Miss O'Connor was generally in sympathy with such views of the Agrarians. When she makes statements such as this one from "The Fiction Writer and His Country" she seems almost to be echoing their beliefs: "The anguish that most of us have observed for some time now has been caused not by the fact that the South is alienated from the rest of the country, but by the fact that it is not alienated enough, that every day we are getting more and more like the rest of the country, that we are being forced out, not only of our many sins but of our few virtues."[13] And certainly one could hardly call a friend of science the creator of Hulga Hopewell, in "Good Country People," who has a Ph.D. in philosophy, a wooden leg, and a willingness to be seduced by a fake Bible salesman who steals the leg and leaves her betrayed and helpless in the hayloft. Hulga underlines this statement in one of the books that she endlessly reads and marks up: "Science, on the other hand, has to assert its soberness and seriousness afresh and declare that it is concerned solely with what-is. Nothing—how can it be for science anything but a horror and a phantasm? If science is right, then one thing stands firm: science wishes to know nothing of nothing. Such is after all the strictly scientific approach to Nothing. We know it by wishing to know nothing of Nothing" (p. 248). The girl, like others of Miss O'Connor's few intellectuals, declares to the Bible salesman, "We are all damned . . . but some of us have taken off our blindfolds and see that there's nothing to see. It's a kind of salvation" (p. 258).[14] Similarly Rayber, in *The Violent Bear It Away*, with all his knowledge seems to be rendered more helpless by all he learns, and falls the semicredulous victim of a lustful child who is not really a spokesman for love but simply for the power of emotion.

"The Displaced Person," a short story that recounts the intrusion into a widow's farm of an efficient and effective displaced person, is typical of the way in which Miss O'Connor's situations can be read in frames not unlike those of the Agrarians. Here the "displaced person" may be taken as symbolic of the mechanical world intruding itself from the outside to disrupt the "order" of a southern farm.[15] Read this way the story is not unlike Robert Penn Warren's "The Patented Gate and the Mean Hamburger,"[16] and yet a careful examination of Miss O'Connor's tone and action make one, I think, suspicious of such a reading, a suspicion confirmed for the reader by the fact that Mrs. McIntyre, the widow who owns the farm, rejects its chance of salvation by Mr. Guizac, effectively destroys him, and declares to Father Flynn, who has been his friend and advocate, " 'as far as I'm concerned . . . Christ was just another D.P.' " (p. 294).

Flannery O'Connor's work is sufficiently similar to that of her contemporaries in the South to justify our feeling that, in one sense at least, she shares not only a common subject but many common concerns. She has other characteristics in common with her southern contemporaries that are worth mentioning. For her, as for them—and, indeed, for any depicter of an agrarian culture—the social unit is the family. For her, as they seemingly did for Faulkner and Wolfe, concrete expressions of meaning seem to come in relatively small actions and limited scenes. Wolfe is most impressive as an artist in his short stories and short novels, and much of Faulkner's best work appeared in brief episodes which were later woven into novels. Miss O'Connor, too, is better as a writer of short stories than she is as a novelist. To examine, for example, *Wise Blood* as a novel after looking at the original appearance of some of its parts as short stories is to question to some degree her wisdom in attempting the larger organization.

She also has an awareness of the caste structures that a relatively fixed social order produces and which have fascinated many southern writers, even though she does not often write of any except her "poor whites." For example, in her story "Revelation," she says:

> Sometimes Mrs. Turpin occupied herself at night naming the classes of people. On the bottom of the heap were most colored people, not the kind she would have been if she had been one, but most of them; then next to them—not above, just away from—were the white-trash; then above them were the home-owners, and above them the home-and-land owners, to which she and Claud belonged. Above she and Claud were people with a lot of money and much bigger houses and much more land. But here the complexity of it would begin to bear in on her, for some of the people with a lot of money were common and ought to be below she and Claud and some of the people who had good blood had lost their money and had to rent and then there were colored people who owned their homes and land as well. There was a colored dentist in town who had two red Lincolns and a swimming pool and a farm with registered white-face cattle on it.[17]

Miss O'Connor's sense that this kind of class distinction is meaningless is made plain here, and such things seem finally to be of much less interest to her than they are to most southern writers.

But these, after all, are largely quibbles. The crucial similarities and differences lie elsewhere. They lie with the concern she has for a religious order, and her most significant differences with her southern contemporaries are in the same area.

The crucial difference between Miss O'Connor and most of her fellow southerners lies in a simple fact, which she seldom passed up an opportunity to emphasize. She was a Catholic novelist in the Protestant South.[18] Indeed she speaks of the writing of fiction in terms of religious vocation, and she declares, "I see from the standpoint of Christian orthodoxy. This means that for me the meaning of life is centered in our Redemption by Christ and what I see in the world I see in its relation to that."[19] Hence the order she sees in the world, the order which redeems it from chaos and gives it community is fundamentally religious. And the tragedy she sees is the failure of the seeking soul to find rest in an adequate God.

The Agrarians who sought an ordered past had sought it in a social world and a political-economic system. Both John Crowe Ransom and Allen Tate, however, had perceived that such an order needed a religious basis, but neither of them believed that such a basis had existed in the South. Ransom's *God Without Thunder* (1930) is an heretical (he assumes that God is an anthropomorphic myth created by man) defense of a certain kind of orthodoxy, the orthodoxy that makes the old Hebraic God of thunder and wrath—unpredictable, awesome, awful, unappeasable—the potent and controlling force in the world. The modern God, on the other hand, Ransom thought to be a product of our age which is incapable of the wonder, the awe, or the sense of mystery which can give meaning to the world.

Tate felt that the South should have been Catholic; his essay on religion in *I'll Take My Stand* is an argument with his fellow southerners against establishing an ordered world that lacks a religious frame. A social order, he felt, must be undergirded and crowned by a firm and ritualistic religion if it is to be good. Tate himself later embraced the Catholic faith, but he knew that both the unified Christendom which he dreamed that the South had had in the past and that which his South knew in the present were not very far from the intense, individualistic, pietistic Protestantism of those like Stonewall Jackson, whose biography Tate had written. It found expression in the nontheological passion of Methodists, Baptists, and Holiness evangelists. The anguish of the soul, he felt, could not be assuaged by the introspective groping of the individual. Yet he was, with the exception of his wife, Caroline Gordon, and Ransom, unique in this persistent cry for a religious structure for his world.

Tate's view of the religion of the South was historically accurate. As James McBride Dabbs has recently noted, "The formal religion of the South did not grow out of its complete life and therefore could not crown that life with meaning."[20] As I have argued elsewhere, the South knew and knows an intense, individualistic puritanism.[21] Even in the Deep South, where the religious culture of New Orleans might have made itself felt, Faulkner, attempting a representation of a theological view in *Light in August,* turns from the ranks of the prolific Baptists and Methodists and makes his religious figures members of the numerically minor sect of Presbyterians, who alone of southern Protestants retained a discernible vestige of a dogma.[22] Thus the region lacked a religious orientation that could establish a meaningful community, while it was justly known as a "Bible Belt" of individual religious fanatics.

It is this aspect of the South—and pretty clearly by only slight extrapolation, of the modern world—which is, I believe, Miss O'Connor's obsessive theme. In what other modern writer is there a comparable pattern to Miss O'Connor's disturbed and desperate seekers? Where else do we find so many men and women for whom, as she expressed it, "belief in Christ is . . . a matter of life and death"? (p. 8).

The fact of Jesus believed in as a continuing divine force is at the root of her world. For the fact of Jesus demands that we do something about

Him. In "A Good Man Is Hard to Find" the old lady asks the murdering Misfit why he doesn't pray, and he gives the modern answer, " 'I don't want no hep. . . . I'm doing all right by myself' " (p. 141). But he later declares of Jesus, " 'He thown everything off balance. If He did what He said, then it's nothing for you to do but thow away everything and follow Him, and if He didn't, then it's nothing for you to do but enjoy the few minutes you got left the best way you can—by killing somebody or burning down his house or doing some other meanness to him. No pleasure but meanness' " (p. 142). In "The Artificial Nigger," Miss O'Connor wrote that Mr. Head

> stood appalled, judging himself with the thoroughness of God, while the action of mercy covered his pride like a flame and consumed it. He had never thought himself a great sinner before but he saw now that his true depravity had been hidden from him lest it cause him despair. He realized that he was forgiven for sins from the beginning of time, when he had conceived in his own heart the sin of Adam, until the present, when he had denied poor Nelson. He saw that no sin was too monstrous for him to claim as his own, and since God loved in proportion as He forgave, he felt ready at that instant to enter Paradise. (pp. 213–214)

Mrs. Shortley, in "The Displaced Person," had "never given much thought to the devil for she felt that religion was essentially for those people who didn't have the brains to avoid evil without it. For people like herself, for people of gumption, it was a social occasion providing the opportunity to sing; but if she had ever given it much thought, she would have considered the devil the head of it and God the hanger-on" (p. 270). "Christ in the conversation," Miss O'Connor says of Mrs. McIntyre, "embarrassed her the way sex had her mother" (p. 291). The mystic Hazel Motes, in *Wise Blood*, is an inverted saint, preaching the "Holy Church of Christ Without Christ," and willing to die like a martyr to deny the power and reality of Jesus.

James McBride Dabbs says, "At the deepest level the Southern white was an individualistic Protestant modern, who did not really believe in community, who did not bring the community before God or hold his membership in it under God, but who faced God in an awful, breath-taking aloneness."[23]

The representation of these lost and passionate seekers becomes naturally a representation of the grotesque. The folks of Miss O'Connor's country are distorted and disturbed because their deepest selves, she believes, seek with undeniable passion a meaning and order which the Protestant South cannot give. "My own feeling," she declared, is that writers who see by the light of their Christian faith will have, in these times, the sharpest eyes for the grotesque, for the perverse, and for the unacceptable. In some cases, these writers may be unconsciously infected with the Manichaean spirit of the times and suffer the much discussed disjunction between sensibility and belief, but I think that more often the reason for this attention to the perverse is the difference between their beliefs and the beliefs of the audience.... The novelist with Christian concerns will find in modern life distortions which are repugnant to him, and his problem will be to make these appear as distortions to an audience which is used to seeing them as natural; and he may well be forced to take ever more violent means to get his vision across to this hostile audience.[24]

A writer's country, she maintained, was both the inner and the outer reality. It seems to me that of her country we may declare its outer self plainly and unmistakably southern, its rage for order common to the twentieth-century southern literary concern, and the reality against which she ultimately judges it to be one which goes far to indict the South for its spiritual sterility, for the way it emasculates its saints and sentimentalizes its poets.

"Our souls," St. Augustine said, "are restless till they find rest in Thee." Flannery O'Connor's restless souls belong to people primitive in mind and Protestant in religion, who with all their difference, share a common, deep, and personal awareness of the awful and awesome presence and power of God in the world. Like Francis Thompson in "The Hound of Heaven," no matter how much they flee "Him down the labyrinthine ways," they cannot deny either His reality or His intolerable demands. Living in a world not ordered to an adequate sense of the power and presence of God, they seek either to deny Him or to pervert Him, and thus they become grotesque and unnatural. The human hunger for love cannot be satisfied with hatred; the human passion for order cannot willingly accept disorder as the principle of its universe; the ultimate dignity of man does not lie in his own hands, and when he tries to take violent hold of it, he destroys himself. That, it seems to me, is the antiexistentialist message that a brave and thoughtful Catholic woman gave to a South hungry, as it has been for a century and a half, for a stable order and a sensible meaning. Because Flannery O'Connor was southern, she used the South as matter and addressed it as audience. But what she said transcends her region and speaks with the authority of art to the great world outside.

Literature and Culture
The Fugitive-Agrarians

The question of the relationship between literature and the culture in which it is produced has been raised in many ways since Taine advanced his theory of literature as the product of "race, epoch, and era";[1] but the development of a sizeable body of distinguished literature in the South in the last forty years has seemed to many to pose the issue in fresh terms. It was stated tauntingly by Donald Davidson when he challenged the sociologists to "account for the appearance in Mississippi, of all places, of William Faulkner, in the three decades between 1920 and 1950."[2] Howard W. Odum and John Maclachlan replied in the *Hopkins Review*,[3] but I think that the group of writers known as the Fugitive-Agrarians are peculiarly suited to examination in such terms and that such an examination will indicate by example certain significant aspects of the relationship of the artist to his culture.

There assembled in Nashville, Tennessee, in the early 1920s a group of young writers of literary genius so startling that they and their works have left what seems to be an indelible mark on American letters and on American culture. The writers were more than a dozen poets and critics—among them John Crowe Ransom, Allen Tate, Donald Davidson, Merrill Moore, and Robert Penn Warren—the place of their assembling was Vanderbilt University, and the occasion was a small magazine which they published called the *Fugitive*.[4]

Astringent wit, philosophic depths clouded by obscurity, high technical skill, and an almost religious devotion to art and to its thoughtful and committed criticism were typical of the group. The very name of their magazine reflected a certain Ishmaelism, a sense of alienation. Tate said, "A Fugitive was quite simply a Poet: the Wanderer, or even the Wandering Jew, the Outcast, the man who carries the secret wisdom of the world."[5] The group was rejecting what Davidson called "poet-laureating, the cheapness and triviality of public taste, even among those supposed to be cultured; the lack of serious devotion to literature, to the arts, to ideas."[6] Other Southern writers were in much the same ferment. As early as 1921 the editors of the New Orleans little magazine the *Double Dealer*, in which William Faulkner's work was first published, declared: "It is high time, we believe, for some doughty, clear-visioned penman to emerge from the sodden marshes of Southern literature. We are sick to death of the treacly sentimentalities with which our well-

intentioned lady fictioneers regale us."[7] The *Fugitive's* editors asserted
that it fled "from nothing faster than from the high-caste Brahmins of
the Old South."[8] But in this flight they produced what Edmund Wilson
called "a new literature that is as free from the flowers of rhetoric as it is
from the formulas of gallantry.... Although it has sloughed off these
demoded trappings, it has kept much of the grace and distinction with
which they were formerly worn."[9]

Several of the best of these writers became members of the group who
in 1930 issued the Agrarian manifesto *I'll Take My Stand,*[10] which argued on economic and political grounds for an agrarian as opposed to an
industrial culture. In 1936 in another manifesto they truculently raised
the question, "Who owns America?"[11] The political-economic doctrines
annunciated in these books have had little effect on modern America;
the relentless march of men into cities has not been checked; science
and technology now "beep" mockingly from outer space; and the
Agrarians' efforts have gained them only the taunting epithet of "Neo-
Confederates."

But unimpaired by this failure and undaunted by this ridicule, several
of these writers have been among the centers of the resurgence of excellence in southern writing which has carried it to greater heights than
it has ever enjoyed before. As poets they have achieved high renown; as
novelists they have gained international standing; as the "New Critics"
they have revolutionized the criticism and the teaching of literature.

Let us examine some of the ways in which this three-part movement
was a response to social and cultural change—being aware that so brief
a statement is necessarily suggestive rather than exhaustive.

First I would remove one issue: certainly the South in this century has
seen a remarkable outpouring of literary talent, the *sine qua non* of any
successful literary movement, and I believe that we cannot yet explain
talent in terms of cultural or environmental factors, although we can
study the direction that talent takes and the degree to which its potential
is realized in terms of such factors. Thus, this accidental occurrence of
great talent in the region being assumed, we can look at cultural conditions as shapers of how talent works.

The Fugitives began in revolt against the literary expression of their
region. The period between 1865 and 1920 might be called the dark night
of southern writing. It was the age of the sentimental local color story, of
the imitative moralistic poem, of the sentimentally exaggerated picture
of the plantation. Before the Civil War the view of the South as a vast
succession of white columned plantations resting on slavery was the
stereotype of abolitionist writers;[12] it hardly existed in Southern writing
until after the Civil War,[13] and then it became a sentimentalized export

The Roots of Southern Writing

that early moved to what Wilbur J. Cash has called "Cloud-Cuckoo Land."[14] The best poet of the period, Sidney Lanier, although he attacked the abstract idea of "Trade" in some of his poetry, generally supported the new economic order and was given to lushly expressed moral sentiments. The literature of the South for half a century had a faint odor of overripeness and glowed unhealthily with the pale phosphorescence of decay. When Ellen Glasgow set out on her career it was in conscious revolt against sentimentality and what she called "evasive idealism." James Branch Cabell, the other serious southern writer between Lanier and the First World War, deserted his region almost entirely for a fantasyland where a desirable order might be realized. The Fugitives began by attacking this literature and by writing a poetry dealing wryly and astringently but also gracefully and decorously with the values of the civilization that preceded the Civil War. Their techniques were those of T. S. Eliot, Hart Crane, the French Symbolistes, and the English metaphysicals, but the controlled rage which gave them vigor came from their revulsion against the writings of the South.

But in a very real sense the Fugitives were also a part of the literary movements of the 1920s in a national as well as a regional way. They were almost a Nashville equivalent of the "lost young men" who spent the "Boom Years" in Paris cafés, published little magazines, and joined with Tristram Tzara in Dada gestures. These young men—Dos Passos, Hemingway, Fitzgerald, Edmund Wilson, Malcolm Cowley, Hart Crane, and many others—rejected the tenets and the facts of capitalistic industrial America and sought in art and the life of the spirit a release for other and—although they did not always know it—older values.[15] Being themselves without strong regional attachments and having gone to Europe when very young, they became cosmopolites, men without a country, and art became for them a religion. For the Fugitives, on the other hand, a religion itself was a lost but desirable reality; they had regional homes; and a powerful cultural myth was operative in them.

Simply expressed, what I am saying is this: the Fugitives represented a spirited aesthetic rejection of the prevailing literature and attitudes of the contemporary South in much the same way that the Paris expatriates represented a rejection of the prevailing literature and attitudes of the industrial and commercial world.

The test came in 1929, when the industrial and economic structure underwent a severe depression and the disaster of the southern farmer, long a fact, could no longer be ignored.[16] The depression made political and economic matters of crucial importance to the literary world, and art no longer being a sufficient religion, the American artist felt that he must embrace political and economic causes. The expatriates moved from

Paris cafés to political conferences and exchanged Dada gestures for political action. The dominant attitude was associated with science and progress, and it was held by the Liberals or Marxists or Proletarians, most of whom had earlier been Paris expatriates or Greenwich Village rebels who now transferred their sights from the *Saturday Evening Post* to the political system.

The compulsion to public action which was a powerful factor in American writing in the 1930s was also operative in the Nashville Fugitives, but where a belief in progress led many Liberals to Marxism, the southern intellectual was drawn in other directions. The South had remained a distinctive region with a distinctive set of attitudes—perhaps, as Harry Ashmore says, it is the only distinctive region left in America.[17] Its distinctiveness was uniquely associated with its agrarian culture.

As early as 1781—long before slavery was an issue—Thomas Jefferson, in his *Notes on the State of Virginia*, wrote: "Those who labour in the earth are the chosen people of God, if ever he had a chosen people, whose breasts he has made his peculiar deposit for substantial and genuine virtue." And he compared the European system of manufactures unfavorably with the American agrarian system, saying, "It is better to carry provisions and materials to workmen there [in Europe], than bring them to the provisions and materials, and with them their manners and principles." It was Jefferson's distrust of large cities and industrial ways, William Peden tells us, that was a major area of disagreement between his party and the Federalists.[18] John Taylor of Caroline in 1803 in *The Arator* defended the agricultural way of life against the support being given by government to manufactures, and in 1814 in his much admired *Inquiry into the Principles and Policy of the Government of the United States,* Taylor asserted that the cultural and moral well-being of America rested with its agricultural people and was being attacked by those who supported capitalistic industrialism, which he called "the system of paper and patronage."[19] This fundamental difference, which was more basic than the slavery issue, wrote a long narrative of tariff fights and slave-free compromises across the first half of our national history, and when efforts at compromise finally failed in 1861, the issue of the war was between these differing concepts of man and his society. Fundamental to the southern system was agriculture and a social system based on stability, tradition, class structure, and the powerful idea of an aristocracy. The northern system was progressive and industrial, with a social system valuing change and revering science. The issues were tried by battle; the victors dictated the peace and imposed their terms by force; but, in 1877, the fifth great crisis and the fourth compromise occurred, as C. Vann Woodward has shown in *Reunion and Reaction*, with the resulting end of Reconstruction and the establishment of a new regime in the South. The effect of this compromise of 1877 was to end the political and economic warfare between the regions. The South was given the principle of "white supremacy" and a promise of a share in the new economic spoils. Thus, Woodward says, "the South became a bulwark instead of a menace to the new order."[20]

It was an age in which, says Lewis Mumford, "the old America was for all practical purposes demolished; industrialism had entered overnight, had transformed the practices of agriculture."[21] But the old order had other qualities which lingered in the memory and the heart of the region after the social fact of the order itself had been demolished, and which together formed a powerful myth of a way of life. I shall merely assert some of these qualities that outlived in the mind the institutions with which they were associated; I shall not attempt to demonstrate them. Among them are the persistence of pessimism and the sense of evil and imperfection which are the most distinctive heritages of the Calvinism which shaped the thought of the region and still forms the philosophical frame within which it thinks and feels; a love for classical learning—a love which predated the devotion to the Greek state which southerners of the 1840s developed in justification of slavery; a sense of place and the soil, which is associated with every agrarian literature and culture which the world has known; a profound but seldom articulated awareness of the interpenetration of the past and the present, so that history becomes a record of inestimable value; a reverence for the family as the basic social unit; a deep sense of the individual dignity of man and a comparatively small regard for his group relations; a tendency to examine the particular rather than to generalize; the ability to live at ease with an unresolved paradox; and a reverence for gracious living and good manners.

The Fugitives were essentially poets, and it was this legend of their land and its past virtues which they chose as their antidote to progress and the theory of class conflict. Their motives were clearly expressed by Stark Young when he wrote in *I'll Take My Stand:*

> If anything is clear, it is that we can never go back, and neither this essay nor any intelligent person that I know in the South desires a literal restoration of the old Southern life, even if that were possible; dead days are gone, and if by some chance they should return, we should find them intolerable. But out of any epoch in civilization there may arise things worth while, that are the flowers of it. To abandon these, when another epoch arrives, is only stupid, so long as there is still in them the breath and flux of life. . . . It would be childish and dangerous for the South to be stampeded and betrayed out of its own character by the noise, force,

and glittering narrowness of the industrialism and progress spreading everywhere, with varying degrees, from one region to another.[22]

Thus the Agrarian way which the Fugitives adopted was, in a sense, a myth of the good order of the past used as a weapon of attack against what they believed to be the bad order of the present.

Such a myth proved to be an effective rallying point for the eager minds of the southern intellectuals caught in the world of economic disaster. It proved to be peculiarly ineffectual in convincing others of the justice or truth of its cause. With the coming of the Second World War its usefulness, even to the southern intellectual, had passed; the urban South was almost at hand, waiting the expedient moment to burst alarmingly upon us. The Agrarians abandoned their economic theory and their political polemics at about the same time that the Liberals against whom they had fought bid their unhappy farewell to the radicalism of the 1930s. But the literature of the South had found in the Agrarian myth a viable legend, a fruitful subject through which the themes of order, of tradition, of grace, and of good manners, of those good and surviving qualities of the Old South could be expressed. And these elements, stripped of their economic and political expressions, have given southern writing depth of meaning, grace of expression, and intensity of feeling unique in our time.

I think that this suggests a broad and very generalized pattern for examining the relationship of literature to its culture. In order to clarify this pattern, allow me to make a useful but by no means mutually exclusive set of divisions and distinguish among three elements in a given author's work: his *talent*, which includes his technical skills, literary conventions, linguistic attitudes and aptitudes; his *subject*, which is the matter that his talent works upon as story, structure of images, or pattern; and, finally, his *theme*, which is the end-product, the often nonconceptualized intention, which is realized through the play of *talent* upon *subject*. I am here following—from afar off and with much variation— Robert Penn Warren's assertions about literature in *Who Owns America?* Mr. Warren has an illuminating paragraph on Milton's *subject* and his *theme* (the idea of *talent* is my addition to Warren's dichotomy) in which he says that "the subject of *Paradise Lost* is the story of the Fall of Man, the story of what happened to Adam and Eve. But the theme is the nature of justice, the relation of human will to Divine Will, the relation of Good to Evil. . . . It is conceivable that Milton might have used another subject, though probably one not as effective, for the vehicle of his theme."[23] In a similar way we might say of Mr. Warren that his *theme* is human guilt and inescapable evil in the nature of man and the world,

The Roots of Southern Writing

that he has used as the vehicle of that theme, various *subjects*, including Huey Long, the Beauchamp-Sharp murder case, and the theological concept of "Original Sin," and that he has expressed this *theme* through these *subjects*, using his various and impressive *talents* as poet, novelist, and dramatist. In a similar way William Faulkner has used his novelistic talent to imprison in stories of impotent perverts, homicidal Negroes, Snopeses, and gallant Confederate soldiers a theme so close to Milton's that we might call the vast Yoknapatawpha County legend a southern *Paradise Lost.*

Now what I am suggesting about the Fugitives is that their theme is drawn from the culture of their region; it is, in fact, the qualities I have equated with the old order which constitute that theme. When, as Agrarians, they espoused an apparent return to Cash's "Cloud-Cuckoo Land," they were in fact using the Old South as *subject* rather than as *theme.* In their attempt to rally the South to stem the tide of materialism and to give it "belief rather than doubt, conviction rather than skepticism, loyalty rather than distrust," as Harry Ashmore has shown,[24] they were making a literary use of economics and politics—they were, indeed, feebly enacting as amateur sociologists what they were later to realize magnificently as art. That their Agrarian effort was unhappy was inevitable.

Yet their response was sensitive and artistically intelligent to the currents of their day. And they have given us a better literature, a more informed criticism, and a greater wealth of good poetry than we might have expected from their half-ludicrous public stances. They have taught us, too, that artists respond to the pressures of their culture, not by making political gestures or by accurate reporting, but by imprisoning through their talent its themes in its subjects. The southern talent has found its themes in a combination of regional tradition and the inner self and its subjects have come from the history and the soil of the South.

Three Views of the Real

> If [a novelist] believes that actions are predetermined by psychic make-up or the economic situation or some other determinable factor, then he will be concerned above all with an accurate reproduction of the things that most immediately concern man, with the natural forces that he feels control his destiny. Such a writer may produce a great tragic naturalism, for by his responsibility to the things he sees, he may transcend the limitations of his narrow vision—*Flannery O'Connor*.[1]

The meaning of a work of art is inextricably interwoven from language, character, action, and form; and our ultimate comprehension of the fundamental value of a work of fiction rests upon our seeing it as an organic whole. In every work of art four elements are present: the subject, which in Aristotle's sense we can view as the thing being imitated; the artist who is using his work as an expression of his personal vision of man; the audience, which through the work of art catches some glimpse of the artist's vision of experience; and finally, the work itself independent of all of these things, an artifact with an objective reality. In these essays I have placed a primary emphasis upon the mimetic quality in southern writing because it seems to me that many critics of contemporary southern fiction have failed to recognize the significant variations in its subject.

I have also made a serious effort to look at the author himself, for, as Wayne Booth has forcefully reminded us,[2] the author is always present in a work of fiction; and even when he thinks he has withdrawn himself, like James Joyce's artist, who "like the God of the creation, remains within or behind or beyond or above his handiwork, invisible, refined out of existence, indifferent, paring his fingernails,"[3] the very fact of his indifference is a part of his reality; and try as he will, fingernail clippings will get mixed in the work. The authors of southern fiction have made relatively little effort to "deal themselves out of the game" as far as the reader is concerned, and they are always present and willing to use any of many kinds of devices to control and to shape the response of the reader. They are there through attitude toward subjects; they are there through direct authorial statement; and they are pervasively there through style.

All authors manipulate language to their own purposes—Miss Glasgow did so wittily; William Faulkner, with incantatory power; and Thomas Wolfe, lyrically and directly through image and adjective. Miss

Glasgow's theme is domestic, and she operates within the relatively closed circle of a small group of families, using as her focus elderly, gracious, ceremonious but ineffectual men and as her central situation the position of marriage and of women and their place in society. William Faulkner deals with a broad spectrum of the social world, however small the rural Mississippi stage is upon which it is enacted, covering, according to his famous map, 2,400 square miles and a population of 6,298 whites and 9,313 Negroes. To that legend he also added, "William Faulkner, sole owner and proprietor"; but throughout the more than twenty volumes of his fiction he has convinced a substantial portion of the reading world that most of the fundamental situations which man faces are somehow duplicated on Faulkner's "postage stamp of earth" and are, therefore, as much theirs as Faulkner's. Thomas Wolfe, on the other hand, was trying to grasp within himself the largest possible range of experience, both real and vicarious; and he defined generic man not as a southerner but as an American so that at last he could say as Walt Whitman did,

> I celebrate myself, and sing myself,
> And what I assume you shall assume,
> For every atom belonging to me as good belongs to you.[4]

Miss Glasgow centered her work in large measure upon the definition of this mannered southern society because she was a resident of the seaboard and an ironic critic of its way of life. Out of its conventions she made the novel of manners and tested the virtues and the vices of her characters by those "memorials of old traditions." Faulkner, tracing the long history of Yoknapatawpha County, moved back into the past and attempted the evocation of legend and the creation of intense symbolic statements. For his characters the past lives with passion and makes enormous demands. Many of his characters are like the Reverend Gail Hightower in *Light in August*, who "grew to manhood among phantoms, and side by side with a ghost. The phantoms were his father, his mother, and an old Negro woman . . . . It was as though the very cold and uncompromising conviction which propped it upright, as it were, between puritan and cavalier, had become not defeated and not discouraged, but wiser" and who hears the galloping horses of his soldier grandfather's company, "the wild bugles and the clashing sabres and the dying thunder of hooves";[5] and out of this past Faulkner has created the materials of a cosmic fable. Thomas Wolfe alone of these writers has felt the democratic pressures which de Tocqueville defined, and he has written more of himself than of his society.

The writers whom we are looking at here have handled the southern past in three radically different ways. Speaking for the Tidewater, Ellen Glasgow has viewed southern history as fact. She had tried to portray in the characters closest to its catastrophe the created illusion that it did not happen, as she did in *The Deliverance*; but she and her characters know that however much defeat might be screened from the consciousness of a dying patrician lady, it could not be screened from her children. She has used the fact of this past as a novelist of manners does—that is, as the means through which a social world is given ironic commentary. She prescribed for the South that she loved and was amused at her now classic formula of "blood and irony" and wrote of it as closer to New England that any other portion of the New World. In her Queenborough novels she portrays the way in which it continues to pay lip service to ideals that have lost their cause for existence and to surrender hope and energy to a social structure whose meaning and justification ended long ago. Thus, like John Marquand's patrician Bostonians or Santayana's Last Puritan, her people represent decayed and ineffectual patricians.

On the other hand the past for William Faulkner has been a world of fable raised almost to the order of myth; and he has used it, as George Snell saw many years ago, as an apocalyptic vision. The Deep South has dealt with the dream of the Tidewater in extravagant terms since the 1830s, and in Faulkner's work this same intense extravagance appears. Passionate and overdrawn, his characters loom not like figures who rode with Stuart or marched with Pickett but like vast shadowy forms who would have been equally at home in the Greek theater and who are closer to Sophocles and Euripides than they are to Stark Young or Margaret Mitchell.

For Thomas Wolfe the past was of much less importance. He declared of the Tidewater gentry, "Their pretense is reduced to pretending that they amounted to so much formerly. And they really amounted to very little."[6] Wolfe's view of the present state of the Low Country and the Tidewater culture is one which Miss Glasgow has treated in her ironic comedies. The pretense regarding what that culture still is has seldom received more effective reduction than it has endured under Miss Glasgow's scalpel. Yet she would have denied, and I think Faulkner for his world too would have denied, that the pretense rested, as Wolfe insisted, on very little. Each—that is, Tidewater and Deep South—knew that an order had existed, a structure had been there in society, and, though it might today be gone, it could not ever be totally and completely forgotten. Of the three only Wolfe believed that past to be of relatively little value.

It is interesting to see how each of these novelists treats the central fact of southern history—that is, the Civil War. There can be little question that each of them sees this war as the watershed in the social and economic history of the South, but each of them also takes a peculiarly different attitude toward it. Miss Glasgow's is ironic. The Civil War cut away the basic roots out of which the Tidewater manners had come; and after the war, these manners and conventions, no longer descriptive of an inner reality, became desiccated and seared. War was thus for her a great accelerator of change. One of her most effective pictures of its meaning is through the character Mrs. Blake in *The Deliverance*. Mrs. Blake, a very elderly and gracious lady, lived on after the war ignorant of its outcome and protected from such disastrous knowledge by her children at great cost to themselves in order that she, unaware of how her world had changed, could, as Miss Glasgow says that she and all Virginia did, "cling, with passionate fidelity, to the ceremonial forms of tradition."[7]

For Thomas Wolfe the Civil War is simply a fact and not a particularly significant one, one perhaps to be forgotten. It does not grieve upon the bones of his own world; and when he turns, as on occasion he does, to a description of those who would insist upon the beauty and the value of the pre–Civil War South, he turns to an ironic treatment of cherished dignity. The picture which he paints of the "refined young gentlemen of the New Confederacy" is one that only a person unsympathetic to both the past and the present South could have uttered.[8] In *You Can't Go Home Again* Wolfe has George Webber say, "Sometimes it seems to me...that America went off the track somewhere—back around the time of the Civil War, or pretty soon afterwards. Instead of going ahead and developing along the line in which the country started out, it got shunted off in another direction—and now we look around and see we've gone places we didn't mean to go. Suddenly we realize that America has turned into something ugly—and vicious—and corroded at the heart of its power with easy wealth and graft and special privilege."[9]

In contrast William Faulkner in *Intruder in the Dust* says: "For every Southern boy fourteen years old, not once but whenever he wants it, there is the instant when it's still not two o'clock on that July afternoon in 1863, the brigades are in position behind the rail fence, the guns are laid and ready in the woods and the furled flags are already loosened to break out and Pickett himself with his long oiled ringlets and his hat in one hand probably and his sword in the other looking up the hill waiting for Longstreet to give the word and it's all in the balance, it hasn't happened yet, it hasn't even begun."[10]

Another way to see a difference clearly demonstrated among the writers using these three Souths as their subject is to compare James Branch Cabell's mocking and ironic autobiography *Let Me Lie*, in which the customs and attitudes of the Tidewater are held up to gently mocking laughter, with William Alexander Percy's autobiography *Lanterns on the Levee*, in which his romantic sense of the beauty and dignity of southern traditional life—even while some of its values and standards are questioned—casts over it some of the glow that Stark Young embodied in *So Red the Rose*. Against this view of the South we might juxtapose the image which Thomas Wolfe used in *The Web and the Rock* to sum up "the whole dark picture of those decades of defeat and darkness." George Webber sees an old house overgrown with grass and weeds so that its paths are no longer passable and no one visits it again, and an old man walks into the house never to come out again. The house shines faintly "like its own ruined spectre, its doors and windows black as eyeless sockets. That was the South. That was the South for thirty years or more." But significantly for Thomas Wolfe his generation has come "into a kind of sunlight of another century. They had come out upon the road again. The road was being paved. More people came now. They cut a pathway to the door again. Some of the weeds were clear. Another house was built . . . and the world was *in*."[11] This house is not unlike Sutpen's mansion in *Absalom, Absalom!* But Faulkner's house is enveloped in flames before the imprisoned past (in the person of Henry Sutpen) can come out into the modern world.

This view of a new South was alien to Miss Glasgow, who could declare, "Noise, numbers, size, quantity, all are exerting their lively or sinister influence. Sentiment no longer suffices. To be Southern, even to be solid, is not enough; for the ambition of the new South is not to be self-sufficing, but to be more Western than the West and more American than the whole of America. Uniformity, once despised and rejected, has become the established ideal. Satisfied for so long to leave the miscellaneous product 'Americanism' to the rest of the country, the South is at last reaching out for its neglected inheritance."[12] She could have been thinking of Thomas Wolfe.

The first of our twentieth-century major southern novelists, Ellen Glasgow, took as her subject the fixed social world of the Tidewater and took as her theme the restrictions placed upon character through the pressure of a decaying, traditionalized, formal society. At one time the society she describes had had grace, dignity, beauty, and honor, but that day had been lost in the early eras of its history. After the Civil War, confronted with the rising lower middle class, it had created itself into a sentimentalized evasion of the world and had made manners a means of excluding reality from the central assumptions by which its citizens lived. Like Jenny Blair Archbald, Miss Glasgow's characters could ignore the true implications of the world in which they lived by falling

The Roots of Southern Writing

back upon a set of conventionalized evasions; but like Jenny, too, this world could step aside from the consequences of its acts only at a tragic cost to its fellow men. Ellen Glasgow knew, as Edith Wharton had known,[13] that a trivial society can be effectively described only in terms of what it destroys. Whatever shadow of evil hangs over her world, it hangs alike over old General Archbald and young Jenny Blair, for each has accepted a system in which the death of the personality is the price of acceptance in the society. In presenting this world, Miss Glasgow has used the well-made realistic novel of manners; and when her voice is heard, as it is on almost every page she wrote, it is a very urbane, witty, and ironic voice, for like Thackeray before her she not only condemns her *Vanity Fair* but is part of what she condemns.

William Faulkner in the lush, semitropical Deep South found material appropriate to gothic treatment and used it to create a symbolic picture of the South as an historical myth and as a cosmic tragedy. His plots are melodramatic structures that are very close to the detective story, as Greek tragedy was, for like the detective story and Greek tragedy the plots move forward to those crucial recognition scenes in which the character comes finally to perceive a truth previously hidden from him.

Thomas Wolfe speaks directly of the piedmont South, a modern world in which the triumph of the middle class has forced a pattern of values primarily in terms of size, cost, and chromium; but he is, despite his criticism of its lack of standards and of beauty, an advocate of the New South, a region willing both to accept and to profit from the general character of his nation; and early in his novels and in his career Wolfe abandoned "hill-pent" Asheville to seek not a regional but a national meaning and to find in himself the common experiences of all men. Hence his books become the loosely constructed autobiographical record of an intense and lyric search for reality as it expresses itself in the inner character of the American. The bardic quality is very clearly in his work, for he approaches himself and his subject primarily as an epic poet and only very partially as a novelist.

These three writers have established, thus, three modes tied in intimate ways to the regions which produced them and viewing in different lights the past history out of which they came. These modes might be defined in any of several different ways. Ellen Glasgow's could well be called the urbane; William Faulkner's, the daemonic; and Thomas Wolfe's, the intense. Viewed in another way, we would see Miss Glasgow as a realist and her approach toward southern society was as ironic. We would see Faulkner as a romanticist and his approach to southern history and society as symbolic and mythic; and we would see Wolfe as an epic lyricist and his view of the southern society outside his self as satiric. Although

Miss Glasgow is correct in asserting that "the truth of art and the truth of life are two different truths,"[14] certainly their artistic uses by these writers define the basic and perhaps ineradicable differences in what we loosely call "The South."

Four years before her death, the gallant lady and militant Christian, Flannery O'Connor, spoke movingly on the difficulty and challenge of being a southern writer and brought the essentially private vision of the novelist into effective relation with the nature of his subject. She said: "The problem for [a southern] novelist will be to know how far he can distort without destroying, and in order not to destroy, he will have to descend far enough into himself to reach those underground springs that give life to his work. This descent into himself will, at the same time, be a descent into his region. It will be a descent through the darkness of the familiar into a world where like the blind man cured in the gospels, he sees men as if they were trees, but walking. This is the beginning of vision, and I feel it is a vision which we in the South must at least try to understand if we want to participate in the continuance of a vital Southern literature. I hate to think that in twenty years Southern writers too may be writing about men in grey flannel suits and may have lost their ability to see that these gentlemen are even greater freaks than what we are writing about now. I hate to think of the day when the Southern writer will satisfy the tired reader."[15]

I feel that neither "the man in the grey flannel suit" nor "the tired reader" is likely to stop the efforts of good writers from all three Souths to find in region, race, religion, and physical reality a viable subject for the statement of unpalatable but enduring truths.

Notes

———— ◆◦•◦◆ ————

The Southerner
as American Writer

Not only does this essay open with a statement of those compulsive contradictions which seem to me to be a part of the essence of the southern experience, it also makes as a whole a summary statement of the positions that are elaborated in the succeeding essays. The essay was written as a part of the symposium, *The Southerner as American*, edited by Charles G. Sellers, Jr. (Chapel Hill, 1960; New York, 1966). The intent of the collection was for nine southerners writing as historians to analyze the complexity of southern history with a view to asserting the continuing similarities that the South has had with the rest of the American nation. They invited me to write an essay on the topic "The Southerner as American Writer," and I was happy to join the eight historians who wrote the other essays: John Hope Franklin, Thomas P. Govan, Charles Grier Sellers, Jr., David Donald, Grady McWhiney, George B. Tindall, L. D. Reddick, and Dewey W. Grantham, Jr. Writing the essay proved to be an instructive and liberating experience for me, for it gave me the opportunity, without becoming a separatist, to deal with the differences that distinguish southern writing. This essay comes closer than any other that I have written to giving a succinct, broad statement of my beliefs about the South and southern writing.

1. Robert Penn Warren, *Segregation: The Inner Conflict of the South* (New York, 1957), p. 15.   2. "The Southern Revival: A Land and Its Interpreters," London *Times Literary Supplement*, September 17, 1954, p. xvi.   3. See Cleanth Brooks, *Modern Poetry and the Tradition* (Chapel Hill, 1939).   4. See Allen Tate, "Tension in Poetry," *Essays of Four Decades* (Chicago, 1968), pp. 56–71.   5. Cotton Mather, *Bonifacius, An Essay Upon the Good, that is to be Devised and Designed* (Boston, 1710), a work popularly known as *The Essays to Do Good*.   6. Richard Beale Davis, *George Sandys* (New York, 1955), pp. 198–226.   7. C. Hugh Holman, "European Influences on Southern American Literature: A Preliminary Survey," *Comparative Literature: Proceedings of the Second Congress of the International Comparative Literature Association*, ed. W. P. Friederich (Chapel Hill, 1959), I, 444–455.   8. *Southern Quarterly Review*, XXIX (1856), 205.   9. See, for example, Henry Wadsworth Longfellow's *Kavanagh: A Tale*, Chap. xx.

10. See John Stafford, *The Literary Criticism of "Young America"* (Berkeley, 1952), and Perry Miller, *The Raven and the Whale* (New York, 1956), for detailed accounts of this literary war and the participation of Poe and Simms in it.   11. "The Gift Outright," *The Poetry of Robert Frost*, ed. Edward Connery Lathem (New York, 1970), pp. 424–425.   12. M. C. S. Oliphant, A. T. Odell, and T. C. D. Eaves, eds., *The Letters of William Gilmore Simms*, 5 vols. (Columbia, S. C., 1952–1956), II, 90.   13. *Letters of Simms*, I, 264.   14. See Jay B. Hubbell, "Literary Nationalism in the Old South," *American Studies in Honor of William Kenneth Boyd*, ed. D. K. Jackson (Durham, 1940), pp. 175–220.   15. W. G. Simms, "The Writings of James Fenimore Cooper," *Views and Reviews in American Literature, History and Fiction*, First Series, ed. C. Hugh Hol-

man (Cambridge, Mass., 1962), pp. 266–268.   16. W. G. Simms, Dedication, *The Damsel of Darien*, 2 vols. (Philadelphia, 1839), I, 9.   17. W. G. Simms, "Literary Statistics of New York," *Southern and Western Monthly Magazine*, II (September 1845), 205–207; Simms, "The National Volume," ibid., I (June 1845), 435–436.   18. W. G. Simms, *The Wigwam and the Cabin* (New York, 1856), pp. 4–5.   19. Allen Tate, "The New Provincialism," *Essays of Four Decades*, pp. 536, 545.

20. Thomas Wolfe, *Of Time and the River* (New York, 1935), pp. 898–899. 21. Thomas Wolfe, *You Can't Go Home Again* (New York, 1941), p. 741.   22. See W. K. Wimsatt, Jr., and Cleanth Brooks, *Literary Criticism: A Short History* (New York, 1957), pp. 3–76.   23. See Robert D. Jacobs, "Poe and the Agrarian Critics," *Southern Renascence: The Literature of the Modern South*, ed. L. D. Rubin, Jr., and R. D. Jacobs (Baltimore, 1953), pp. 35–46.   24. W. G. Simms, "Modern Prose Fiction," *Southern Quarterly Review*, XV (April 1849), 41–83.   25. Bernard Smith, *Forces in American Criticism* (New York, 1939), p. 128.   26. Allen Tate, "The New Provincialism," *Essays of Four Decades*, p. 543.   27. William P. Trent, *William Gilmore Simms* (Boston (1892).   28. *Letters of Simms*, I, 256, 259. The letter originally appeared in the *Magnolia*, III (August 1841), 376–380.   29. C. Vann Woodward, "The Irony of Southern History," *Southern Renascence*, p. 65.

30. Alexis de Tocqueville, *Democracy in America,* trans. Henry Reeve, rev. Francis Bowen (New York, 1957), II, 78.   31. W. G. Simms, *The Cassique of Kiawah* (New York, 1859), p. 207.   32. W. G. Simms, *Charlemont* (New York, 1856), p. 292. 33. Ellen Glasgow, *The Woman Within* (New York, 1954), p. 42.   34. Ellen Glasgow, *A Certain Measure* (New York, 1943), p. 144.   35. Ibid., p. 155.   36. Ibid., p. 175.   37. Ibid., p. 250.   38. William Faulkner, *Go Down, Moses* (New York, 1942), p. 345.   39. Walt Whitman, *Democratic Vistas*, in *The Poetry and Prose of Walt Whitman* (New York, 1949), p. 816n.

40. Nathaniel Hawthorne, *The Scarlet Letter*, ed. Newton Arvin (New York, 1950), p. 274. It is worthy of note that Hawthorne is the American writer to whom Faulkner has most often been compared; see, for example, Randall Stewart, "Hawthorne and Faulkner," *College English*, XVII (February 1956), 258–262.   41. John P. Kennedy, *Swallow Barn* (1832), Chap. XLVI. This entire chapter is worthy of close attention for the student interested in the attitude of antebellum southern writers on the slavery issue.   42. William Faulkner, *Light in August* (New York, 1932), p. 239.   43. Robert Penn Warren, "Original Sin: A Short Story," *Selected Poems 1923–1943* (New York, 1944), p. 23. 44. Allen Tate, "The Wolves," *Poems: 1922–1947* (New York, 1948), pp. 110–111. 45. Ellen Glasgow, *A Certain Measure*, p. 188.

Simms and the Wider World
Views and Reviews

That I have done more work on William Gilmore Simms than on any other writer except Thomas Wolfe would seem not unusual for a South Carolinian. To me, however, it has always been surprising. As a graduate student, under the direction of Gregory Lansing Paine, I began work in 1947 on a dissertation dealing with the American historical novel—a choice that joined my interest in the novel with my interest in history. Having, as graduate students do, taken all the world for my province, I soon found my forces too small to defend its territorial boundaries. So, also as most graduate students do, I narrowed my field, in my case to American novels dealing with the Revolution. When that proved too large, I confined myself, to my surprise but not to my sorrow, to William Gilmore Simms's Revolutionary Romances.

The Roots of Southern Writing

The five essays that follow are all results but only indirectly products of that dissertation. My interest in Simms as an historical romancer extended to an interest in his criticism and his poetry and from there to a concern with the shape and meaning of his literary career. I am still pursuing that interest.

The following essay was written as an introduction to an edition of Simms's *Views and Reviews in American Literature, History and Fiction*, First Series, which I prepared for the John Harvard Library and which was published by the Harvard University Press in 1962. Although it comes relatively late in my study of Simms, I am using it as the first of the Simms essays because it presents an overview of Simms's career to the mid-1840s and discusses some of the tensions that an antebellum southern writer experienced. In the preparation of the John Harvard Library edition of *Views and Reviews*, I had the valuable guidance of Howard Mumford Jones, then editor of the Library.

1. *The Sense of the Beautiful. An Address* (Charleston, 1870). 2. Edd Winfield Parks, *William Gilmore Simms As Literary Critic* (Athens, 1961) is the only extended study in print of Simms's criticism. Raymond C. Palmer's dissertation, "The Prose Fiction Theories of William Gilmore Simms" (Indiana University, 1946); C. Hugh Holman's dissertation, "William Gilmore Simms's Theory and Practice of Historical Fiction" (University of North Carolina, 1949); and Edward T. Herbert's dissertation, "William Gilmore Simms As Editor and Literary Critic" (University of Wisconsin, 1957) are all unpublished. Bernard Smith, in *Forces in American Criticism* (New York, 1939), pp. 125–131, is one of the few historians of American criticism to take Simms seriously. 3. See H. H. Clark, "Changing Attitudes in Early American Criticism," *The Development of American Literary Criticism*, ed. Floyd Stovall (Chapel Hill, 1955), pp. 15–74. Simms reflected, apparently often unconsciously, most of the critical issues and movements of literary criticism in America before 1850. 4. Parks, *Simms As Critic*, p. 110. 5. The title page of each carries the date 1845, although the First Series volume appeared in 1846 and the Second Series volume in 1847. These were paperbound books; they were also offered for sale bound together in cloth in one volume in 1847. 6. Parks (in *Simms As Critic*, p. 112) states that these volumes gained "a certain unity but at the expense of a fair representation of Simms's critical views." 7. See Advertisement, *Views and Reviews in Amrican Litrature, History and Fiction*, First Series, ed. C. Hugh Holman (Cambridge, Mass., 1962), p. 5. 8. *Criticism in America* (Norman, 1956), p. 96. 9. *Forces in American Criticism*, p. 126.

10. "Simms," *Homes of American Authors* (New York, 1853), p. 262. 11. There is no adequate biographical study of Simms. The only book-length biography by William P. Trent (Boston, 1892), although incomplete, sometimes in error in fact and often poor in historical and critical judgment, is still the most nearly reliable treatment. A. S. Salley's biographical sketch in *The Letters of William Gilmore Simms*, ed. Mary C. S. Oliphant, A. T. Odell, and T. C. D. Eaves, 5 vols. (Columbia, S. C., 1952–1956), I, lix–lxxxix, contains much new information but is not always accurate and should be used with care. The *Letters* and their extensive annotation form an invaluable repository of information on Simms's life between 1832 and 1870. The data on Simms's life in this essay are drawn primarily from these sources. 12. *Letters*, I, 160; *Southern Bivouac*, I (October 1885), 261; *International Magazine*, V (1852), 433. 13. Trent, *Simms*, pp. 12–13. Trent is paraphrasing a manuscript "Personal Memorabilia" by Simms. 14. *Charleston and Her Satirists; A Scribblement* (Charleston, 1848), pp. 6, 11. 15. *The Golden Christmas* (Charleston, 1852), p. 20. 16. Charleston *City Gazette*, March 9, 1830. 17. Ibid., March 7, 1832. 18. Ibid., May 8, 1832. 19. Trent, *Simms*, pp. 62–65.

20. *Guy Rivers* (New York, 1855), p. 9. 21. On November 25, 1832, in a letter to James Lawson, he called South Carolina "this, once high, but now damnably defiled

scene of brutal prostitution and tyranny" and expressed the belief that "her name and star place [should be] blotted out, and her territory divided among the contiguous & more loyal states" (*Letters*, I, 47).   22. On Charleston and Jeffersonianism see the excellent brief discussion by Henry Adams, *History of the United States of America during the First Administration of Thomas Jefferson* (New York, 1899), I, Chap. v. On the nullification controversy, see C. S. Boucher, *The Nullification Controversy in South Carolina* (Chicago, 1916) and Frederic Bancroft, *Calhoun and the South Carolina Nullification Movement* (Baltimore, 1928).   23. "Mrs. Trollope and the Americans," *American Quarterly Review*, XII (September 1832), 109–133; reprinted in modified form in *Views and Reviews*, Second Series, pp. 1–56.   24. *Magnolia*, III (January, February 1841), 1–6, 69–74.
25. *Notes on the State of Virginia*, ed. William Peden (Chapel Hill, 1954), pp. 64–65.
26. *Monthly Review*, LXXVIII (1788), 377, 459.   27. See William B. Cairns, *British Criticism of American Writings, 1783–1815* (University of Wisconsin Studies in Language and Literature, No. 1; Madison, 1918) and *British Criticism of American Writings, 1815–1833* (University of Wisconsin Studies in Language and Literature, No. 14; Madison, 1922).   28. Alexis de Tocqueville, *Democracy in America*, trans. Henry Reeve and ed. Phillips Bradley (New York, 1957), II, 411–436, 505–506.   29. Longfellow's clearest statement on the subject is in Chapter xx of his novel *Kavanagh* (1849).
30. *Notions of the Americans* (Philadelphia, 1828), Letter XXIII. The similarity of Cooper's sentiments to those of Alexis de Tocqueville in Part II, Book 1, Chapter XII, of *Democracy in America* is notable.   31. "American Literature," *Southern Review*, VII (August 1831), 443.   32. Preface, *The Marble Faun* (Boston, 1883), p. 15.
33. Simms, "The Writings of James Fenimore Cooper," *Views and Reviews*, p. 267.
34. See Benjamin T. Spencer, *The Quest for Nationality* (Syracuse, 1957), for an extended treatment of these movements in American literary history.   35. Simms, "The Four Periods of American History," *Views and Reviews*, pp. 75–86.   36. *Count Julian* was published in 1845, but it was written in 1837–1838 as a sequel to *Pelayo* and was lost in transit for five years.   37. Commodity prices, based on the Warren-Pearson wholesale price index for all commodities—New York 1910–1914 equal to 100—fell from 110 in 1838 to 75 in 1843 and then rose to 82 in 1848. (See Richard B. Morris, *Encyclopedia of American History*, New York, 1953, pp. 508–509.)   38. Frank Luther Mott, *A History of American Magazines, 1741–1850* (Cambridge, Mass., 1938), pp. 354–363.   39. *One Hundred and Fifty Years of Publishing 1785–1935* [Lea and Febiger] (Philadelphia, 1935), pp. 25–26.
40. Letter to James Henry Hammond, August 16, 1841, *Letters*, I, 271.   41. Letter to James Henry Hammond, December 24, 1847, *Letters*, II, 385.   42. Earl L. Bradsher, *Mathew Carey: Editor, Author, and Publisher* (New York, 1912), p. 93.   43. The phrase was coined by John L. O'Sullivan in the *Democratic Review*, an "official" organ of the Young America group. (See Arthur M. Schlesinger, Jr., *The Age of Jackson*, Boston, 1946, p. 427.)   44. Detailed studies of the Young America group and its literary wars in the 1840s may be found in John Stafford, *The Literary Criticism of "Young America": A Study in the Relationship of Politics and Literature, 1837–1850* (Berkeley and Los Angeles, 1952) and Perry Miller, *The Raven and the Whale: The War of Words and Wits in the Era of Poe and Melville* (New York, 1956).   45. *Knickerbocker Magazine*, VII (February 1836), 169; VII (January 1836), 37; XII (November 1838), 416.
46. See, for example, the *Knickerbocker* reviews of *The Yemassee* (V, April 1835, 341–343) and of *The Partisan* (VI, December 1835, 577).   47. *Magnolia*, III (January, February, 1841), 1–6, 69–74.   48. *Ibid.*, (February 1841), 72.   49. *Knickerbocker*, XVIII (November 1841), 462.
50. *Ibid.*, XX (August 1842), 200. Earlier exchanges may be found in ibid., XIX (May 1842), 496, and *Magnolia*, IV (June 1842).   51. *Southern Literary Messenger*, X (January, March, June, August, 1844), 7 17, 137 151, 340–349, 449–469. The March and June articles are two parts of one long letter. Benjamin T. Spencer (*The Quest for Nationality*, p. 145) calls this series of articles "one of the most cogent arguments for copyright before the Civil War."   52. Letter to James Fenimore Cooper, April 10,

1844, *Letters*, v, 380.   53. x (January 1844), 33–39.   54. Letter to James Lawson, March 26, 1844, *Letters*, I, 410.   55. Letter to George F. Holmes, November 18, 1844, *Letters*, I, 442.   56. *Broadway Journal*, II (August 30, 1845), 121.   57. John C. Guilds, "William Gilmore Simms as Magazine Editor to 1845" (unpublished dissertation, Duke University, 1954), p. 236.   58. Letter to Evert A. Duyckinck, February 11, 1845, *Letters*, II, 29.   59. See Stafford, *Literary Criticism of "Young America,"* pp. 23–24; Miller, *The Raven and the Whale*, pp. 135–167; Randall Stewart, "Hawthorne's Contributions to *The Salem Advertiser*," *American Literature*, v (January 1934), 328–329. A surprising amount of information on this series is to be found in T. O. Mabbott's introduction to the Facsimile Text Society edition of *The Raven and Other Poems* by Edgar A. Poe (New York, 1942), pp. vi–xviii.

60. Miller suggests that Duyckinck's motive was to give Simms's essay on "Americanism in Literature" wider circulation. (See *The Raven and the Whale*, p. 154).

61. Letter to Evert A. Duyckinck, August 7, 1845, *Letters*, II, 95.   62. Letter to Evert A. Duyckinck, October 19, 1845, *Letters*, II, 106; Letter to Evert A. Duyckinck, October 28, 1845, *Letters*, II, 110.   63. Mabbott, Introduction to *The Raven*, pp. xi, xiv.

64. Letter to Evert A. Duyckinck, November 13, 1845, *Letters*, II, 118; Letter to Evert A. Duyckinck, October 19, 1845, *Letters*, II, 106; Letter to Evert A. Duyckinck, October ruary 9, 1846, *Letters*, II, 142.   65. *Letters*, II, 142n.   66. Letter to Evert A. Duyckinck, June 29, 1846, *Letters*, II, 170.   67. *Letters*, II, 265n. The book bore the date 1845 on its title page, however.   68. Whitman clipped this essay when it first appeared as a review of the work of Cornelius Mathews in the *Southern Quarterly Review*, VI (October 1844), 307–342, wrote on its margin "Very Fine," and kept it. (See Spencer, *The Quest for Nationalism*, p. 220).   69. *North American Review*, LXIII (October 1846), 357–381.

70. "Editor's Table," *Knickerbocker*, XXVIII (November 1846), 450–454.

71. *Yankee Doodle*, I (October 24, 1846), 33.   72. *Literary World*, II (October 23, 1847), 282.   73. *Knickerbocker*, xxx (December 1847), 556.   74. "A National Literature, 1837–1855," *American Literature*, VIII (May 1936), 158.   75. Stewart, "Hawthorne's Contributions to *The Salem Advertiser*," pp. 331–332. This review would have been even more unfavorable if Hawthorne had been as frank in it as he was in a letter of April 30, 1846, to Duyckinck, accompanying the manuscript of the review: "I know well enough what I like, but am always at a loss to render a reason. Mr. Simms I do not like at all" (ibid., p. 330).   76. Frank Luther Mott, *Golden Multitudes* (New York, 1947), pp. 306–308.   77. Perhaps the best summaries of Scott's theories of the historical novel are those by George Saintsbury, in "The Historical Novel," *Essays in English Literature, 1780–1860*, 2nd ser. (London, 1895), pp. 303–383; Georg Lukács, *The Historical Novel* (Boston, 1963); however, there is no real substitute for Scott's prefaces and his General Introduction to the Waverley Novels in the revised edition of *Waverley*.   78. C. Hugh Holman, "The Influence of Scott and Cooper on Simms," *American Literature*, XXIII (May 1951), 203–218. Reprinted in this volume.   79. *The Yemassee* (New York, 1835), I, vi, vii. Parks (*Simms As Literary Critic*, p. 110) finds this distinction between novel and romance to be Simms's only contribution to critical theory.

80. Spencer, *The Quest for Nationalism*, p. 96.   81. xl (February–June 1850), 107–118, 161–169, 243–251, 320–326, 397–411; XLI (July–December 1850), 13–27, 89–100, 162–179, 205–219, 286–298, 332–352.   82. XIV (July 1848), 37–77; (October 1848), 261–337.   83. *Southern Quarterly Review*, XXII (July 1852), 203–220.

84. *Southern Quarterly Review*, n.s., v (January 1852), 262. The attribution to Simms is uncertain, although he wrote practically all the brief notices in the *Southern Quarterly Review* at this time.   85. Trent, *Simms*, passim; Smith, *Forces in American Criticism*, pp. 125–131; Vernon L. Parrington, *Main Currents in American Thought* (New York, 1927), II, 125–136.   86. Clement Eaton, in *Freedom of Thought in the Old South* (Durham, 1940), traces in detail the development of this defensive attitude in the antebellum South.   87. His most infamous statement on the subject is his long essay in *The Pro-Slavery Argument* (Charleston, 1852, and Philadelphia, 1853), pp. 175–285.

This essay was, in fact, a review of Harriet Martineau's *Society in America* which was published in 1837 as "The Morals of Slavery" (*Southern Literary Messenger*, III, November, 1837, 641–657) and reprinted in pamphlet form in Richmond in 1838 as *Slavery in America*.   88. Schlesinger, *Age of Jackson*, pp. 375–380.   89. Letter to George F. Holmes, August 15, 1842, *Letters*, I, 319.

William Gilmore Simms's Picture
of the Revolution as a Civil War

This essay, my first essay on Simms, was published in the *Journal of Southern History*, xv (November 1949), 441–462. It is concerned with the historicity of Simms's Revolutionary Romances. It seems to me to throw light on the antebellum writer's sense of class and upon his concept of realism. The prime model for these historical romances was Sir Walter Scott, and the attributes of Scott's fiction are everywhere discernible in Simms's romances. As I try to point out, it is Simms's excessive reverence for history which gets him in trouble—a characteristic not uncommon for southerners.

1. W. Gilmore Simms, *The Partisan* (New York, 1882), p. v. In the order of publication these novels are *The Partisan* (1835); *Mellichampe* (1836); *The Kinsmen* (1841), better known as *The Scout*, the title of the revised edition; *Katharine Walton* (1851); *The Sword and the Distaff* (1852), better known as *Woodcraft*, the title of the revised edition; *The Forayers* (1855); and *Eutaw* (1856). In terms of the events which they chronicle, their order is *The Partisan, Mellichampe, Katharine Walton, The Scout, The Forayers, Eutaw,* and *Woodcraft*.   2. Simms, *The Forayers* (Chicago, 1885), p. 5.
3. William P. Trent, *William Gilmore Simms* (Boston, 1892), p. v.   4. He wrote, "A sober desire for history—the unwritten, the unconsidered, but veracious history—has been with me, in this labour, a sort of principle" (Simms, *The Partisan*, p. vii).
5. Edward F. Hayward, "Some Romances of the Revolution," in *Atlantic Monthly*, LXIV (1889), 628. This ten-page article attempted to point out Simms's importance as a portrayer of southern history, but it has been largely ignored.   6. V. L. Parrington, *Main Currents in American Thought*, 3 vols. (New York, 1927–1930), III.   7. Simms, *The Yemassee* (New York, 1937), p. 6.   8. Simms, *Mellichampe* (Chicago, 1885), p. 6.   9. Simms, *Vasconselos* (New York, 1882), p. 2.
10. Simms, *Katharine Walton* (Chicago, 1885), p. 3.   11. Simms, *Mellichampe*, p. 2.   12. Simms, *The Life of Francis Marion* (New York, 1844). This was probably the most popular book that he wrote. Frank Luther Mott, in *Golden Multitudes: The Story of Best Sellers in the United States* (New York, 1947), p. 319, lists it as a "better seller" for the 1840–1850 decade.   13. Simms, *The Life of Nathanael Greene* (New York, [1849]). 14. Simms, *Marion*, p. [vi].   15. Every work listed in the bibliography on "The War in the South (1776–1780)," in C. H. Van Tyne, *The American Revolution, 1776–1783* (New York, 1905, p. 350), that was available when Simms wrote appears in the note in *Marion*.   16. Trent, *Simms*, p. 106.   17. Simms, *Marion*, p. [vi]. This collection was later published as *Documentary History of the American Revolution*, edited by Robert W. Gibbes, 3 vols. (New York, 1853–1857).   18. Simms, *The History of South Carolina* (Charleston, 1860), p. 2. This work, originally published in 1840, was a public school textbook.   19. Trent, *Simms*, pp. 191, 211. In the dedicatory letter in *The Forayers*, Simms wrote to Jamison, "You will find . . . that I have borrowed freely from your notes."
20. Simms acknowledges a debt to Johnson for information in the dedication of *Woodcraft* (Chicago, 1885), p. 4.   21. Simms, *History*, pp. 1–5.   22. Simms, *The*

Partisan, p. vii.   23. Simms, *Mellichampe*, p. 2.   24. Simms, "History for the Purposes of Art," in *Views and Reviews in American Literature, History and Fiction*, First Series, ed. C. Hugh Holman (Cambridge, Mass., 1962), p. 56.   25. Ibid., p. 57.

26. John E. Farrior, in "The Use of Historical Characters by William Gilmore Simms in His Romances of the Revolution" (M. A. thesis, University of North Carolina, 1944), made a painstaking and admirably thorough examination of Simms's historical personages, comparing them with what was said of them in the sources Simms employed. He found that in no place where Simms made pretensions to accurate presentation of historical character or events was he in disagreement with the sources he used.   27. See Jay B. Hubbell, "Literary Nationalism in the Old South," in *American Studies in Honor of William Kenneth Boyd*, ed. D. K. Jackson (Durham, 1940), pp. 175–220, for a detailed discussion of this movement.   28. Simms, *The Wigwam and the Cabin* (New York, 1882), pp. 4–5. Trent says, "Simms did lay a foundation for Southern literature by following the universal, not sectional, principle of literary art which requires that a man should write spontaneously and simply about those things he is fullest of and best understands" (*Simms*, p. 105).   29. Simms, *The Partisan*, p. vii.

30. Simms, *The Wigwam and the Cabin*, p. 430n.   31. Simms, *Katharine Walton*, p. 2.   32. Simms, *Woodcraft*, p. 3.   33. Trent, *Simms*, pp. 8–9; Simms, *The Wigwam and the Cabin*, p. 2.   34. [Simms], "Ellet's Women of the Revolution," in *Southern Quarterly Review*, xvxii (1850), 351–352.   35. Simms, *Mellichampe*, p. 3. 36. [Simms], "Ellet's Women of the Revolution," p. 351.   37. W. A. Schaper, in "Sectionalism and Representation in South Carolina," in American Historical Association *Annual Report*, 1900, 2 vols. (Washington, 1901), I, 354, said: "If the local history of South Carolina were as well known as that of Massachusetts is, our historians would not have been obliged to draw so largely upon Boston for their material in writing the history of the opposition to the British tea tax." In 1900 Schaper could also say, "South Carolina is the least written about and the least understood of all the States that have played an important part in our history" (ibid., p. 239).   38. For detailed discussions of this formula and its evolution see George Saintsbury, "The Historical Novel," in *Essays in English Literature, 1780–1860*, 2nd series (London, 1895), pp. 303–383; Edward Wagenknecht, *Cavalcade of the English Novel* (New York, 1943), pp. 163–169; Louis Maigron, *Le roman historique à l'époque romantique: essai sur l'influence de Walter Scott* (Paris, 1912), pp. 99–234; James T. Hillhouse, *The Waverley Novels and Their Critics* (Minneapolis, 1936); Jacques Barzun, *Romanticism and the Modern Ego* (Boston, 1944), pp. 85–86; Louis Reynaud, *Le romantisme: ses origines anglo-germaniques* (Paris, 1926), pp. 177–184; Ernest A. Baker, *The History of the English Novel*, 10 vols. (London, 1934–1939), VI, 207–226; Georg Lukács, *The Historical Novel* (Boston, 1963), pp. 19–88. 39. Simms, "History for the Purposes of Art," pp. 45–46.

40. Ibid., p. 263; Simms, "Modern Prose Fiction," in *Southern Quarterly Review*, xv (1849), 82.   41. Simms, "Modern Prose Fiction," p. 83.   42. Simms, *The Partisan*, p. 57.   43. Simms, *Eutaw* (New York, [1869]), p. 478.   44. Simms, *The Scout* (New York, 1854), p. 12.   45. Ibid., p. 29.   46. Simms, *The Forayers*, p. 55.   47. Ibid., p. 170.   48. Simms, *Eutaw*, p. 68.   49. Simms, *The Scout*, pp. 12–13.

50. Simms has often been accused, quite unjustly, of a jingoistic patriotism in these books. Typical of this approach to Simms is E. E. Leisy's implication that Simms's presentation of the "patriotic ardor of South Carolina" was too favorable. Introduction to J. P. Kennedy, *Horse-Shoe Robinson* (New York, 1937), p. xxiv.   51. Parrington, *Main Currents in American Thought*, II, 134.   52. Simms, *Mellichampe*, p. 6.   53. Simms, *The Partisan*, p. 53.   54. Simms, *The Scout*, p. 12.   55. Ibid., p. 159.   56. Simms, *The Forayers*, pp. 265–266.   57. Simms, *The Scout*, p. 140.   58. Ibid., p. 345. 59. Simms, *Eutaw*, p. 81.

60. Simms, *Mellichampe*, pp. 310–314.   61. Ibid., p. 2. Actually Brown was treated even more cruelly than Barsfield reports himself as being treated. See Edward McCrady, *The History of South Carolina in the Revolution, 1775–1780* (New York, 1901), pp.

35–36.   62. Simms, *Mellichampe*, p. 2.   63. Simms, *The Scout*, p. 55.   64. See
Philip Davidson, "The Southern Backcountry on the Eve of the Revolution," in Avery
Craven, ed., *Essays in Honor of William E. Dodd* (Chicago, 1935), pp. 1–15, for a succinct
discussion of the Up Country groups.   65. Rosser H. Taylor, *Ante-Bellum South
Carolina: A Social and Cultural History* (Chapel Hill, 1942), p. 3.   66. For the low
status of the overseer see ibid., pp. 81–83.   67. F. L. Owsley, Introduction in Blanche
Henry Clark, *The Tennessee Yeomen, 1840–1860* (Nashville, 1942), p. xiii. Simms's
use of such a division between 1835 and 1856 would indicate that the conception,
at least as it is applied to the South Carolina Low Country in the late eighteenth century, was not exclusively "of abolitionist parentage," as Owsley suggests here.
68. Omitted from this tabulation are the many figures from recorded history who act
in or walk across the pages of the novels; for, as already noted, Simms employed these
characters in expository, not narrative or dramatic, sections of the books. Omitted also
are the many dozens of minor fictional characters who crowd the works until they seem
to be teeming with life.   69. For descriptions of this class see Paul H. Buck, "Poor
Whites of the Old South," in *American Historical Review*, xxxi (1925–1926), 41–54, and
Guion G. Johnson, *Ante-Bellum North Carolina* (Chapel Hill, 1937), pp. 67–73.

    70. Such a character distribution could be explained as a reflection of Simms's intense
sympathy for the American cause and the excessive deference he is alleged to have paid
the Charleston aristocracy; see Russell Blankenship, *American Literature as an Expression of
the National Mind* (New York, 1931), pp. 235–237. I believe, however, that in the light
of his other expressions such an interpretation may be safely ignored.   71. Simms,
History, p. 179.   72. Simms, *The Forayers*, p. 109.   73. Simms, *Eutaw*, pp. 492–
494.   74. Simms, *The Partisans*, p. 153.   75. Simms, *The Forayers*, pp. 140–141.
76. Simms, *Eutaw*, p. 189.   77. Ibid., p. 221.   78. Simms, *The Forayers*, p. 414.
79. Shields McIlwaine, *The Southern Poor-White from Lubberland to Tobacco Road*
(Norman, 1939), pp. 27–32.

    80. Ima H. Herron, *The Small Town in American Literature* (Durham, 1939), pp.
314–318.   81. John H. Nelson, *The Negro Character in American Literature*, in
University of Kansas *Humanistic Studies*, iv, No. 1 (Lawrence, 1926), pp. 24–44.
82. Stirling Brown, *The Negro in American Fiction* (Washington, 1937), p. 10.
83. Simms, "Works of the Imagination," in *Magnolia*, n.s., i (1842), 52.   84. Simms,
"Modern Prose Fiction," p. 53.

The Influence of Scott
and Cooper on Simms

In this essay I attempt to evaluate the contributions of the two major English
and American historical novelists on Simms's Revolutionary Romances.
Where the preceding one was a study primarily of the content of these historical novels, this one is a study of their form. The essay also gives in summary
statement my conclusions about the nature of the Scott novel, a form of
great importance to southern writing. It was published in *American Literature*, xxiii (May 1951), 203–218.

    1. Grant C. Knight, in *The Novel in English* (New York, 1931), pp. 116–117, gives
a succinct statement of this view, saying that Simms "was a frank imitator of Cooper,
doing for Marion's guerilla warfare what the northerner had done for the Revolution and
the western movement." A similar view is expressed in John Erskine, *Leading American
Novelists* (New York, 1910), pp. 131–177; William P. Trent, *William Gilmore Simms*
(Boston, 1892), pp. 110, 241, 316, 329–330; Carl Van Doren, *The American Novel*

1789–1939, rev. ed. (New York, 1940), pp. 50–55; Arthur Hobson Quinn, *American Fiction: An Historical and Critical Survey* (New York, 1936), pp. 114–123; and Alexander Cowie, *The Rise of the American Novel* (New York, 1948), pp. 228–246.   2. Vernon L. Parrington, *Main Currents in American Thought* (New York, 1927), II, 125–136; Walter Fuller Taylor, *A History of American Letters* (New York, 1936), pp. 216–218; Russell Blankenship, *American Literature as an Expression of the National Mind*, rev. ed. (New York, 1949), pp. 235–237; Bernard Smith, *Forces in American Criticism* (New York, 1939), pp. 125–131; and Fred Lewis Pattee, *The First Century of American Literature 1770–1870* (New York, 1935), pp. 427–433.   3. Notably Ernest E. Leisy, in *The American Historical Novel* (Norman, 1950), pp. 12–13, 35–36, 106–107. Leisy asserts the existence of mutual influences without discussing their nature.   4. Other important ones were William Godwin, the British dramatists, and Thomas Carlyle. Simms acknowledged Godwin's influence in a letter of December 1846, reprinted in part in *Passages from the Correspondence and Other Papers of Rufus W. Griswold* (Cambridge, Mass., 1898), pp. 80–86; and *The Letters of William Gilmore Simms,* ed. Mary C. S. Oliphant, A. T. Odell, and T. C. D. Eaves, 5 vols. (Columbia, S. C., 1952–1956), II, 220–233. For the influence of the dramatists, see C. Hugh Holman, "Simms and the British Dramatists," *PMLA*, LXV (June 1950), 346–359; reprinted in this volume. Carlyle's influence, although clearly present, has not been examined in detail; see, however, Rollin G. Osterweis, *Romanticism and Nationalism in the Old South* (New Haven, 1949), pp. 33–35.   5. *The Partisan* (1835); *Mellichampe* (1836); *The Kinsmen* (1841), renamed *The Scout* in later editions; *Katharine Walton* (1851); *The Sword and the Distaff* (1852), renamed *Woodcraft* in later editions; *The Forayers* (1855); and *Eutaw* (1856). All references to these works are to the edition published by A. C. Armstrong (New York, 1882) from the plates of the Redfield revised edition (New York, 1853–1856); see "Works of William Gilmore Simms," *Literary World*, XIII (October 21, 1882), 351–352.   6. In a letter to R. W. Griswold, December, 1846, *Correspondence of Griswold,* pp. 80–86; *Letters*, II, 220–233. 7. Even Hampton M. Jarrell, who in "William Gilmore Simms: Realistic Romancer" (unpublished dissertation, Duke University, 1932) is the strongest defender of Simms's Border Romances, says, "The Revolutionary romances as a group are Simms's most important work" (p. 186).   8. See H. Butterfield, *The Historical Novel, an Essay* (Cambridge, 1924); George Saintsbury, "The Historical Novel," in *Essays in English Literature, 1780–1860*, 2nd ser. (London, 1895), pp. 303–382; Ernest A. Baker, *The History of the English Novel* (London, 1934–1939), VI, 207–226; Louis Maigron, *Le roman historique à l'époque romantique: essai sur l'influence de Walter Scott* (Paris, 1912), pp. 99–234; and Lillie D. Loshe, *The Early American Novel* (New York, 1907), pp. 82–86.   9. Riverside edition (Boston, 1923), p. xi.

10. "The Historical Novel," p. 341.   11. *Le Romantisme: ses origines anglo-germaniques* (Paris, 1926), p. 184.   12. *Views and Reviews in American Literature, History and Fiction,* First Series, ed. C. Hugh Holman (Cambridge, Mass., 1962), p. 262. 13. Ibid., p. 57.   14. Review of Scott's *Tales of My Landlord, Quarterly Review,* XVI (January 1817), 431. The attribution to Scott appears settled; see James T. Hillhouse, *The Waverley Novels and Their Critics* (Minneapolis, 1936), p. 17n.   15. Grace Landrum, "Scott and His Literary Rivals in the Old South," *American Literature,* II (November 1930), 256–276.   16. See "Bulwer's Genius and Writings," *Magnolia,* n.s., I (December 1842), 329–337; "James' Novels," ibid. (July 1842), 52–56, which is severely critical; "Modern Prose Fiction," *Southern Quarterly Review,* XV (April 1849), 41–83, which in part contrasts Bulwer-Lytton unfavorably with Scott.   17. *Views and Reviews,* p. 268. 18. "Modern Prose Fiction," p. 83.   19. *Views and Reviews,* pp. 45–46.

20. *The Yemassee* (New York, 1937), p. 5.   21. "Modern Prose Fiction," p. 82. 22. Ibid., p. 83.   23. Gregory L. Paine, ed., *The Deerslayer* (New York, 1927), pp. xxiv–xxv.   23. Tremaine McDowell, ed., *The Spy* (New York, 1931), p. xx. Cf., however, James Grossman, *James Fenimore Cooper* (New York, 1949), p. 27, for the view that Cooper is inaccurate.   25. *Leading American Novelists,* p. 62.   26. Thomas R.

Lounsbury, *James Fenimore Cooper* (Boston, 1882), p. 49.   27. Grossman, p. 40. Lounsbury calls *Lionel Lincoln* "one of Cooper's most signal failures" (p. 50). 28. *Views and Reviews*, p. 274.   29. Ibid., p. 276.

30. Ibid., p. 274.   31. Ibid.   32. Ibid., pp. 272, 275. This criticism antedates James Russell Lowell's similar statement, in *A Fable for Critics*, ll. 1031–1044, by three years.   33. Page 148.   34. *Views and Reviews*, pp. 269–270, 272–273.   35. *Main Currents*, II, 135.   36. *Views and Reviews*, pp. 260–262.   37. Ibid., p. 268. 38. Ibid., p. 265.   39. Page 43.

40. *Views and Reviews*, p. 274.   41. *The Forayers*, p. 4.   42. *Main Currents*, II, 134–135.   43. For a detailed examination of the accuracy of Simms's portrayal of historical and social forces, see C. Hugh Holman, "William Gilmore Simms' Picture of the Revolution as a Civil Conflict," *Journal of Southern History*, XV (November 1949), 441– 462; reprinted in this volume. John E. Farrior, in "The Use of Historical Characters by William Gilmore Simms in His Romances of the Revolution" (M. A. thesis, North Carolina, 1944), compared Simms's novels with what was given in the sources he used and found that he was in disagreement with his sources in no place where he claimed historical accuracy.   44. Simms wrote quite acceptable biographies of Francis Marion (1844), Captain John Smith (1846), the Chevalier Bayard (1847), and Nathanael Greene (1849), and a textbook *History of South Carolina* (1840), which, in greatly revised form, is still in use in the public schools of that state.   45. *The Wigwam and the Cabin* (New York, 1882), p. 430n.   46. *Views and Reviews*, p. 56.   47. See *Confession* (New York, 1882), p. 8.   48. These are: the battle of Camden, Chaps. XL–XLIII of *The Partisan*, 32 pages; the last attack and relief of Fort Ninety-Six, Chap. XXV, *The Scout*, 10 pages; actions at Biggin Church, Quinby, and Shubrick's, Chaps. XXV–XXIX, *Eutaw*, 26 pages; the battle of Eutaw Springs, Chap. XLII, *Eutaw*, 16 pages.   49. *Vasconselos* (New York, 1882), p. 1.

50. For example, Cowie, in *The Rise of the American Novel*, says, "Seen as a whole, the Revolutionary romances lack a good focus of the reader's hopes and affections . . . there is no single character comparable in power and interest to Natty Bumppo" (pp. 234–235). 51. *Main Currents*, II, 133.   52. Ibid., p. 135.   53. Parrington, *Main Currents*, II, 136, 125–126. Shields McIlwaine, in *The Southern Poor-White from Lubberland to Tobacco Road* (Norman, 1939), p. 27, says, "The ready market for romance seduced him into wasting his fine energy . . . his desire for home approval partially dictated his use of aristocrats for major rôles, although . . . his true forte [was] 'the rough-hewn and the half-polished specimens of backwoods humanity.' "   54. *A Literary History of England*, ed. Albert C. Baugh (New York, 1948), p. 1216.   55. Quoted in Edward Wagenknecht, *Cavalcade of the English Novel* (New York, 1943), p. 168.   56. Introduction, *The Waverley Pageant* (New York, 1932), p. xxv. Cf. Parrington's statement that Simms "lived in a world of unreality, of social and economic romanticism, that was forever benumbing his strong instinct for reality" (*Main Currents*, II, 136).   57. *Romanticism and the Modern Ego* (Boston, 1944), pp. 85–86.   58. See Hillhouse, *The Waverley Novels*, pp. 228–331.   59. *Views and Reviews*, p. 268.

60. Ibid., pp. 266, 291.   61. Ibid., p. 267

Simms and the British Dramatists

The two preceding essays attempt to define the content and the form of the historical novel as Simms practiced it. This essay turns to a consideration of Simms's method of handling characters and scenes in his historical romances. It demonstrates that his methods of characterization are drawn from the British drama, an immensely popular form of entertainment in the eighteenth- and nineteenth-century South. The essay was published in *PMLA*, LXV (June 1950), 346–359.

1. Vernon L. Parrington, *Main Currents in American Thought* (New York, 1927), II, 130–133.   2. See note 18 below. Hampton M. Jarrell, "Falstaff and Simms's Porgy," *American Literature*, III (May 1931), 204–212, gives the most detailed statement of this view.   3. *The Partisan* (1835); *Mellichampe* (1836); *The Kinsmen* (1841), renamed *The Scout* in all later editions: *Katharine Walton* (1851): *The Sword and the Distaff* (1852), renamed *Woodcraft* in all later editions; *The Forayers* (1855); and *Eutaw* (1856). Further references to these books are to the editions published in New York by A. C. Armstrong in 1882, from the plates of the Redfield edition.   4. William P. Trent, *William Gilmore Simms*, American Men of Letters series (Boston, 1892), pp. 135, 310. 5. *A Supplement to the Plays of William Shakespeare* (New York, 1848).   6. Trent, *Simms*, pp. 71, 145.   7. For a detailed study of drama in Charleston before 1860, see W. Stanley Hoole, *The Ante-bellum Charleston Theatre* (University of Alabama Press, 1946).   8. See Jay B. Hubbell, *The Last Years of Henry Timrod* (Durham, 1941), pp. 54, 76.   9. "A Note on Simms's Novels," *American Literature*, II (May 1930), 173–174.
10. "Modern Prose Fiction," *Southern Quarterly Review*, XV (April 1849), 62.
11. *Simms*, p. 109.   12. *The Yemassee* (Boston, 1961), pp. 5–6.   3. "History for the Purposes of Art," *Views and Reviews in American Literature, History and Fiction*, First Series, ed. C. Hugh Holman (Cambridge, Mass., 1962), pp. 78, 81.   14. Induction, *Every Man Out of His Humor*.   15. *Confession; or, The Blind Heart* (New York, 1882), pp. 5–10. Here Simms also warns that the controlling passion employed must not be used to the exclusion of all else in the character.   16. In Etherege's *The Man of Mode*; he affects disgust for England after traveling in France, believes himself to be an invincible lady-killer, and delights in his clothing. He became a model for a long line of fops in Restoration comedy.   17. Pages 223–225. Cf. *School for Scandal*, I, i, and II, ii. 18. See Jarrell for the most detailed statement; see also Parrington, II, 131–132; Carl Van Doren, *The American Novel 1789–1939*, rev. ed. (New York, 1940), p. 54; Alexander Cowie, *The Rise of the American Novel* (New York, 1948), pp. 233–234, 790n.; and for an early statement, Edward F. Hayward, "Some Romances of the Revolution," *Atlantic Monthly*, LXIV (November 1889), 632.   19. See Parrington, II, 130–131.
20. Trent, *Simms*, p. 203.   21. See particularly *Woodcraft*, pp. 278–287. 22. Cf. his criticism of Cooper's novels in "The Writings of James Fenimore Cooper," *Views and Reviews*, pp. 258–292, with his own practice in the historical novel.   23. Review of *The Partisan* in *Complete Works*, ed. James A. Harrison (New York, 1902), VIII, 151; originally published in the *Southern Literary Messenger*, II (January 1836), 117–121. 24. *Leading American Novelists* (New York, 1910), p. 153. Since Porgy's conversational method changes little after his first appearance in 1835, it could not be derived from, but would have to anticipate, the minstrel show. Carl Wittke, in *Tambo and Bones: A History of the American Minstrel Stage* (Durham, 1930), p. 41, says, "Probably the first public presentation of what may be called a real minstrel show took place in the Bowery Amphitheatre in New York City in 1843."   25. *Maule's Curse: Seven Studies in the History of American Obscurantism* (Norfolk, Conn., 1938), p. 44.

William Gilmore Simms
and the "American Renaissance"

In a sense in this essay I pick up Simms's career where it is left off in "Simms and the Wider World" and inquire into why a man of such great and versatile talent produced a relatively sterile body of work at that very period in his career when he seemed best equipped to realize artistic triumphs. What happened to Simms, I believe, happened to most antebellum southern writers to some degree, and Simms, as man of talent rather than genius, becomes almost an exemplum of the dangers of sectionalism. A genius would have created great art from the tensions that weakened Simms.

This essay was first presented as a paper at the American Studies Program at the College of William and Mary, Williamsburg, Virginia, on July 13, 1961. Portions of it appear in modified form in my introduction to Simms's novel *The Yemassee* (Riverside Edition, Boston, 1961). The original paper here given was published in the *Mississippi Quarterly*, xv (Summer 1962), 126–137.

The Novel in the South

This essay is a summary introduction to one aspect of the twentieth-century southern novel. In it I attempt a brief summary of some general qualities of the South and then make a series of short analyses of the work of Ellen Glasgow, James Branch Cabell, Thomas Wolfe, William Faulkner, and Robert Penn Warren. Thus it foreshadows much of what is to come in the remaining essays in this volume. Its general nature was dictated in part at least by the circumstances of its composition. I wrote it at the request of Robert E. Spiller and recorded it for a Voice of America series in 1961. It was published by the Voice of America as a pamphlet in Literature Series 9, entitled "The Rebirth of the South: Wolfe, Faulkner, Warren." The essay also was published in a slightly modified form as "The Novel in the South" in *A Time of Harvest: American Literature, 1910–1960*, edited by Robert E. Spiller (New York: Hill and Wang, 1962).

The View from the Regency Hyatt

This essay complements "The Novel in the South" in two respects: it presents another aspect of the twentieth-century southern novel and it deals with another type of southern novelist. Only Thomas Wolfe plays any important part in both essays. I wrote this piece as a talk presented at a symposium on the continuing relevance of southern literature at Davidson College, Davidson, North Carolina, in March 1968. The other symposium members were Louis D. Rubin, Jr., who spoke on the continuing relevance of southern literature, and Walter Sullivan, who spoke on the southern renascence and the Joycean aesthetic. The organizer and moderator of the symposium was George Core. The proceedings were published as *Southern Fiction Today: Renascence and Beyond*, edited by George Core (Athens: University of Georgia Press, 1969).

1. "The New Provincialism," *Collected Essays* (Denver, 1959), pp. 292–293.
2. "After Ten Years," *Tobacco Road*, Modern Library Edition (New York, 1940), pp. [viii–ix].   3. "T. S. Stribling, Critic's Almanac, April 18, 1926," in *The Spyglass:*

Views and Reviews, 1924–1930, ed. John T. Fain (Nashville, 1963), pp. 13–14.   4. Joseph Blotner, *William Faulkner's Library—A Catalogue* (Charlottesville, 1964), p. 54.
5. *The Letters of Thomas Wolfe*, ed. Elizabeth Nowell (New York, 1956), p. 700.
6. "Boom Town" in the May 1934 *American Mercury*, and "The Company," in the January 11, 1938, *New Masses*.   7. *The Letters of Thomas Wolfe to His Mother*, ed. C. Hugh Holman and Sue Fields Ross (Chapel Hill, 1968), p. 42.   8. *Call It Experience* (New York, 1951), pp. 101–102.   9. Ibid., p. 32.
    10. *A Good Man Is Hard to Find and Other Stories* (New York, 1955), p. 243.
11. See Leonard Lutwack, "Mixed and Uniform Prose Styles in the Novel," in *The Theory of the Novel*, ed. Philip Stevick (New York, 1967), pp. 209–219.   12. "A Collection of Statements," in *The Added Dimension: The Art and Mind of Flannery O'Connor*, ed. Melvin J. Friedman and Lewis A. Lawson (New York, 1966), p. 243.   13. Ibid., p. 239.

Ellen Glasgow: The Novelist
of Manners as Social Critic

This essay was presented originally as the second lecture in the ninth series of the Eugenia Dorothy Blount Lamar Memorial Lectures, at Mercer University, in Macon, Georgia, on November 15, 1965. It was published in its present form in *Three Modes of Modern Southern Fiction: Ellen Glasgow, William Faulkner, Thomas Wolfe* (Athens: University of Georgia Press, 1966). The theme upon which these lectures were based was that there are three quite distinct southern regions—Atlantic coastal plain, Piedmont and mountains, and Gulf coastal plain—and that each has produced a distinct kind of culture, has had a distinct history, and is generally represented in a definite and peculiar mode. The idea, although a schema that omits much that differentiates the subregions and also much that binds them into a unity, has proved fruitful to me in my efforts to understand the literature of the southeastern regions. I think it is more succinctly expressed in my treatment of Miss Glasgow than it is in the other lectures of that series. The idea reappears in this volume in "Her Rue With a Difference" and "Three Views of the Real."

    1. Ellen Glasgow, *The Sheltered Life* (Garden City, 1932), p. 98.   2. Henry Adams, *The United States in 1800* (Ithaca, 1955), p. 107. (A reprint of Chapters i-vi of Adams's *History of the United States During the Administrations of Jefferson and Madison*, 9 vols., Boston, 1889–1891.)   3. Thomas J. Wertenbaker, *The Golden Age of Colonial Culture* (Ithaca, 1959), p. 3.   4. John Pendleton Kennedy, *Swallow Barn; or, A Sojourn in the Old Dominion* (New York, 1962), p. 27.   5. Thomas Nelson Page, *The Old South: Essays Social and Political* (New York, 1927), p. 5.   6. Ellen Glasgow, *A Certain Measure* (New York, 1943), p. 155.   7. Edward Wagenknecht, *The Cavalcade of the American Novel* (New York, 1952), p. 348.   8. Glasgow, *A Certain Measure*, p. 135. 9. Ibid., p. 142.
    10. Ibid., p. 4.   11. Daniel W. Patterson, "Ellen Glasgow's Plan for a Social History of Virginia," *Modern Fiction Studies*, v (Winter 1960), 353–360; and the reply by Oliver L. Steele, "Ellen Glasgow, Social History, and the 'Virginia Edition,'" *Modern Fiction Studies*, vi (Summer 1961), 173–176.   12. Glasgow, *The Sheltered Life*, p. 26. 13. Glasgow, *A Certain Measure*, p. 5.   14. H. Blair Rouse, ed., *Letters of Ellen Glasgow* (New York, 1958), p. 342.   15. Glasgow, *A Certain Measure*, p. 75.   16. Ibid., p. 28.   17. Ibid., pp. 237, 238.   18. Glasgow, *The Sheltered Life*, p. 193.

Notes   213

19. Ellen Glasgow, *The Romantic Comedians* (Garden City, 1926), p. 2. 20. Ibid., pp. 3–4. 21. Ibid., p. 3. 22. Ibid., pp. 20, 218. 23. Ibid., p. 251. 24. Glasgow, *A Certain Measure*, pp. 209–210. 25. Rouse, *Letters of Ellen Glasgow*, p. 232. 26. Ibid., p. 124. 27. Glasgow, *The Sheltered Life*, p. 152. 28. Ibid., pp. 163–164. 29. Ibid., p. 283.

30. Rouse, *Letters of Ellen Glasgow*, pp. 124, 262. 31. Glasgow, *A Certain Measure*, pp. 224–225. 32. Glasgow, *The Sheltered Life*, p. 155. 33. Glasgow, *A Certain Measure*, p. 147.

The Dark, Ruined Helen of his Blood
Thomas Wolfe and the South

I have done more work on Thomas Wolfe than on any other writer, and the three essays which I present here show three aspects of that work. "The Dark, Ruined Helen of his Blood" was written at the request of Louis D. Rubin, Jr., for the volume *South: Modern Southern Literature in Its Cultural Setting*, edited by Louis D. Rubin, Jr., and Robert D. Jacobs (Garden City, N.Y.: Doubleday, 1961). Mr. Rubin's invitation to write on Wolfe and the South—a subject with which he had dealt brilliantly himself—gave me an opportunity to look at Wolfe's work and career with reference to his southern origins and also to test my growing concept of a southern literary tradition by applying it to Wolfe. The essay has been reprinted in *Thomas Wolfe: Three Decades of Criticism*, edited by Leslie A. Field (New York: New York University Press, 1968).

1. *Writers in Crisis* (Boston, 1942), p. 196. 2. "A Note on the Hamlet of Thomas Wolfe," *Selected Essays* (New York, 1958), p. 183. 3. "One's-Self I Sing." 4. New York, 1936, p. 92. 5. *The Wigwam and the Cabin* (New York, 1856), pp. 4–5. 6. *South*, ed. L. D. Rubin and Robert D. Jacobs (Garden City, 1961), p. 43. 7. New York, 1935, p. 93. 8. *Segregation* (New York, 1957), p. 15. 9. "Agrarianism in Southern Literature: The Period Since 1925," *Georgia Review*, XI (1957), 157.

10. "The New Provincialism," *Essays of Four Decades* (Chicago, 1968), p. 543.
11. *On Native Grounds* (New York, 1942), p. 468. 12. *American Fiction, 1920–1940* (New York, 1941), p. 211. 13. "Rhetoric in Southern Writing: Wolfe," *Georgia Review*, XII (1958), 82. 14. New York, 1939, pp. 245–246. 15. Introduction, *I'll Take My Stand* (New York, 1930), p. xx. 16. New York, 1941, p. 393. 17. "The Irony of Southern History," *Southern Renascence*, ed. Louis D. Rubin, Jr., and Robert D. Jacobs (Baltimore, 1953), p. 65. 18. *The Woman Within* (New York, 1954), p. 42.

The Loneliness at the Core

This essay was written for a series, "Re-Assessment: 1955," published in the *New Republic*. Being given the opportunity to do this essay by Robert Evett, then book editor of the *New Republic*, proved to be a very fortunate circumstance for me. As the essay recounts, it brought me back to Thomas Wolfe after an interlude in which I had rejected his work, and it launched me on what has proved to be a very fruitful and rewarding interest. But the essay is included here not only for its importance to me personally but also because it is a record of a southerner's experience with Wolfe, a report on the accuracy of Wolfe's treatment of a portion of the South, and a linking of Wolfe to Sterne's *Tristram Shandy*, an always popular work in the South from the eighteenth century on. The essay originally appeared in the *New Republic*, cxxxiii (October 10, 195), 16–17. It has been reprinted in *Writing from Experience*, edited by R. C. Palmer, J. A. Lowrie, and J. F. Speer (Ames: Iowa State College Press, 1957); in *The Idea of an American Novel*, edited by L. D. Rubin, Jr., and J. R. Moore (New York: Thomas Y. Crowell Co., 1961); in *Experience and Expression*, edited by R. C. Palmer, J. A. Lowrie, and J. F. Speer (New York: Scribner's, 1962); in *The World of Thomas Wolfe*, edited by C. H. Holman (New York: Scribner's, 1962); and in *Studies in Look Homeward, Angel*, edited by Paschal Reeves (Columbus, Ohio: Charles E. Merrill, 1970).

Europe as a Catalyst for Thomas Wolfe

This essay was written for a program on southern writers in Europe, arranged by Nathalia Wright, for a meeting of the South Atlantic Modern Language Association, in Charlotte, North Carolina, in November 1966. It seems to me that Wolfe, in his hunger for the homeland during his European jaunts, is particularly like the southerner rather than the easterner or mid-westerner. The essay was published in *Essays in American and English Literature Presented to Bruce Robert McElderry, Jr.*, edited by Max F. Schulz (Athens: Ohio University Press, 1967).

1. Nathalia Wright, *American Novelists in Italy, The Discoverers: Allston to James* (Philadelphia, 1966), and Van Wyck Brooks, *The Dream of Arcadia: American Writers and Artists in Italy, 1760–1915* (New York, 1958). 2. George M. Reeves, *Thomas Wolfe et l'Europe* (Paris, 1955), pp. 83, 142. In another monograph, Daniel L. Delakas, *Thomas Wolfe, la France, et les romanciers français* (Paris, 1950), also takes this view. Neither Reeves nor Delakas sees the issue as a simple one, and both put Wolfe's work apart from that of the expatriates. Reeves, for example, while he asserts that Wolfe's experience is like that of "La Génération perdue," declares his work to lie "en dehors du principal courant littéraire de son époque" (p. 83). 3. Malcolm Cowley, *Exile's Return: A Literary Odyssey of the 1920's* (New York, 1951), pp. 9, 291–292. 4. *Thomas Wolfe's Purdue Speech: "Writing and Living,"* ed. William Braswell and Leslie A. Field (Purdue University, 1964), pp. 36–37. 5. These biographical data are assembled from *The Letters of Thomas Wolfe to His Mother*, ed. C. Hugh Holman and Sue Fields Ross (Chapel Hill, 1968); *The Letters of Thomas Wolfe*, ed. Elizabeth Nowell (New York, 1956); Elizabeth Nowell, *Thomas Wolfe: A Biography* (New York, 1960); Richard S. Kennedy, *The Window of Memory* (Chapel Hill, 1962); and Delakas, *Thomas Wolfe, la France, et les romanciers français*, which has a very useful "Tableau Chronologique de la Vie de Wolfe" on pp. 143–147, which is very detailed on Wolfe's European travels. 6. An almost unbelievable listing of cities he visited is given in the "Tableau Chronologique" in Delakas. The postcards listed in the "Calendar of Wolfe's Letters to His Mother" in *The Letters of Thomas Wolfe to His Mother*, pp. xvii–xxii, also help one to see his coverage of Europe. 7. Kennedy (*The Window of Memory*, pp. 97–106) has a good account of this work. 8. Wolfe, *Of Time and the River* (New York, 1935), pp. 858–859. 9. Wolfe, *The Story of a Novel* (New York, 1936), p. 31.

10. Wolfe, *The Web and the Rock* (New York, 1939), pp. 692–693.   11. *The Story of a Novel*, pp. 30–31, 35–36, 37–38.   12. Nowell, *Thomas Wolfe*, p. 168. 13. *Of Time and the River*, p. 329.   14. *The Letters of Thomas Wolfe*, to Maxwell E. Perkins, July 17, 1930, pp. 240–245. This is a very important letter, which deserves examination in its totality, and is too richly instructive to be reduced to the brief summary I have given of it.   15. In *The Short Novels of Thomas Wolfe*, ed. C. Hugh Holman (New York, 1961), pp. 233–278, in the form in which it was published in the *New Republic*, LXXXX (March 10, 17, 24, 1937), 132, 136, 159–164, 202–207. A longer version appears in Wolfe's *You Can't Go Home Again* (New York, 1941), pp. 634–704. 16. Bella Kussy, "The Vitalist Trend and Thomas Wolfe," in *The World of Thomas Wolfe*, ed. C. Hugh Holman (New York, 1962), p. 110. The essay originally appeared in *Sewanee Review*, L (July–September 1942), 306–324.   17. See Bruce R. McElderry, Jr., *Thomas Wolfe* (New York, 1964), pp. 64–66, where he comments on similarities between Wolfe and Mark Twain. See also McElderry's article, "The Durable Humor in *Look Homeward, Angel*," *Arizona Quarterly*, XI (1955), 123–128.   18. Cowley, in *Exile's Return*, is excellent on the ideals of this group.   19. *Of Time and the River*, p. 135. The material on Hatcher's class—almost all of it satiric—occurs in pp. 130–135, 167–175, 282–304, 309–324. 20. Ibid., pp. 698–699.   21. Wolfe, *The Hills Beyond* (New York, 1941), p. 186. 22. See, among many possible places, *The Letters of Thomas Wolfe*, pp. 262–266, particularly his description of Fitzgerald "in the Ritz Bar where he was entirely surrounded by Princeton boys, all nineteen years old, all drunk, and all half-raw" (p. 263).   23. *The Letters of Thomas Wolfe*, p. 67: "I'm going to Heaven in September [1924]. That is, to England."   24. Ibid., p. 71.   25. Ibid., p. 74.   26. *The Web and the Rock*, pp. 302–303.   27. *The Letters of Thomas Wolfe*, p. 92.   28. Ibid., p. 93.   29. *You Can't Go Home Again*, pp. 703–704. I have attempted to describe in more detail Wolfe's reaction to Germany in my article "Thomas Wolfe's Berlin," *Saturday Review*, L (March 11, 1967), 66, 69, 90. 30. *The Letters of Thomas Wolfe*, pp. 192–193.   31. *The Letters of Thomas Wolfe to His Mother*, p. 94.   32. *The Story of a Novel*, pp. 92–93.   33. In "Thomas Wolfe: Biography in Sound, An NBC Radio Broadcast," published in the *Carolina Quarterly*, Fall 1956, p. 9.

The Unity of Faulkner's
Light in August

This essay was first prepared for presentation on an American Literature program, arranged by Theodore Hornberger, at the annual meeting of the Modern Language Association, in Washington, D.C., in December 1956. It was published in an expanded form in *PMLA*, LXXIII (March 1958), 155–166. I am publishing it now in the same form as that in which it appeared in *PMLA*, although two points need to be made about it: There is great debate over whether Joe Christmas was thirty-three at the time of his death, as I assert here, or thirty-six, as others have argued. The real issue is whether "the road that ran for eighteen years," from Joe's fifteenth year, ran to his entry into Jefferson or to his death three years later. There is no conclusive evidence, although I obviously believe it to be thirty-three rather than thirty-six. In the second place this essay is heavily annotated, largely because at the time I wrote it I had grown weary of Faulkner critics who ape each other without credit. If I were doing the piece over, I would greatly reduce the footnotes, although in its present form they serve a purpose. Much has been written about *Light in August* since this essay was finished in 1957, but I have not added to the notes in order to include material not available to me at the time of writing. The essay has been reprinted in two collections of articles on *Light in August*, one edited by Olga Vickery (San Francisco, 1971) and the other by M. Thomas Inge (Columbus, Ohio, 1971).

1. Introduction, *The Portable Faulkner*, ed. Malcolm Cowley (New York, 1946), p. 18; "The Stone and the Crucifixion: Faulkner's *Light in August*," in *William Faulkner: Two Decades of Criticism*, ed. Frederick J. Hoffman and Olga W. Vickery (Michigan State College, 1951), pp. 205–217. Between these two extremes a great variety of attitudes have been held. Irving Howe, although he praises the novel, feels that it "suffers from a certain structural incoherence" resulting from its use of "a triad of actions" (*William Faulkner: A Critical Study*, New York, 1952, pp. 153, 149). Conrad Aiken believes that it fails because Faulkner's excessive concern with formal technique is not here "matched with the characters and the theme" ("William Faulkner: The Novel as Form," *Faulkner: Two Decades of Criticism*, p. 145). George M. O'Donnell also feels that the novel is a failure "because of the disproportionate emphasis upon Christmas—who ought to be the antagonist but who becomes, like Milton's Satan, the read protagonist in the novel" ("Faulkner's Mythology," ibid., p. 57).   2. Harry M. Campbell and Ruel E. Foster find unity in the book through an interplay of its incidents in terms of their contribution to "a successful metaphysical conceit" (*William Faulkner: A Critical Appraisal*, Norman, 1951, pp. 68ff.). William V. O'Connor believes that it achieves unity through its pervasive concern with southern Protestant mores ("Protestantism in Yoknapatawpha County," in *Southern Renascence: The Literature of the Modern South*, ed. Louis D. Rubin, Jr., and Robert D. Jacobs, Baltimore, 1953, pp. 153–169). (This essay is reprinted in an abridged and modified form as Chapter VI of O'Connor, *The Tangled Fire of William Faulkner*, Minneapolis, 1954, pp. 72–87.) Jacobs sees the book as centered in the tragedy of human isolation ("Faulkner's Tragedy of Isolation," *Southern Renascence*, pp. 170–191). Carl Benson finds its theme in man's tragic search for community ("Thematic Design in *Light in August*," *South Atlantic Quarterly*, LIII, 1954, 540–555). In an interesting but largely ignored examination of the novel just three years after its publication, James W. Linn and H. W. Taylor advanced the provocative idea that *Light in August* is a "counterpoint of stories," and said, "Through this ... device ... the novelist can, without any distortion of the individual elements of the material, still express his inner vision, his most personal intuitions, not in so many sentences, but in a design, which, like the structure of music, represents nothing but is a sort of meaning in itself" (*A Foreword to Fiction*, New York, 1935, p. 157).   3. "The Design and Meaning of *Absalom! Absalom!*" PMLA, LXX (December 1955), 904.
4. O'Connor, *Southern Renascence*, p. 169.   5. For example, Richard H. Rovere says, "Although it seems indisputable to me that some sort of connection [between Christ and Joe Christmas] was in Faulkner's mind at one point or another, I cannot believe that there is much profit ... in exploring the matter very deeply or in using it to interpret the novel" (Introduction, *Light in August*, Modern Library edition, New York, 1950, p. xiii). Richard Chase says, "Faulkner seems not to sense exactly how the Christ theme should be handled, sometimes making it too overt and sometimes not overt enough. His attempts to enlarge Joe's character by adducing a willed mythology remind one of Melville's similar attempts in *Pierre*" (*Faulkner: Two Decades of Criticism*, p. 212). Carl Benson says, "I am not certain as to just how far we may push the Christ-Christmas parallel" (*South Atlantic Quarterly*, LIII, 552). Irene C. Edmonds states: "One feels that he had a very definite connection in his mind between Christmas and Christ. The vagueness with which he establishes the connection suggests that the magnitude of his theme was too great for the limits of his imaginative powers to assimilate. ... One feels that Faulkner, a Southerner, when confronted by the enormity of his attempt to liken a man with Negro blood in his veins to Christ, could not find the moral courage to make the analogy inescapably clear. So it remained a suggestion, trailing away into the obfuscation of It-Could-or-Could-Not-Have-

Been" ("Faulkner and the Black Shadow," *Southern Renascence*, p. 196). Beekman W. Cottrell's article, "Christian Symbolism in 'Light in August,' " *Modern Fiction Studies*, II (Winter 1956–1957), 207–213, which takes seriously Faulkner's use of Christian materials in the novel, appeared after the present study had been accepted for publication. However, Cottrell's approach, although illuminating and provocative, is so different from mine that in only one respect, indicated in note 24, would it have altered my case appreciably. Three other studies have appeared since this essay was written, but they would not have modified seriously the reading given here: John L. Longley, Jr., "Joe Christmas: The Hero in the Modern World," *Virginia Quarterly Review*, XXXIII (1957), 233–249; Ilse D. Lind, "The Calvinistic Burden of *Light in August*," *New England Quarterly*, XXX (1957), 307–329; and Alfred Kazin, "The Stillness of 'Light in August,' " *Partisan Review*, XXIV (1957), 519–538.   6. Ward L. Miner, in *The World of William Faulkner* (Durham, 1952), pp. 139–141; Robert M. Adams, in "Poetry in the Novel: Or Faulkner Esemplastic," *Virginia Quarterly Review*, XXIX (1953), 419–434; and Carvel Collins, in a review of *A Fable* in the *New York Times Book Review* (August 1, 1954, p. 1) have called attention to Faulkner's use of the Holy Week in *The Sound and the Fury* (1929). George K. Smart has shown that the very early newspaper sketches assembled in *Mirrors of Chartres Street* used materials from the Christ story ("Faulkner's Use of Religious Terms," a paper read before the Southeastern American Studies Association, Daytona Beach, Florida, November 26, 1955).   7. "The Art of Fiction XII: William Faulkner," *Paris Review*, IV (Spring 1956), 42.   8. "*A Fable:* The Novel as Myth," *College English*, XVI (1955), 475. Significantly Faulkner has called Joyce and Mann the two great European men of his time and has said, "You should approach Joyce's *Ulysses* as the illiterate Baptist preacher approaches the Old Testament: with faith" (*Paris Review*, p. 46).   9. *Light in August* (New York, 1932). All page references are to this edition of the novel. (The Modern Readers Series edition, published by New Directions, apparently duplicates the 1932 edition by photoreproduction.)

10. *Southern Renascence*, pp. 175–176.   11. Ibid., p. 176.   12. Irene C. Edmonds's objection that Faulkner is here indulging in the fallacious "tragic mulatto" theme (*Southern Renascence*, pp. 196–197) seems justified. However, it seems also true that Faulkner's use of "black blood" has here transcended the level of racial qualities, whether true or false, and has been universalized to all mankind.   13. Joseph Campbell, *The Hero With a Thousand Faces* (New York, 1956), pp. 121–122. It it this aspect of Faulkner's work that seems to bother Edith Hamilton most in her "Faulkner: Sorcerer or Slave?" *Saturday Review*, XXXV (July 12, 1952), 8–10, 39–41.   14. See headnote and text, "Barbey Ellen," in Willard Thorp, *A Southern Reader* (New York, 1955), pp. 618–620, for this ballad in its southern version.   15. *The 1936 Census of Religious Bodies*, Bureau of the Census (Washington, 1941), I, 234–237, shows for Mississippi 150,000 communicants in the Southern Baptist Church, 322,362 in the Negro Baptist Church, 107,245 in the Methodist Church, and only 18,445 in the Presbyterian Church.   16. See ibid., II, 1382, 1402–1403.   17. Ibid., II, 1402–1403, and esp. p. 1444.   18. "Ode to the Confederate Dead," ll. 53–55.   19. *Portable Faulkner*, p. 15.

20. *World of William Faulkner*, p. 143.   21. Norman H. Pearson, in "Lena Grove," *Shenandoah*, III (Spring 1952), 3–7, has the provocative idea that Lena is the "leaf-fringed legend" and the "foster-child of silence and slow time" of Keats's "Ode to a Grecian Urn."

22. The passage reads:

I think I could turn and live with animals, they're so placid and self-contain'd,
I stand and look at them long and long.
They do not sweat and whine about their condition,
They do not lie awake in the dark and weep for their sins,
They do not make me sick discussing their duty to God,
Not one is dissatisfied, not one is demented with the mania of owning things,
Not one kneels to another, nor to his kind that lived thousands of years ago,
Not one is respectable or unhappy over the whole earth. (ll. 684–691)

23. See Campbell, *The Hero With a Thousand Faces*, pp. 109–126, 297–302.

24. Faulkner, Nobel Prize Address, *The Faulkner Reader* (New York, 1959), pp. 3–4.

25. "A Sight in Camp in the Daybreak Gray and Dim," ll. 14–15.

Absalom, Absalom!
The Historian as Detective

The idea for this essay was suggested to me by some students in a discussion at Davidson College on the occasion on which "The View from the Regency Hyatt" was presented. I explored the idea further for a presentation before an American Studies Institute at Southwestern Louisiana University, in Lafayette, Louisiana, the following summer. It found its present form for publication in the *Sewanee Review*, LXXIX (Autumn 1971), 542–553.

My joint interests in historical fiction and the detective story unite in this piece in an effort to express the intensity and the complexity of the southern writer's involvement with his past.

Her Rue with a Difference

This essay was written at the request of Lewis A. Lawson that I write on Flannery O'Connor and the southern literary tradition for a commemorative volume on Miss O'Connor which he and Melvin J. Friedman were editing. In this piece I continued testing my concept of the southern literary tradition by applying it to writers of distinction, and here I added a new aspect to my view of the southern experience, that of geographical differences. These differences proved useful to me in the preparation of my *Three Modes of Modern Southern Fiction* (Athens: University of Georgia Press, 1966), where I greatly elaborated them. They are, however, expressed clearly and succinctly here. The essay was published in *The Added Dimension: The Art and Mind of Flannery O'Connor*, edited by Melvin J. Friedman and Lewis A. Lawson (New York: Fordham University Press, 1966).

All page references in the text are to *Three by Flannery O'Connor* (New York, 1964). 1. "The Old Manse," *Mosses from an Old Manse*, in the Riverside Edition of *The Complete Works of Nathaniel Hawthorne* (Boston, 1883), II, 13. 2. "Flannery O'Connor's *Wise Blood*," *Critique*, II (Fall 1958), 3. 3. "The Fiction Writer and His Country," in *The Living Novel, a Symposium*, ed. Granville Hicks (New York, 1957), p. 159. 4. Ibid. 5. Ibid., p. 160. 6. James G. Leyburn, in *The Scotch-Irish: A Social History* (Chapel Hill, 1962), describes in great detail the migration, settlement, and customs of this group, which is very important to the understanding of the South but which is seldom looked at. Of particular usefulness to me have been his treatments of Scotch-Irish settlements and frontier society (pp. 184–295). 7. The Reverend Mr. Woodmason's journal has been edited by Richard J. Hooker and published as *The Carolina Backcountry on the Eve of the Revolution* (Chapel Hill, 1953). This primary document emphasizes the almost unbelievable difference between the Low-Country and Up-Country southerner. 8. *The Grotesque: An American Genre and Other Essays* (Carbondale, 1962), pp. 13, 6. 9. Ibid., p. 5.

10. Twelve Southerners, *I'll Take My Stand* (New York, 1930), p. ix.   11. Louis
D. Rubin, Jr., "Southern Literature: The Historical Image," in *South: Modern Southern
Literature in Its Cultural Setting*, ed. Louis D. Rubin, Jr., and Robert D. Jacobs (Garden
City, 1961), pp. 29–47.   12. Allen Tate, in "The Agrarians Today: A Symposium,"
Shenandoah, IIII (Summer 1952), 28–29.   13. "The Fiction Writer and His Country,"
p. 159.   14. Bartlett C. Jones, in "Depth Psychology and Literary Study," *Midcontinent
American Studies Journal*, V (Fall 1964), 50–56, gives an interesting and illuminating
Freudian reading of this story, while never losing sight of Miss O'Connor's non-Freudian
intention in writing the tale.   15. Louis D. Rubin, Jr., suggests, although he does not
accept, such a reading. See Rubin's review, "Two Ladies of the South," *Sewanee Review*,
LXIII (Autumn 1955), 671–681; his article, "Flannery O'Connor: A Note on Literary
Fashions," *Critique*, 11 (Fall 1958), 11–18; and his volume *The Faraway Country* (Seattle,
1963), p. 238, where he says that the Displaced Person "has irretrievably disrupted the
customary patterns of Southern rural society."   16. In Robert Penn Warren, *The Circus
in the Attic and Other Stories* (New York, 1947).   17. "Revelation," *Sewanee Review*,
LXXIII (Spring 1964), 181–182, and *Everything That Rises Must Converge* (New York,
1965), pp. 195–196.   18. See, for example, her essays, "Catholic Novelists and their
Readers" and "The Fiction Writer and His Country," in *Mystery and Manners* (New York,
1969), pp. 169–190, 25–35.   19. "The Fiction Writer and His Country," pp. 161–262.
20. *Who Speaks for the South?* (New York, 1964), p. 113.   21. "The Southerner
as American Writer," in *The Southerner as American*, ed. Charles G. Sellers, Jr. (Chapel
Hill, 1960), p. 193. Reprinted in this volume.   22. C. Hugh Holman, "The Unity of
Faulkner's *Light in August*," *PMLA*, LXXIII (March 1958), 155–166. Reprinted in this
volume.   23. *Who Speaks for the South?*, p. 258.   24. "The Fiction Writer and His
Country," pp. 162–163.

Literature and Culture: The Fugitive-Agrarians

This essay and the one that follows it seem to me to bring together most of
the themes and attitudes that I have tried to express in this volume. The
present essay attempts to relate the "Nashville group" to the main currents
of southern life and experience and to show that both their intentions and
their basic metaphor have intimate links with the South of the past and the
recent present. Indeed these poets, critics, and novelists represent in a sense
an epitome of the southern attitudes, a distillation of the southern response to
the national experience. "Literature and Culture" was presented as a paper
before the Southern Sociological Society, at its annual meeting, in Asheville,
North Carolina, in April 1958. It was published in *Social Forces*, XXXVII (October 1958), 15–19.

1. Hippolyte Taine, *Histoire de la littérature anglaise* (Paris, 1864).   2. "Why the
Modern South Has A Great Literature," *Still Rebels, Still Yankees and Other Essays* (Baton
Rouge, 1957), pp. 159–179.   3. Odum, "On Literature and Southern Culture," reprinted in *Southern Renascence: The Literature of the Modern South*, ed. Louis D. Rubin,
Jr., and Robert D. Jacobs (Baltimore, 1953), pp. 84–100; Maclachlan, "No Faulkner in
Metropolis," reprinted in ibid., pp. 101–111.   4. The best account of this group is
Louise Cowan, *The Fugitive Group* (Baton Rouge, 1959).   5. "The Fugitive—1922–
1925," *Princeton University Library Chronicle*, III (1942), 78–79.   6. From an unpublished letter of May 10, 1939, quoted by Frederick J. Hoffman, Charles Allen, and
Carolyn F. Ulrich, in *The Little Magazine: A History and a Bibliography* (Princeton, 1947),

p. 121.   7. "Southern Letters," *Double Dealer*, 1 (1921), 214.   8. John M. Bradbury, *The Fugitives: A Critical Account* (Chapel Hill, 1958), p. 13.   9. *The Shores of Light: A Literary Chronicle of the Twenties and Thirties* (New York, 1952), pp. 193–194.

10. Twelve Southerners, *I'll Take My Stand: The South and the Agrarian Tradition* (New York, 1930).   11. Edited by Herbert Agar and Allen Tate (Boston, 1936).
12. See Howard R. Floan, *The South in Northern Eyes, 1831 to 1861* (Austin, 1958).
13. See Francis Pendleton Gaines, *The Southern Plantation: A Study in the Development and the Accuracy of the Tradition* (New York, 1925).   14. Wilbur J. Cash, *The Mind of the South* (New York, 1941).   15. Described in detail in Malcolm Cowley, *Exile's Return: A Literary Odyssey of the 1920's* (New York, 1951).   16. At the height of the Boom farmers were receiving only 15 percent of the national income. Quoted in Norman Foerster, *American Poetry and Prose*, 4th ed. (Boston, 1957), p. 1196.   17. *An Epitaph for Dixie* (New York, 1958), particularly pp. 172–189.   18. Thomas Jefferson, *Notes on the State of Virginia*, ed. William Peden (Chapel Hill, 1955), pp. 164–165, 292.
19. Reprinted in *The Literature of the South*, ed. Richmond C. Beatty, Floyd C. Watkins, and Thomas Daniel Young, rev. ed. (Chicago, 1968), pp. 69–85.

20. *Reunion and Reaction* (Boston, 1951), passim. The quotation is from p. 246.
21. Quoted in Norman Foerster, *American Poetry and Prose*, 3rd ed. (Boston, 1948), p. 936.   22. *I'll Take My Stand*, p. 328.   23. *Who Owns America?*, pp. 268–269.
24. *Epitaph for Dixie*, pp. 177–178.

Three Views of the Real

This essay seems to me to sum up much of what I want to say about the fiction of the Southern Renascence. Although it repeats some material used earlier in this volume, I hope—and believe—that it so juxtaposes that material to other elements in the southern literary experience that it takes on special significance. I am using "Three Views of the Real" as the conclusion to this volume because it expresses clearly, I think, the sense I have tried to communicate of the interrelatedness of southern writing with the southern experience and the southern land. Objection has been raised to my principal point in the essay—that of three Souths—in that it does not take into consideration the South of Tennessee and Kentucky. I think it does, although not specifically, and I believe that the preceding essay on the Fugitive-Agrarians fits clearly into the general pattern outlined here.

"Three Views of the Real" was first presented as the concluding lecture in the Ninth Mercer University Lamar Memorial Lectures on November 16, 1965. It was published in its present form in *Three Modes of Modern South Fiction: Ellen Glasgow, William Faulkner, Thomas Wolfe* (Athens: University of Georgia Press, 1966).

1. Flannery O'Connor, "Some Aspects of the Grotesque in Southern Literature," *Mystery and Manners: Occasional Prose*, ed. Sally and Robert Fitzgerald (New York, 1969), p. 41.   2. Wayne C. Booth, *The Rhetoric of Fiction* (Chicago, 1961). The division of a work of art into four elements is drawn from Meyer Abrams, *The Mirror and the Lamp* (New York, 1953).   3. James Joyce, *A Portrait of the Artist as a Young Man*, in *The Portable James Joyce*, ed. Harry Levin (New York, 1947), pp. 481–482.   4. Walt Whitman," "Song of Myself," ll. 1–3.   5. William Faulkner, *Light in August* (New York, 1932), pp. 415, 422.   6. Thomas Wolfe, *The Web and the Rock* (New York, 1939), p. 15.   7. Ellen Glasgow, *A Certain Measure* (New York, 1943), p. 27.   8. Wolfe, *The Web and the Rock*, p. 242.   9. Thomas Wolfe, *You Can't Go Home Again* (New York, 1941), p. 393.

10. William Faulkner, *Intruder in the Dust* (New York, 1948), pp. 194–195.
11. Wolfe, *The Web and the Rock*, pp. 245–246.   12. Glasgow, *A Certain Measure*, p. 145.   13. Edith Wharton, *A Backward Glance* (New York, 1934), p. 207.
14. Glasgow, *A Certain Measure*, p. 213.   15. O'Connor, "Some Aspects of the Grotesque in Southern Literature," p. 50.

Index

In the following index, proper names are used throughout as the key entries. Works by an author and characters created by an author are listed under the author's name.

Abrams, Meyer H. 221

Adams, Henry 108, 204, 213; WORKS: *History of the United States During the Administrations of Jefferson and Madison*, 108, 213; *History of the United States of America During the First Administration of Thomas Jefferson*, 204; *The United States in 1800*, 213

Adams, John Quincy 20

Adams, Robert M. 218

Addison, Joseph 61, 109; CHARACTERS: de Coverley, Sir Roger, 109

Aeschylus 169, 176; WORKS: *Oresteia*, 169, 173

Agar, Herbert 221; WORKS: *Who Owns America?*, 188, 192, 221

Agrarians 17, 97, 101, 103, 118, 120, 128, 129, 130, 136, 177, 181, 182, 183, 192, 193

Aiken, Conrad 217

Aiken, South Carolina 81

Alabama 24

Alberta, Canada 173

Album, The (magazine) 16

Allen, Charles 220

Allston, Washington 215

American Mercury (magazine) 102

American Quarterly Review 21

Anderson, Sherwood 89

André, Major John 52

Anglophile criticism 26

Antaeus 121

Archdale, John 36

Arcturus, The (magazine) 26

Aristotle 6, 116, 194; WORKS: *Poetics*, 6

Armstrong, A. C. (and Son, publishers) 209, 211

Arnold, Benedict 18

Arnold, Matthew 97; WORKS: "The Function of Criticism at the Present Time," 97

Arvin, Newton 202

Ashepoo River 69

Asheville, North Carolina 118, 136, 146, 199

Ashley River 108, 109

Ashmore, Harry 190, 193, 221

Aswell, Edward 145

Atlanta, Georgia 96, 106

Atreus, House of 169

Auden, W. H. 170

Augusta, Georgia 36, 44

Auld, J. B. 26

Austen, Jane 109–110, 116

Austria 140, 141

Baker, Ernest A. 207, 209

Baker, George Pierce 118

Baldwin, Joseph Glover 8, 75

Balfour, Nesbitt 37

Balzac, Honoré de 121, 124, 169

Bancroft, Frederic 204

Bancroft, George 36

"Barbara Allen" 156

Barnwell District, South Carolina 27, 77

Barzun, Jacques 59, 207, 210

Basso, Hamilton 90

Baugh, Albert C. 210

Bayard, the Chevalier 210

Beach, Joseph Warren 127, 214

Beatty, Richmond C. 221

Beauchampe-Sharpe murder case 24, 94, 193

Beaumont, Francis 61, 62

Benjamin, Park 24, 77, 79

Benson, Carl 217

Bergson, Henri 124

Berlin, Germany 143

"Bible Belt" 184

Biltmore Estate (Asheville, North Carolina) 119
Bird, Robert Montgomery 32
Blair, James 20
Blankenship, Russell 208, 209
Blotner, Joseph 213
Boone, Daniel 18
Booth, Wayne 194, 221
Boston, Massachusetts 109, 196
Boucher, C. S. 204
Bowen, Francis 202
Boyd, James 119
Boynton, H. W. 79; WORKS: *Annals of American Bookselling*, 79
Bradbury, John M. 221
Bradley, Phillips 204
Bradsher, Earl L. 204
Braswell, William 215
Bridge, Horatio 28; WORKS: *A Journal of an African Cruiser*, 28
British Monthly Review 21–22
Broadway Journal 26, 29
Brome, Richard 62
Brooks, Cleanth 2, 7, 168, 201, 202
Brooks, Preston 82
Brooks, Van Wyck 215
Brother Jonathan (magazine) 24
Brown, Charles Brockden 32
Brown, Colonel Thomas 44, 207
Brown, Stirling 49, 208
Bryant, William Cullen 19, 25, 76, 203
Buck, Paul H. 208
Buffon, Count de 21
Bulwer-Lytton, Edward 52, 73, 79, 80, 209; CHARACTERS: Guloseton, Sir, 72, 73; WORKS: *Pelham*, 72
Butterfield, H. 209
Byrd, William 109, 179; WORKS: *History of the Dividing Line*, 179; *A Journey to the Land of Eden*, 179

Cabell, James Branch 88, 111, 112, 124, 125, 189, 197, 212; WORKS: *The Biography of the Life of Manuel*, 88, 111; *The Cords of Vanity: A Comedy of Shirking*, 111; *The Cream of the Jest: A Comedy of Evasions*, 89, 111; *Let Me Lie*, 197; *The Rivet in Grandfather's Neck: A Comedy of Limitations*, 89, 111
Cable, George Washington 179
Cabot, John 18
Cairns, William B. 204
Caldwell, Erskine 1, 8, 12, 90, 97, 99, 100, 103, 104, 105, 106, 177, 180, 212, 213; CHARACTERS: Lester, Jeeter, 99; WORKS: *Call It Experience*, 103, 213; *God's Little Acre*, 104; "Kneel to the Rising Sun," 104, 105; *Tobacco Road*, 99, 103, 212; *Trouble in July*, 104
Calhoun, John Caldwell 1, 34, 85, 127, 204
Calvinism 10, 132, 151, 152, 157, 158, 179, 191
Cambridge, Massachusetts 173
Camden, South Carolina 36, 37
Campbell, Harry M. 217
Campbell, Joseph 155, 218, 219
Canada 171
Cape Fear, North Carolina 44
Capote, Truman 1, 177
Carey, Mathew 204
Caribbean 179
Carlyle, Thomas 16, 18, 28, 209; WORKS: *On Heroes, Hero-Worship, and the Heroic in History*, 18
Carr, John Dickson 169
Carroll, B. R. 36, 206; WORKS: *Historical Collections of South Carolina*, 36
Cash, Wilbur J. 96, 127, 189, 193, 221; WORKS: *The Mind of the South*, 96, 221
Cervantes Saavedra, Miguel de 70; CHARACTERS: Sancho, 70; WORKS: *Don Quixote*, 70, 73
Chapel Hill, North Carolina xii, 96, 118, 119, 136
Chapman, George 62
Charles Scribner's Sons (publishers) 141
Charles II 108
Charleston, South Carolina 16, 19, 20, 27, 35, 36, 37, 38, 39, 55, 61, 77, 78, 80, 83, 84, 108
Charleston (South Carolina) Theatre 77, 80

Charlotte, North Carolina 96

Chase, Richard 149, 217

Cheever, George B. 29; WORKS: *Wanderings of a Pilgrim under the Shadow of Mont Blanc*, 29

Chester, Pennsylvania 178

Chew, Samuel C. 58

Chicago, Illinois 107

Chopin, Kate 179

Christ 93, 105, 149, 150, 151, 152, 153, 157, 158, 164, 165, 167, 182, 184, 185

Christie, Agatha 169

Cibber, Colley 61

City Gazette (Charleston, South Carolina) 20, 21

Clark, Blanche Henry 208

Clark, H. H. 203

Clark, Lewis Gaylord 25, 26, 27

Clavers, Mary 29; WORKS: *Western Clearings*, 29

Clemens, Samuel Langhorne, see Mark Twain

Clinton, Sir Henry 37

Clytemnestra 176

Coleridge, Samuel Taylor 1, 16, 18

Coligny, Gaspard de 18

Collins, Carvel 218

Comte, Auguste 10

Concord, Massachusetts 1

Congreve, William 62

Cooke, John Esten 75, 77; WORKS: *Leather Stocking and Silk*, 77; *The Virginia Comedians*, 77

Cooper, James Fenimore 4, 7, 19, 22, 23, 25, 27, 32, 34, 50, 52–55, 57–60, 61, 72, 76, 79, 83, 201, 204, 205, 208–210; CHARACTERS: Birch, Harvey, 53, 60; Bumppo, Natty, 53, 60; Cow-Boys, 52; Hawkeye, 53, 60; Hutter, Hetty, 59; Jacopo, 53; the Pilot, 53; Polwarth, 72, 73; Sitgreaves, Dr., 59; Skinners, 52; Wharton, Henry, 53; WORKS: *The Bravo*, 53; *The Crater*, 83; *The Deerslayer*, 52, 57, 59, 209; "land rents" trilogy, 54; *Home As Found*, 83; *The Last of the Mohicans*, 77; *Leatherstocking Tales*, 79; *A Letter to His Countrymen*, 34;

Lionel Lincoln, 52, 53, 72, 210; *The Littlepage Manuscripts*, 83; *The Monikins*, 83; *Notions of the Americans*, 22–23, 204; *The Spy*, 32, 52, 53, 54, 57, 59, 209

Cooper River 108

Core, George xiii, 212

Cornwallis, Charles 39, 82

Cortes, Hernando 18, 19; WORKS: *The Dispatches of Hernando Cortes*, 18

Cottrell, Beekman W. 218

Courier (Charleston, South Carolina) (newspaper) 16

Cowan, Louise 220

Cowie, Alexander 209, 210, 211

Cowley, Malcolm 139, 149, 161, 189, 215, 216, 217, 218, 221

Cowpens, South Carolina 37

Craddock, Charles Egbert 179

Crane, Hart 189

Creek Indians 19

Crete 124

Crockett, Davy 80

Cumberland, Richard 61

Cummins, Maria 75

Czechoslovakia 140

Dabbs, James McBride 184, 185, 220

Daniels, Jonathan 118

Darley, F. O. C. 77

Darwin, Charles Robert 10

Davidson, Donald 7, 101, 130, 187, 212, 220

Davidson, Philip 208

Davis, Richard Beale 201

Dekker, Thomas 61, 62

Delakas, Daniel L. 215

DeLeon, Dr. Edwin 27; WORKS: "Cheap Literature: Its Character and Tendencies," 27

Democratic Review 26

Denmark 140

De Soto, Hernando 18, 33

DeVoto, Bernard 135; WORKS: "Genius is Not Enough," 135

Dew, Thomas R. 84

Dickens, Charles 30, 79, 91

Disneyland 87

Disraeli, Benjamin 79
Dodd, William E. 208
Dolmetsch, Carl xiii
Donald, David 201
Dos Passos, John 89, 189
Dostoevski, Fyodor 91
Double Dealer (magazine) 89, 187
Drayton, John 36
Dryden, John 2, 62
Duyckinck, Evert A. 3, 4, 26, 27, 28, 29, 30, 31, 84, 205
Duyckinck, George L. 3, 26

Eaton, Clement 85, 205; WORKS: *Freedom of Thought in the Old South*, 85, 205
Eaves, T. C. D. 201, 203, 209
Edmonds, Irene C. 217–218
Eliot, Thomas Stearns 11, 99, 139, 189
Elizabeth I 56, 98, 108
Ellery Queen's Mystery Magazine 169
Emerson, Ralph Waldo 28, 75
England 140, 141, 145, 146
Erskine, John 52, 72, 208, 209, 211
Etherege, Sir George 62, 211; CHARACTERS: Sir Fopling Flutter, 66; WORKS: *The Man of Mode*, 211
Euripides 167, 196; WORKS: *Orestes*, 176
Eutaw Springs, Battle of 37
Evett, Robert xiii, 214

Fain, John T. 213
Farquhar, George 61
Farrell, James T. 89
Farrior, John E. 207, 210
Faulkner, William 1, 8, 11, 12, 13, 90, 92, 93, 94, 95, 97, 101, 102, 103, 114, 117, 121, 124, 125, 127, 131, 132, 149–176, 177, 180, 182, 184, 187, 193, 194, 195, 196, 197, 198, 199, 202, 212, 213, 216–219, 220, 221, 222; CHARACTERS: Allen, Bobbie, 152, 155, 156, 157; Bon, Charles, 168, 170–175 passim; Bond, Jim, 175; Brown, 152, 163; Bunch, Byron, 150, 151, 159, 160, 163, 164, 166; Bundrens, 11, 97; Burch, Lucas, 150, 163; Burden, Joanna, 150–162 passim;

Christmas, Joe, 13, 93, 149–167; Clytie, 175; Coldfield, Miss Rosa, 168, 169, 171; Compson, General, 171; Compson, Mr., 168, 169, 171, 172, 173; Compson, Quentin, 14, 92, 93, 132, 168–175 passim; Grimm, Percy, 151, 154; Grove, Lena, 149, 150, 151, 159, 162–167 passim; Halliday, 152; Hightower, Gail, 149–167 passim, 195; Hightower, Mrs., 162; Hines, Eupheus, 157, 160, 165; Hines, Milly, 150, 165; Hines, Old Mrs., 159, 160, 165, 166; Judith, 173, 174; McCannon, Shreve, 168–176 passim; McCaslin, Ike, 11, 13, 131, 132; McEachern, Simon, 151, 152, 156, 157, 158, 160; McEachern, Mrs., 151, 152; McEacherns, 155; Snopeses, 97, 102, 103, 174, 193; Stevens, Gavin, 154, 165; Sutpen, Henry, 168–175 passim, 198; Sutpen, Thomas, 92, 168, 169, 174, 179; Tom, 174; WORKS: *Absalom, Absalom!*, 92, 102, 168–176, 179, 198; *As I Lay Dying*, 11, 92; *The Bear*, 13, 132; "Delta Autumn," 11, 131; *A Fable*, 93, 149, 150, 165; 218; *Go Down, Moses*, 202; *Intruder in the Dust*, 169, 197, 222; *Knight's Gambit*, 169; *Light in August*, 12, 13, 93, 149–167, 184, 195, 202, 217, 218, 220, 221; *Mirrors of Chartres Street*, 218; *New Orleans Sketches*, 93; Nobel Prize Address, 176, 219; *The Sound and the Fury*, 12, 14, 92, 93, 132, 171, 218
Felton, Cornelius C. 30
Field, Leslie A. 214, 215
Fielding, Henry 52
Fitzgerald, F. Scott 89, 145, 189, 216
Fitzgerald, Sally and Robert 221
Flaubert, Gustave 147
Fletcher, John 61, 62
Floan, Howard R. 221
Florence, Alabama 100–101
Florida 41, 43
Foerster, Norman 221
Ford, John 93
Forrest, Edwin 25, 61

Fort Motte, South Carolina 36
Fort Ninety-Six, South Carolina 37
Fort Watson, South Carolina 36
"47 Workshop" 118
Foster, Ruel E. 217
France 139, 140, 141, 146
France, Anatole 88
Franklin, John Hope 201
Freneau, Peter 20
Freud, Sigmund 93, 114, 161, 220
Friederich, W. P. 201
Friedman, Melvin J. 213, 219
Froissart, Jean 55, 87
Frost, Robert 3, 201; WORKS: "The Gift
    Outright," 3, 201
Fugitive-Agrarians 99, 187–193
Fugitive, The (magazine) 7, 89, 187,
    188

Gaea 121
Gaines, Francis Pendleton 221
Garrick, David 61
Gates, Horatio 36, 37, 39
Gates, Mrs. Jane Miller Singleton 38
Geismar, Maxwell 118, 214
George III 18
Georgetown, South Carolina 36
Georgia 24, 76, 97, 177, 178, 179
Georgia, University of 106
Germany 102, 139, 140, 141, 143, 146
Gibbes, Robert W. 206
Glasgow, Ellen 8, 10, 14, 88, 89, 92,
    102, 108–117, 124, 125, 131, 189, 194,
    195, 196, 197, 198, 199, 200, 202, 212,
    213–214, 221, 222; CHARACTERS: Arch-
    bald, General, 112, 114, 115, 199;
    Archbald, Jenny Blair, 115, 198, 199;
    Blake, Mrs., 197; Honeywell, Judge
    Gamaliel, 113; Littlepage, Mr., 116;
    Oakley, Dorinda, 112; Upchurch,
    Mrs., 114; WORKS: *Barren Ground*,
    10, 88, 112; *A Certain Measure*, 202,
    213, 214, 221, 222; *The Deliverance*,
    196, 197; Queensborough novels,
    112, 115, 196; *In This Our Life*, 112;
    The Miller of Old Church, 88; *The
    Romantic Comedians*, 112, 113, 114,
    214; *The Sheltered Life*, 112, 113,
114, 115, 213, 214, *They Stooped to
    Folly*, 112, 113, 115, 116; *Vein of
    Iron*, 88, 112; *The Woman Within*,
    202, 214
Glenn, James 36
Godey's Lady's Book (magazine) 33, 78
Godwin, William 23, 24, 209
Goldsmith, Oliver 116
Gordon, Caroline 1, 117, 177, 184, 219
Govan, Thomas P. 201
Grady, Henry 96
Grahame, James 36
Granby, South Carolina 36
Grantham, Dewey W., Jr. 201
Grau, Shirley Ann 1
Great Valley 178
Great Western (ship) 24
Greene, General Nathanael 36, 37, 39,
    82, 83, 210
Greene, Robert 62
Greenwich Village, New York City 90,
    190
Griffith, Benjamin W., Jr. xiii
Griswold, Rufus W. 209
Grossman, James 53, 54, 209, 210
Guilds, John C. 205

Hamilton, Edith 218
Hammond, James Henry 84, 204
Hardy, Thomas 88, 112
Harper & Brothers (publishers) 81
Harper, William 84
Harris, George Washington 8, 75; CHAR-
    ACTERS: Lovingood, Sut, 75, 76
Harrison, James A. 211
Harvard College 14, 30, 75, 118, 144,
    168, 170
Hawthorne, Nathaniel 12, 23, 28, 29,
    31–32, 33, 75, 80, 83, 85–86, 105,
    177, 202, 204, 205, 219; CHARACTERS:
    Dimmesdale, Arthur, 12; WORKS:
    The Marble Faun, 204; *Mosses from
    an Old Manse*, 29, 219; "The Old
    Manse," 219; *The Scarlet Letter*, 33,
    80, 202
Hayne, Paul Hamilton 61, 77
Hayne, Robert Y. 20
Hayward, Edward F. 206, 211

Headley, J. T. 28, 29; WORKS: *The Alps and the Rhine,* 29; *Letters from Italy,* 28
Hegel, Georg Wilhelm 120, 128
Helen 121
Hemingway, Ernest 78, 89, 189
Henry VIII 62
Henry, Dr. Robert 2
Heracles 121
Herbert, Edward T. 203
Herron, Ima H. 48, 208
Hewatt, Alexander 36
Heywood, John 62
Hicks, Granville 219
Hillhouse, James T. 207, 209, 210
Hoagland, Kathleen, 148
Hobkirk's Hill, Battle of 37
Hoffman, Charles Fenno 94
Hoffman, Frederick J. 217, 220
Holmes, Abiel 36
Holmes, George F. 205, 206
Homer 21, 150
Hooker, Richard J. 219
Hoole, W. Stanley 211
Hopkins Review 187
Hornberger, Theodore 216
Horry, General Peter 36, 206
Howe, Irving 150, 217
Howells, William Dean 88
Hubbell, Jay B. 201, 207, 211

Inge, M. Thomas 217
Irving, Washington 3, 25, 26, 76, 110; WORKS: *Bracebridge Hall,* 110
Italy 139, 140

Jackson, Andrew 17, 19, 20, 21, 34, 184, 204; "Old Hickory," 19, 20
Jackson, D. K. 201, 207
Jacobs, Robert D. 152, 202, 214, 217, 218, 220
Jamaica 66
James I 50, 56, 108
James, G. P. R. 52
James, Henry xii, 88, 134, 139, 147, 209, 215
James River 108, 110
Jamestown, Virginia, 2, 18, 108

Jamison, David F. 36, 206
Jarrell, Hampton M. 70, 71, 209, 211
Jason 121
Jefferson, Thomas 1, 17, 20, 21, 90, 127, 190, 204, 221; WORKS: *Notes on the State of Virginia,* 21, 190, 204, 221
Johnson, Guion G. 208
Johnson, Joseph 36, 72, 206; WORKS: *Traditions and Reminiscences of the Revolution in South Carolina,* 36
Johnston, E. W. 23, 204
Jones, Bartlett C. 220
Jones, Howard Mumford xiii, 203
Jones, William A. 26
Jonson, Ben 62, 65, 68, 73, 74, 211; WORKS: *Every Man Out of His Humor,* 211
Journal of Southern History xi
Joyce, James 91, 97, 99, 100, 102, 105, 134, 135, 150, 194, 212, 218, 221; WORKS: *A Portrait of the Artist as a Young Man,* 134, 194, 221; *Ulysses,* 135, 150, 218

Kansas 82
Kant, Emmanuel 2
Kartiganer, Donald M. 174
Kazin, Alfred 127, 214, 218
Keats, John 218; WORKS: "Ode to a Grecian Urn," 218
Kelley, Edith Summers 102; WORKS: *Weeds,* 102
Kennedy, John Pendleton 13, 16, 33, 75, 76, 77, 79, 81, 82, 110, 202, 207, 213; CHARACTERS: Meriwether, Frank, 13; WORKS: *Horse-Shoe Robinson,* 33, 76, 79, 81, 82, 207; *Rob of the Bowl,* 79; *Swallow Barn,* 13, 76, 110, 202, 213
Kennedy, Richard S. 215
Kentucky 24, 94, 102
Kings Mountain, North Carolina 37
Kirkland, Mrs. Caroline, see Mary Clavers
Knickerbocker Magazine, The 3, 4, 25, 26, 27, 30, 31, 84, 123
Knickerbocker writers 25, 30, 31, 110
Knight, Grant C. 208

The Roots of Southern Writing

Kohler, Dayton 150, 218
Kronos 121
Ku Klux Klan 101
Kussy, Bella 143, 216

Lamar, Eugenia Dorothy Blount 213
Landrum, Grace 209
Lanier, Sidney 7, 130, 189; WORKS: *The Science of English Verse,* 7
Lathem, Edward Connery 201
Lawrence, D. H. 134; WORKS: *Sons and Lovers,* 134
Lawson, James 203, 205
Lawson, John 25
Lawson, Lewis A. xiii, 213, 219
Lea and Blanchard (publishers) 25
Leary, Lewis 75; WORKS: *Contemporary Literary Scholarship,* 75
Lee, Nathaniel 61
Legaré, Hugh Swinton 23
Leisy, Ernest E. 207, 209
Levin, Harry 221
Lewis, Sinclair 89, 91, 99, 100, 103, 105; WORKS: *Main Street,* 100
Leyburn, James G. 219
Library of American Books 17, 28, 29, 30, 31
"Library of Choice Reading" 28
Lillo, George 61
Lincoln, Benjamin 36
Lind, Ilse D. 149, 168, 217, 218
Linn, James W. 217
Literary World 3, 30, 31, 84
Little Rock, Arkansas 151
London 2, 98, 141, 143, 145
Long, Huey 193
Longfellow, Henry Wadsworth 3, 22, 26, 28, 123, 201, 204; WORKS: *Kavanagh: A Tale,* 201, 204
Longley, John L., Jr. 218
Longstreet, Augustus Baldwin 7, 8, 75, 76, 77, 179; WORKS: *Georgia Scenes,* 7, 12, 76, 77, 179
Longstreet, General James 197
Los Angeles, California 107
Loshe, Lillie D. 209
Louis xi 56
Lounsbury, Thomas R. 209–210

Low Country (South Carolina) 35, 37, 41, 44, 45, 55, 109, 117, 178, 196
Lowell, James Russell 210
Lowrie, J. A. 215
"Lubberland" 109
Lukács, Georg xii, 169, 205, 207
Lutwack, Leonard 213

Mabbott, T. O. 205
McCrady, Edward 207
McCullers, Carson 1, 177, 180
McDowell, Tremaine 209
McElderry, Bruce Robert, Jr. 216
McIlwaine, Shields 48, 208, 210
Maclachlan, John 187, 220
McLane, Louis 20
McWhiney, Grady 201
Magnolia, The (magazine) 4, 8, 21, 26, 27
Maigron, Louis 207, 209
Maine 142
Malory, Sir Thomas 55
Mann, Thomas 150, 180, 218; WORKS: *Doctor Faustus,* 150
Marion, General Francis 24, 36, 37, 41, 55, 56, 69, 82, 83, 210; "the Swamp Fox," 36
Mark Twain 97 144, 216; WORKS: *The Innocents Abroad,* 144
Marlowe, Christopher 62
Marquand, John P. 196
Marston, John 93
Martineau, Harriet 84, 206; WORKS: *Travels in America,* 84
Marx, Karl 10, 134, 190
Mary Queen of Scots 56
Massachusetts 111
Massinger, Philip 61, 62
Mather, Cotton 2, 201; WORKS: *Bonifacius, An Essay Upon the Good, that is to be Devised and Designed* [known as *The Essays to Do Good*], 201
Mathew Carey (publisher) 25
Mathews, Cornelius 4, 26, 27, 28, 29, 30, 205; WORKS: *Big Abel and the Little Manhattan,* 26, 29, 30; *The Career of Puffer Hopkins,* 26

Matthiessen, F. O. xii, 75, 76, 85; WORKS: *American Renaissance*, 75

Maugham, William Somerset 134; WORKS: *Of Human Bondage*, 134

Melville, Herman 4, 12, 26, 29, 30, 34, 75, 85, 204, 217; CHARACTERS: Ahab, 34; WORKS: *Moby Dick*, 4, 34; *Pierre*, 217; *Typee*, 29

Mencken, H. L. 99

Metaphysical poets 189

Mexico 18, 19

Middleton, Thomas 61, 62

Milledgeville, Georgia 105

Miller, Perry 201, 204, 205

Milton, John 21, 22, 62, 192, 193, 217; WORKS: *Paradise Lost*, 192, 193

Miner, Ward L. 162, 218

Mississippi 19, 24, 92, 96, 166, 168, 170, 172, 174, 179, 187, 195

Mississippi River, 87

Mississippi, University of 77

Mitchell, Margaret 96, 196

Montreux, Switzerland 143

Moore, J. R. 215

Moore, Merrill 187

Morning Post (Boston, Massachusetts) 30–31

Morris, Richard B. 204

Mott, Frank Luther 204, 205, 206

Moultrie, William 36

Muller, Herbert 134

Mumford, Lewis 191

Munich, Germany 141

Murphree, Mary Noailles, see Charles Egbert Craddock

Murphy, Arthur 61

Murrell, John A. 24

Napoleon Bonaparte 110

Nashville, Tennessee 89, 187, 189

Nelson, Admiral Horatio 110

Nelson, John H. 48–49, 208

New Castle, Delaware 178

"New Critics" 1, 6, 7, 18, 188

New-England Magazine 77

New Haven, Connecticut 90

New Masses (magazine) 102

New Orleans, Louisiana 19, 184, 187

New World (magazine) 79

New York City xii, 4, 25, 26, 28, 76, 80, 84, 102, 107, 110, 123, 141, 146

New York Commercial Advertiser 76

New York Times 76

Niebuhr, Reinhold 14

North American Review 30

North Carolina 109, 118, 145, 178, 179

North Carolina, University of xii, 118

Notion (Boston, Massachusetts) (magazine) 24, 79

Nowell, Elizabeth 213, 215, 216

O'Connor, Flannery 1, 100, 104, 105, 106, 107, 177–186, 194, 200, 213, 219–220, 221; CHARACTERS: Flynn, Father, 182; Guizac, Mr., 105, 182; Head, Mr., 185; [Head], Nelson, 185; Hopewell, Hulga, 181; McIntyre, Mrs., 105, 182, 185; Misfit, The, 185; Motes, Hazel, 107, 185; Rayber, 182; Shortley, Mrs., 185; Turpin, Claud, 183; Turpin, Mrs., 183; WORKS: "The Artificial Nigger," 185; "The Displaced Person," 104, 105, 182, 185, 220; *Everything That Rises Must Converge*, 220; "The Fiction Writer and His Country," 181, 219, 220; "Good Country People," 181; *A Good Man Is Hard To Find*, 104, 185, 213; *Mystery and Manners*, 220; "Revelation," 183, 220; *The Violent Bear It Away*, 182; *Wise Blood*, 107, 180, 182, 185, 219

O'Connor, William Van 180, 217, 219, 222; WORKS: "The Grotesque: An American Genre," 180, 219

Odell, A. T. 201, 203, 209

O'Donnell, George M. 217

Odum, Howard W. 96, 187, 220

Oliphant, Mary C. S. 201, 203, 209

Omaha, Nebraska 14

Orangeburg, South Carolina 36, 37, 42

Osterweis, Rollin G. 209

O'Sullivan, John L. 204

Otway, Thomas 61

Ovid 2; WORKS: *Metamorphoses*, 2

Owsley, F. L. 208

Oxford Book of English Verse 146

Page, Thomas Nelson 96, 110, 179, 213; WORKS: *In Ole Virginia,* 110; *Red Rock,* 110
Paine, Gregory Lansing 52, 202, 209
Palmer, Raymond C. 203, 215
Panic of 1837 24, 78
Paris, France 90, 141, 142, 143, 145, 146, 189, 190
Paris Review 153, 155, 163, 164, 165
Parks, Edd Winfield 16–17, 203, 205
Parrington, Vernon L. 35, 41, 54, 55, 58, 73, 83, 84, 205, 206, 207, 209, 210, 211
Pattee, Fred Lewis 209
Patterson, Daniel W. 213
Paulding, James Kirke 4, 32
Pearson, Norman H. 218
Peden, William 190, 204, 221
Peele, George 62
Pennsylvania 178
Percy, William Alexander 198; WORKS: *Lanterns on the Levee,* 198
Perkins, Maxwell 119, 121, 123, 135, 216
Peru 24
Peterloo Massacre 110
Philadelphia, Pennsylvania 76, 178
Phillips, John 61
Pickett, General George Edward 196, 197
Plato 6; WORKS: *Republic,* 6
PMLA xi
Pocahontas 18, 66
Poe, Edgar Allan 3, 4, 6, 7, 10, 11, 16, 26, 28, 29, 30, 72, 76, 77, 78, 180, 201, 202, 204, 205, 211; WORKS: "Marginalia," 26; *The Narrative of Arthur Gordon Pym,* 78–79; "Philosophy of Composition," 7; "Rationale of Verse," 7; *The Raven and Other Poems,* 29, 205; *Tales,* 28, 30
Pope, Alexander 2
Porter, Katherine Anne 1, 90
Poseidon 121
Prescott, William Hickling 18; WORKS: *History of the Conquest of Mexico,* 18

Pritchard, John Paul 18, 203
Pro-Slavery Argument, The 84, 205
Proust, Marcel 91, 124; WORKS: *Remembrance of Things Past,* 134
Purdue University 139

Queen, Ellery 169
Quinn, Arthur Hobson 209

Racine, Jean Baptiste 21
Ramsay, David 36
Ransom, John Crowe 1, 7, 183, 184, 187; WORKS: *God Without Thunder,* 183
Rawdon, Lord Francis 37, 39
Raynal, Abbé 21
Reddick, L. D. 201
Reeve, Henry 22, 202, 204
Reeves, George M., Jr. 139, 215; WORKS: *Thomas Wolfe et l'Europe,* 139, 215
Reeves, Paschal 215
Regency Hyatt House 96, 106, 107
Renaissance (American) 75–86
Renaissance (English) 61, 62
Restoration 61, 65, 66
Reynaud, Louis 51, 207
Richardson, Samuel 52
Richmond, Virginia 88, 108, 111, 113
Rivers, William J. 36
Roberts, George 24, 79
Robin Hood 58
Rochester, John Wilmot 62
Rock, Virginia 126, 214
Rockefeller, John D. 109
Rome, Italy 90
Roosevelt, Franklin Delano 97
Ross, Sue Fields xiii, 213, 215
Rotary Club 146
Rouse, H. Blair 213, 214
Rovere, Richard H. 217
Rowe, Nicholas 61
Rubin, Louis D., Jr. xii, xiii, 97, 107, 124, 135, 202, 212, 214, 215, 217, 220
Russell's Bookshop 77

Sabine, Lorenzo 33, 81; WORKS: *The American Loyalists,* 33, 81
St. Augustine 186

St. Catharine's, South Carolina 44
St. Paul 153
Saintsbury, George Edward Bateman
51, 205, 207, 209
Salem (Massachusetts) *Advertiser*
(newspaper) 31–32
Salley, A. S. 203
Sandys, George 2
Santayana, George 196
Saturday Evening Post (magazine) 144,
190
Savannah Convention on Southern Lit-
erature 78
Sayers, Dorothy 169
Schaper, W. A. 207
Schlesinger, Arthur M., Jr. 204, 206
Schoolcraft, Henry R. 18
Schulz, Max F. 215
Scotch-Irish 10, 178, 179
Scott, Sir Walter 32, 33, 39, 40, 50–60,
61, 62, 79, 80, 81, 169, 205, 206, 207,
208–210; CHARACTERS: Elizabeth I,
56; Friar Tuck, 72, 73; James I, 56;
Louis XI, 56; Mary Queen of Scots,
56; Merrilies, Meg, 59; Norma of the
Fitful Head, 59; WORKS: *The Abbot*,
52; *The Fortunes of Nigel*, 50, 51;
Guy Mannering, 59; *The Heart of
Midlothian*, 39; *Ivanhoe*, 39, 52, 57;
Kenilworth, 52, 57; *The Pirate*, 59;
Quentin Durward, 57; *Redgauntlet*,
39; *Tales of My Landlord*, 209;
Waverley, 205; Waverley Novels,
32, 50, 51, 57, 59, 60, 205, 209;
Woodstock, 39
Sedgwick, Catherine Maria 28; WORKS:
Home, 28
Sellers, Charles Grier, Jr. 201, 220
Shakespeare, William 21, 22, 61, 62, 64,
70, 72, 80, 84, 95, 97, 98, 120, 162;
CHARACTERS: Coleville of the Dale,
Sir, 70; Falstaff, 61, 69, 70, 71, 72,
73, 74; Ford, Mistress, 71; Hamlet,
95, 120, 132; Iago, 64; Page, Mis-
tress, 71; Parolles, 72, 73; Quickly,
Mistress, 71; Richard III, 64; Shy-
lock, 65; Wrotham, Sir John, 72;
WORKS: *Henry IV*, 162; *The Merry

Wives of Windsor, 70, 71; *Sir John
Oldcastle*, 71; *Timon of Athens*, 61
Sheridan, Richard Brinsley 61, 67;
CHARACTERS: Backbite, Sir Benjamin,
67; Crabtree, 67; WORKS: *The School
for Scandal*, 67, 211
Shiloh, Tennessee 173
Shirley, James 62
Simms, William Gilmore xi, 3, 4, 5, 6,
7, 8, 10, 16–86, 94, 123, 179, 201,
202–212, 214; CHARACTERS: Avinger,
Widow, 45; Balfour, Colonel, 67;
Ballou, Jim, 66; Bannister, Supple
Jack, 40, 42, 58, 66; Barry, Major
Harry, 67; Barsfield, 43; Berkeley,
Janet, 57; Black Riders, 66, 67; Blod-
git, Mother, 66; Blodgits, 58; Blonay,
Mother, 48; Blonay, Ned, 63; Blo-
nays, 58; Bostwick, Dory, 68; Bost-
wick, Sam, 48, 58, 71; Conway, Clar-
ence 57; Conway, Edward, 57;
Crockett, Davy, 80; Eveleigh, Mrs.,
68, 71; Floyd, Hurricane Nell, 58,
59, 64, 66; Ford, Mother, 42, 45;
Frampton, 41, 45; Griffin, Mrs. 71;
Griffins, 45; Harvey, Moll, 67; Hell-
Fire Dick, 41, 47, 58, 77; Hillhouse,
Surgeon, 66, 73; Huck, Christian,
41; Humphries, 65; Inglehardt, 45,
48, 64; M'Kewn, 45, 48, 71; M'Mahon, Captain, 67; Mellichampe, Ernest, 57; Mellichampe, Max, 43;
Middleton, Flora, 57, 66; Millhouse,
Sergeant, 68, 71; Muggs, 42, 44; Nelson, Lady, 65; Nelson, Sherrod, 46,
65; Oakenburg, Dr., 59, 66; Porgy,
Captain, 57, 61, 62, 68, 69, 70, 71,
72, 73, 77; Rawdon, Francis, 37, 39,
66; Sinclair, Colonel, 46, 47; Sinclair,
Willie, 57, 63; Singleton, Major
Robert, 46, 57, 65; Stockton, Lieutenant, 44, 67; Thumbscrew, 58;
Travis, Bertha, 57, 62, 63; Travis,
Henry, 62, 63; Travises, 45; Walton,
Colonel, 41, 46; Walton, Katharine,
57, 65, 67; Williamson, General Andrew, 41; WORKS: Border Romances,
8, 24, 179, 209; Revolutionary Ro-

mances, xi, 50, 55, 57, 58, 59, 60, 61, 62, 66, 69, 73, 77, 80, 81, 82, 83, 202, 206, 208, 209; "Americanism in Literature," 17, 205; "The American Sagas of the Northmen," 30; *Beauchampe*, 24, 78; *Border Beagles*, 24; "Bulwer's Genius and Writings," 209; "Caloya; or The Loves of the Driver," 8; "The Case of Major André," 30; *The Cassique of Kiawah*, 33, 202; *Charlemont*, 24, 202; *Charleston and Her Satirists; A Scribblement*, 203; *Confession; or, The Blind Heart*, 24, 25, 210, 211; "Cortes and the Conquest of Mexico," 18; *Count Julian*, 79, 204; *The Damsel of Darien*, 24, 25, 202; "Daniel Boon," 18; "The Domestic Manners of the Americans by Mrs. Trollope," 30, 204; "Ellet's Women of the Revolution," 207; "The Epochs and Events of American History as Suited to the Purposes of Art in Fiction," 17, 31, 207, 211; *Eutaw*, 33, 37, 40, 41, 45, 46, 48, 56, 57, 58, 59, 64, 66, 70, 77, 81, 83, 206, 207, 208, 209, 210, 211; *The Forayers*, 33, 37, 40, 41, 45, 46, 48, 55, 57, 58, 62, 64, 66, 80, 83, 206, 207, 208, 209, 210, 211; "The Four Periods of American History," 204; *The Golden Christmas*, 203; *Guy Rivers*, 23, 76, 179, 203; *History of South Carolina*, 36, 46, 206, 208, 210; *The Humors of Glen Eberly*, 71; "The Humourous in American and British Literature," 30; "International Copyright Law," 27; "James' Novels," 209; *Katharine Walton*, 33, 35, 37, 41, 57, 67, 71, 78, 80, 83, 206, 207, 209, 211; *The Kinsman*, 24, 25, 206, 209, 211; *The Life of Francis Marion*, 206, 210; *The Life of Nathanael Greene*, 206, 210; "Literary Statistics of New York," 202; "Literature and Art Among the American Aborigines," 18; *Martin Faber*, 23; *Mellichampe*, 24, 35, 36, 37, 39, 43, 51, 56, 57, 72, 81, 206, 207, 208, 209, 211; "Memorial on Copyright," 27; *Michael Bonham*, 61, 80; "Modern Prose Fiction," 202, 207, 208, 209, 211; "The National Volume," 202; *Norman Maurice*, 61, 80; *The Partisan*, 24, 35, 36, 40, 41, 45, 48, 55, 56, 57, 58, 59, 63, 65, 66, 69, 72, 76, 81, 204, 206, 207, 208, 209, 210, 211; *Pelayo*, 24, 204; "Personal Memorabilia," 203; *Richard Hurdis*, 24; *The Scout*, 24, 37, 40, 42, 56, 57, 66, 69, 81, 206, 207, 208, 209, 210, 211; *The Sense of the Beautiful: An Address*, 16, 203; "South Carolina in the Revolutionary War," 33, 82; "Southern Literature," 21, 26; *Southward, Ho!*, 80; *Supplement to Shakespeare's Plays*, 72, 211; *The Sword and the Distaff*, 33, 80, 206, 209, 211; *Vasconselos*, 33, 80, 206, 210; *Views and Reviews in American Literature, History and Fiction*, First Series and Second Series, 16–34, 85, 201, 202, 203, 204, 207, 209, 210, 211; "Weems, the Biographer and Historian," 30; *The Wigwam and the Cabin*, 4, 28, 29, 202, 207, 210, 214; *Woodcraft*, 33, 36, 37, 38, 45, 48, 56, 57, 59, 62, 70, 71, 72, 77, 80, 83, 206, 207, 209, 211; *Works*, 80; "Works of the Imagination," 208; "The Writings of James Fenimore Cooper," 19, 201, 204, 211; *The Yemassee*, 24, 32, 50, 55, 58, 76, 77, 78, 83, 84, 204, 205, 209, 211, 212

Simms's Magazine 28

Simonini, Rinaldi xiii

Sirius (ship) 24

Smart, George K. 218

Smith, Bernard 6, 19, 202, 203, 205, 209

Smith, Captain John 210

Snell, George 196

Social Forces xi

Sophocles 176, 196

South Carolina xii, 20, 24, 27, 33, 35, 36, 37, 38, 39, 40, 41, 42, 43, 44, 47, 48, 49, 55, 56, 77, 81, 82, 84, 85, 109, 123, 178

South Carolina, University of 84
Southern and Western Magazine 28
Southern Literary Gazette 20
Southern Literary Messenger 27, 76
Southern Quarterly Review 2, 33, 77, 82
Southern Review 23
Southworth, Mrs. E. D. E. N. 75
Spain 24
Speer, J. F. 215
Spencer, Benjamin T. 31, 32, 204, 205
Spencer, Herbert 10
Spiller, Robert E. xiii, 212
Stafford, John 201, 204, 205
Steele, Oliver L. 213
Steele, Richard 109
Stein, Gertrude 89
Sterne, Laurence 137, 138, 215; CHAR-
    ACTERS: Shandy, Mrs., 137; Shandy,
    Tristram, 137, 138; Shandy, Walter,
    137, 138; Toby, Uncle, 137, 138;
    WORKS: *Tristram Shandy*, 137, 215
Stevens, Wallace 169; WORKS: "Thirteen
    Ways of Looking at a Blackbird," 169
Stevick, Philip 213
Stewart, Dugald 2
Stewart, Randall 202, 205
Stout, Rex 169
Stovall, Floyd 203
Stowe, Harriet Beecher 96; CHARACTERS:
    Cassy, 96; Legree, Simon, 96; Uncle
    Tom, 96; WORKS: *Uncle Tom's Cab-
    in*, 96
Stratford, England 97, 98
Stribling, T. S. 90, 100, 101, 102, 103,
    212; CHARACTERS: Jones, Railroad,
    100; Vaiden, Miltiades, 101; Vaidens,
    100, 101; WORKS: *Birthright*, 100;
    Bright Metal, 100, 102; *The Forge*,
    100, 101; *The Store*, 100, 101; *Teef-
    tallow*, 100, 101, 102; *Unfinished
    Cathedral*, 100, 101
Stuart, General Jeb 196
Styron, William 1, 11, 125; CHARACTERS:
    Loftis, Peyton, 11; WORKS: *Lie Down
    in Darkness*, 11, 125
Sullivan, Walter 97, 99, 212
Sumner, Charles 82; WORKS: "Crime
    Against Kansas," 82

Sumter, Thomas 41, 56, 82
Switzerland 140, 143

Taine, Hippolyte xii, 187, 220
Tariff of 1828 20
Tarleton, Banastre 36, 37
Tate, Allen 1, 2, 5, 7, 14, 98, 106, 117,
    125, 126, 132, 159, 175, 181, 183, 184,
    187, 201, 202, 212, 214, 218, 220,
    221; WORKS: *Ode to the Confederate
    Dead*, 125, 218; "The Wolves," 14,
    132, 202
Taylor of Caroline, John 190, 221;
    WORKS: *The Arator*, 190; *Inquiry
    into the Principles and Policy of the
    Government of the United States*,
    190
Taylor, General Zachary 21, 30
Taylor, H. W. 217
Taylor, Rosser H. 45, 208
Taylor, Walter Fuller 209
Tennessee 19, 100, 101, 163, 166–167,
    177, 178, 179
Tennyson, Alfred Lord 161, 162
Tetractys Club 26
Texas 80, 124
Thackeray, William Makepeace 79, 137,
    199; WORKS: *Vanity Fair*, 199
Thompson, Francis 186; WORKS: "The
    Hound of Heaven," 186
Thomson, James 61
Thoreau, Henry David 75, 123
Thorp, Willard 218
Tidewater (Virginia) 106, 108, 109,
    110, 111, 113, 116, 117, 178, 179,
    196, 197, 198
Times Literary Supplement (London)
    1
Timrod, Henry 13, 16, 61, 75, 77, 211
Tindall, George B. xiii, 201
Tocqueville, Comte Alexis de 9, 10, 22,
    121, 195, 202, 204; WORKS: *Democra-
    cy in America*, 22, 202, 204; "In-
    fluence of Democracy on the Action
    of Intellect in the United States," 22
Tolstoy, Leo N. 124
Trafalgar 110
Trent, William Peterfield 62, 72–73, 84,

The Roots of Southern Writing

202, 203, 205, 206, 207 208, 211

Trevett, Russell 26

Trollope, Mrs. Francis Milton 21, 30, 204; WORKS: *Domestic Manners of the Americans*, 21, 30, 204

Tucker, Nathaniel Beverley 77, 82

Turner, Arlin xiii

Twelve Southerners 129, 220, 221; WORKS: *I'll Take My Stand*, 129, 184, 188, 191–192, 214, 220, 221

Tzara, Tristram 189

Ulrich, Carolyn F. 220

Up Country (South Carolina) 37, 39, 45, 55

Vanbrugh, Sir John 62

Van Buren, Martin 21

Vanderbilt University 97, 120, 181, 187

Vanderbilts 119

Van Doren, Carl 208–209, 211

Van Tyne, C. H. 206

Venice 53

Vickery, Olga W. 168, 217

Virgil 21

Virginia 77, 88, 96, 108, 111, 112, 113, 124, 142, 178, 179, 197

Virginia Quarterly Review 5

Virginia, University of 169

Voltaire 21

Wagenknecht, Edward 207, 210, 213

Walpole, Hugh 59, 210

Warner, Susan 75

Warren, Robert Penn 1, 7, 8, 11, 12, 14, 90, 94, 95, 96, 120, 125, 126, 127, 132, 182, 187, 192, 201, 202, 212, 214, 220, 221; CHARACTERS: Beaumont, Jeremiah, 94; Burden, Jack, 94; Stark, Willie, 11, 12, 94; Starr, Amantha, 12; WORKS: *All the King's Men*, 11, 12, 94; "The Ballad of Billie Potts," 14, 125; *Band of Angels*, 12, 94, 96; *Brother to Dragons*, 95; *The Cave*, 95; *The Circus in the Attic and Other Stories*, 220; "Original Sin: A Short Story," 14, 132, 193, 202; "The Patented Gate and the

Mean Hamburger," 182; *World Enough and Time*, 94, 125

Washington, George 52

Wateree River 37

Watkins, Floyd C. 127, 214, 221

Webster, Daniel 20

Webster, John 62, 93

Welty, Eudora 1, 90, 180

Wendell, Barrett 75; WORKS: *Literary History of America*, 75

Wertenbaker, Thomas J. 109, 213

Whaley, Grace W. 61–62, 211

Wharton, Edith 199, 222; WORKS: *A Backward Glance*, 222

Whitman, Walt 12, 30, 75, 90, 121, 122, 147, 164, 167, 195, 202, 205, 214, 218, 219, 221; WORKS: *Democratic Vistas*, 12, 202; *Franklin Evans*, 79; *Leaves of Grass*, 147; "One's-Self I Sing," 214; "A Sight in Camp in the Daybreak Gray and Dim," 219; "Song of Myself," 164, 195, 218, 221

Whittier, John Greenleaf 28

Wilde, Oscar 88

Wiley and Putnam (publishers) 17, 28, 29, 30

William III 108

William and Mary, College of 77, 84

Williams, Horace 120

Williams, Tennessee 177, 180

Williamsburg, Virginia 77, 108, 109

Willis, N. P. 24; WORKS: *Corsair* (magazine), 24

Wilmot, Robert 62

Wilson, Edmund xii, 76, 188, 189, 221

Wimsatt, W. K., Jr. 202

Winchester, Jonas 24; WORKS: *New World* (magazine), 24

Winters, Yvor 72, 211

Wittke, Carl 211

Wolfe, Thomas 5, 11, 14, 90, 91, 92, 93, 94, 95, 100, 102, 103, 105, 106, 117, 118–148, 182, 194, 195, 196, 197, 198, 199, 202, 212, 213, 214–216, 221, 222; CHARACTERS: Bland, Judge Rumford, 106, 120; Crane, Nebraska, 120; Gant, Ben, 136; Gant, Eliza, 120, 136, 138; Gant, Eugene, 5, 120, 125,

126, 134, 135, 136, 137, 138, 140, 141, 145; Gant, Helen, 120, 137; Gant, W. O., 120, 126, 136, 138; Hatcher, Professor, 144; Jack, Esther, 120; James, Laura, 127, 137; Joyners, 123; Maw, Aunt, 129; Pentland, Bascom, 120; Pentlands, 123; Starwick, Francis, 120, 145; Webber, George, 119, 120, 128, 129, 130, 145, 146, 197, 198; WORKS: "Boom Town," 102, 103, 213; "Chickamauga," 125; "The Company," 213; *From Death to Morning*, 120; "God's Lonely Man," 145; *The Hills Beyond*, 120, 125, 216; "The House That Jack Built," 102; "I Have a Thing to Tell You," 91, 102, 143; *Look Homeward, Angel*, 91, 102, 118, 120, 127, 134–141 passim, 215, 216; *Of Time and the River*, 91, 120, 123, 125, 126, 130, 142, 143, 145, 202, 214, 215, 216; "The Party at Jack's," 91; "Passage to England," 140; *A Portrait of Bascom Hawke*, 91; *Purdue Speech: "Writing and Living,"* 215; *The Story of a Novel*, 119–132 passim, 141, 143, 147, 214, 215, 216; *The*

Web and the Rock, 91, 118, 119, 120, 128, 141, 198, 214, 216, 221, 222; *The Web of Earth*, 91; *You Can't Go Home Again*, 91, 102, 105, 120, 129, 130, 131, 132, 143, 197, 202, 214, 216, 221

Woodmason, The Reverend Charles 178, 219; WORKS: *The Carolina Backcountry on the Eve of the Revolution*, 219

Woodward, C. Vann 9, 10, 131, 190–191, 202, 214, 221; WORKS: *Reunion and Reaction*, 190–191, 221
World War I 98, 139, 189
World War II 107, 110, 192
Wright, Nathalia 215
Wycherley, William 62

Yankee Doodle (magazine) 30
Yorktown, Virginia 37, 83
"Young America" group 3, 4, 17, 25, 26, 27, 28, 30, 31, 34, 84, 123
Young, Stark 96, 191, 196, 198, 221; WORKS: *So Red the Rose*, 198
Young, Thomas Daniel 221

Zola, Emile 124